CAMBRIDGE

CHECKPOINTS

2018–2022

Year 11 (Stage 6) Chemistry

- Sample examination questions
- Questions arranged by topic
- Suggested responses to questions

Dr Roger Slade & Maureen Slade

CAMBRIDGE
UNIVERSITY PRESS

Shaftesbury Road, Cambridge CB2 8EA, United Kingdom

One Liberty Plaza, 20th Floor, New York, NY 10006, USA

477 Williamstown Road, Port Melbourne, VIC 3207, Australia

314–321, 3rd Floor, Plot 3, Splendor Forum, Jasola District Centre, New Delhi – 110025, India

103 Penang Road, #05–06/07, Visioncrest Commercial, Singapore 238467

Cambridge University Press is part of the University of Cambridge & Assessment, a department of the University of Cambridge.

We share the University's mission to contribute to society through the pursuit of education, learning and research at the highest international levels of excellence.

www.cambridge.org

First published 2018
20 19 18 17 16 15 14 13 12 11 10 9 8 7 6 5

Printed in Australia by Ligare Book Printers.

A catalogue record for this book is available from the National Library of Australia at www.nla.gov.au

ISBN 978-1-108-43530-7 Paperback

Additional resources for this publication at www.cambridge.edu.au/GO

Cambridge University Press & Assessment acknowledges the Australian Aboriginal and Torres Strait Islander peoples of this nation. We acknowledge the traditional custodians of the lands on which our company is located and where we conduct our business. We pay our respects to ancestors and Elders, past and present. Cambridge University Press & Assessment is committed to honouring Australian Aboriginal and Torres Strait Islander peoples' unique cultural and spiritual relationships to the land, waters and seas and their rich contribution to society.

Contents

Introduction

This book is a collection of over 580 practice questions for Chemistry Preliminary Course. This book covers the four modules of Properties and Structure of Matter, Introduction to Quantitative Chemistry, Reactive Chemistry and Drivers of Reactions. Both multiple choice and extended response questions have been included.

Within each area of study, the questions have been grouped under a number of major headings, for example 'Properties of Matter' and 'Atomic Structure and Atomic Mass'. At the end of each chapter, a short test has been prepared. These are designed to allow students to complete a test on the whole of a module.

Questions should be attempted once the relevant theory has been completed. Answers have been included at the end of the book.

Periodic Table of the Elements

Atomic Number Symbol Relative Atomic Mass

							1 H 1.01	
3 Li 6.94	4 Be 9.01							
11 Na 22.99	12 Mg 24.31							
19 K 39.10	20 Ca 40.08	21 Sc 44.96	22 Ti 47.90	23 V 50.94	24 Cr 52.00	25 Mn 54.94	26 Fe 55.85	27 Co 58.93
37 Rb 85.47	38 Sr 87.62	39 Y 88.91	40 Zr 91.22	41 Nb 92.91	42 Mo 95.94	43 Tc (98)	44 Ru 101.07	45 Rh 102.91
55 Cs 132.91	56 Ba 137.34	57 La 138.91	72 Hf 178.49	73 Ta 180.95	74 W 183.85	75 Re 186.21	76 Os 190.21	77 Ir 192.22
87 Fr (223)	88 Ra (226)	89 Ac (227)	104 Rf (261)	105 Db (262)	106 Sg (263)	107 Bh (262)	108 Hs (265)	109 Mt (266)

Lanthanides	58 Ce 140.12	59 Pr 140.91	60 Nd 144.24	61 Pm (147)	62 Sm 150.35	63 Eu 151.96
Actinides	90 Th 232.04	91 Pa (231)	92 U 238.03	93 Np (237)	94 Pu (242)	95 Am (243)

Numbers in parentheses are mass numbers of the most stable isotope of that element

								2 **He** 4.00
			5 **B** 10.81	6 **C** 12.01	7 **N** 14.01	8 **O** 16.00	9 **F** 19.00	10 **Ne** 20.18
			13 **Al** 26.98	14 **Si** 28.09	15 **P** 30.97	16 **S** 32.06	17 **Cl** 35.45	18 **Ar** 39.95
28 **Ni** 58.71	29 **Cu** 63.55	30 **Zn** 65.37	31 **Ga** 69.72	32 **Ge** 72.59	33 **As** 74.92	34 **Se** 78.96	35 **Br** 79.91	36 **Kr** 83.80
46 **Pd** 106.42	47 **Ag** 107.87	48 **Cd** 112.40	49 **In** 114.82	50 **Sn** 118.69	51 **Sb** 121.75	52 **Te** 127.60	53 **I** 126.90	54 **Xe** 131.30
78 **Pt** 195.09	79 **Au** 196.97	80 **Hg** 200.59	81 **Tl** 204.37	82 **Pb** 207.19	83 **Bi** 208.98	84 **Po** (210)	85 **At** (210)	86 **Rn** (222)

64 **Gd** 157.25	65 **Tb** 158.92	66 **Dy** 162.50	67 **Ho** 164.93	68 **Er** 167.26	69 **Tm** 168.93	70 **Yb** 173.04	71 **Lu** 174.97
96 **Cm** (247)	97 **Bk** (247)	98 **Cf** (251)	99 **Es** (254)	100 **Fm** (257)	101 **Md** (258)	102 **No** (259)	103 **Lr** (260)

Data Table 1

Avogadro's constant	6.022×10^{23} mol^{-1}
Volume of 1 mole of ideal gas: at 100 kPa and at 0°C	22.71 L mol^{-1}
at 25°C	24.79 L mol^{-1}
Ionisation constant for water at 25°C, K_w	1.0×10^{-14}
Specific heat capacity of water	4.18×10^3 J kg^{-1} K^{-1}
$pH = -\log_{10}[H^+]$	
$\Delta H = -mC\Delta T$	

Data Table 2 **Standard Reduction Potentials**

Half-reaction	E°
$Li^{+}(aq) + e^{-} \rightleftharpoons Li(s)$	−3.02 V
$K^{+}(aq) + e^{-} \rightleftharpoons K(s)$	−2.94 V
$Ba^{2+}(aq) + 2e^{-} \rightleftharpoons Ba(s)$	−2.91 V
$Ca^{2+}(aq) + 2e^{-} \rightleftharpoons Ca(s)$	−2.87 V
$Na^{+}(aq) + e^{-} \rightleftharpoons Na(s)$	−2.71 V
$Mg^{2+}(aq) + 2e^{-} \rightleftharpoons Mg(s)$	−2.34 V
$Al^{3+}(aq) + 3e^{-} \rightleftharpoons Al(s)$	−1.68 V
$Mn^{2+}(aq) + 2e^{-} \rightleftharpoons Mn(s)$	−1.18 V
$H_2O(l) + e^{-} \rightleftharpoons \frac{1}{2}H_2(g) + OH^{-}(aq)$	−0.83 V
$Zn^{2+}(aq) + 2e^{-} \rightleftharpoons Zn(s)$	−0.76 V
$Cr^{3+}(aq) + 3e^{-} \rightleftharpoons Cr(s)$	−0.74 V
$Fe^{2+}(aq) + 2e^{-} \rightleftharpoons Fe(s)$	−0.44 V
$Cr^{3+}(aq) + e^{-} \rightleftharpoons Cr^{2+}(aq)$	−0.41 V
$Cd^{2+}(aq) + 2e^{-} \rightleftharpoons Cd(s)$	−0.40 V
$Co^{2+}(aq) + 2e^{-} \rightleftharpoons Co(s)$	−0.28 V
$Ni^{2+}(aq) + 2e^{-} \rightleftharpoons Ni(s)$	−0.23 V
$Sn^{2+}(aq) + 2e^{-} \rightleftharpoons Sn(s)$	−0.14 V
$Pb^{2+}(aq) + 2e^{-} \rightleftharpoons Pb(s)$	−0.13 V
$H^{+}(aq) + e^{-} \rightleftharpoons \frac{1}{2}H_2(g)$	0.00 V
$S(s) + 2H^{+}(aq) + 2e^{-} \rightleftharpoons H_2S(g)$	+0.14 V
$Sn^{4+}(aq) + 2e^{-} \rightleftharpoons Sn^{2+}(aq)$	+0.15 V
$SO_4^{2-}(aq) + 4H^{+}(aq) + 2e^{-} \rightleftharpoons SO_2(aq) + 2H_2O(l)$	+0.16 V
$Cu^{2+}(aq) + 2e^{-} \rightleftharpoons Cu(s)$	+0.34 V
$\frac{1}{2}O_2(g) + H_2O(l) + 2e^{-} \rightleftharpoons 2OH^{-}(aq)$	+0.40 V
$Cu^{+}(aq) + e^{-} \rightleftharpoons Cu(s)$	+0.52 V
$\frac{1}{2}I_2(s) + e^{-} \rightleftharpoons I^{-}(aq)$	+0.54 V
$\frac{1}{2}I_2(aq) + e^{-} \rightleftharpoons I^{-}(aq)$	+0.62 V
$\frac{1}{2}O_2(g) + H^{+}(aq) + e^{-} \rightleftharpoons \frac{1}{2}H_2O_2(aq)$	+0.68 V
$Fe^{3+}(aq) + e^{-} \rightleftharpoons Fe^{2+}(aq)$	+0.77 V
$Ag^{+}(aq) + e^{-} \rightleftharpoons Ag(s)$	+0.80 V
$\frac{1}{2}Br_2(l) + e^{-} \rightleftharpoons Br^{-}(aq)$	+1.08 V
$\frac{1}{2}Br_2(aq) + e^{-} \rightleftharpoons Br^{-}(aq)$	+1.10 V
$\frac{1}{2}O_2(g) + 2H^{+}(aq) + 2e^{-} \rightleftharpoons H_2O(l)$	+1.23 V
$\frac{1}{2}Cl_2(g) + e^{-} \rightleftharpoons Cl^{-}(aq)$	+1.36 V
$\frac{1}{2}Cr_2O_7^{2-}(aq) + 7H^{+}(aq) + 3e^{-} \rightleftharpoons Cr^{3+}(aq) + 7/2H_2O(l)$	+1.36 V
$\frac{1}{2}Cl_2(aq) + e^{-} \rightleftharpoons Cl^{-}(aq)$	+1.40 V
$MnO_4^{-}(aq) + 8H^{+}(aq) + 5e^{-} \rightleftharpoons Mn^{2+}(aq) + 4H_2O(l)$	+1.51 V
$Au^{+}(aq) + e^{-} \rightleftharpoons Au(s)$	+1.68 V
$\frac{1}{2}H_2O_2(aq) + H^{+}(aq) + e^{-} \rightleftharpoons H_2O(l)$	+1.77 V
$\frac{1}{2}F_2(g) + e^{-} \rightleftharpoons F^{-}(aq)$	+2.89 V

Chapter 1

Properties and Structure of Matter

Multiple Choice Items

(1) Properties of Matter

Question 1
Which one of the following lists contains only pure substances?

(A) Water, molten iron, carbon dioxide gas
(B) Air, molten iron, copper(II) sulfate solution
(C) Salt, oxygen gas, iron(II) chloride solution
(D) Oxygen gas, nitrogen gas, air

Question 2
A student is required to separate a mixture of charcoal and sugar. Which one of the following alternatives best summarises the method that would allow the separation of the mixture and retention of both components?

	Step 1	Step 2	Step 3
(A)	Addition of water	Decantation	Crystallisation
(B)	Addition of water	Filtration	Evaporation and crystallisation
(C)	Sieving	Addition of water	Evaporation
(D)	Sedimentation	Addition of water	Distillation

Question 3
When a solution of barium nitrate is added to a solution of sodium sulfate, an insoluble white precipitate of barium sulfate is formed. The BEST way of separating the barium sulfate from the solution would be

(A) evaporation.
(B) distillation.
(C) filtration.
(D) crystallisation.

Question 4
Which one of the following does NOT contain homogeneous substances?

	Substance 1	Substance 2
(A)	Carbon dioxide gas	Air
(B)	A solution of copper(II) nitrate	Molten iron
(C)	Oil and water	Sand and water
(D)	A solder made from tin and lead	Water

Question 5
Which one of the following techniques could **not** be used to separate two insoluble solids?

(A) Filtration
(B) Magnetic separation
(C) Sedimentation
(D) Sieving

Question 6
The boiling temperatures of some gases found in air are given in the table below.

Gas	Boiling point (°C)	Gas	Boiling point (°C)
argon	–186	nitrogen	–196
carbon dioxide	–78	oxygen	–183

If a sample of liquid air containing all these gases at –200°C is warmed, the first gas to distill from the mixture would be

(A) argon.
(B) carbon dioxide.
(C) nitrogen.
(D) oxygen.

Question 7
A mixture of zinc oxide and wet sand weighs 11.62 g. After drying, 2.53 g of zinc oxide and 7.25 g of sand remain. The percentage of water in the original mixture is closest to

(A) 15.8%
(B) 18.8%
(C) 25.4%
(D) 84.2%

Question 8
The correct name for the compound with the formula $MgBr_2$ is

(A) magnesium bromine.
(B) magnesium bromite.
(C) magnesium bromate.
(D) magnesium bromide.

Question 9
A compound of iron and oxygen has the formula Fe_2O_3. The correct name for this compound is

(A) iron(II) oxide.
(B) iron trioxide.
(C) iron(III) oxide.
(D) iron oxide.

Question 10
The correct formula for sodium sulfate is

(A) Na_2S
(B) $NaSO_3$
(C) $NaSO_4$
(D) Na_2SO_4

Question 11
The correct formula for copper(II) oxide is

(A) Cu_2O
(B) CuO_2
(C) CoO
(D) CuO

Question 12

1.000 g of substance A was reacted with a number of different chemicals as shown in the flow chart below. After each reaction a product was obtained, which was purified, dried and weighed. The mass of each product is shown.

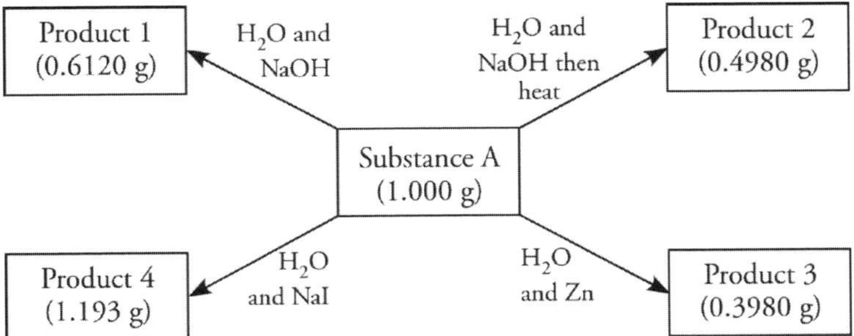

Substance A and the four products are thought to contain the same element. Which product is most likely to be the pure element?

(A) Product 1
(B) Product 2
(C) Product 3
(D) Product 4

Question 13

Some of the properties of four elements are shown in the table below.

Property	Element 1	Element 2	Element 3	Element 4
melting point (°C)	98	–39	1085	113
boiling point (°C)	883	357	2572	445
electrical conductivity (MS m^{-1})	21	1.0	58.4	10^{-21}
thermal conductivity (J s^{-1} m^{-1} K^{-1})	141	8.3	401	0.27
density (g mL^{-1})	0.97	13.53	8.96	2.07

Which element is most likely to be a non-metal?

(A) Element 1
(B) Element 2
(C) Element 3
(D) Element 4

Question 14

Some properties of four compounds (W, X, Y and Z) are given in the table below. All four compounds are insoluble in water.

Property	W	X	Y	Z
melting point (°C)	–116	–23	119	–93.7
boiling point (°C)	34.5	76.7	218	3.6
density (g mL^{-1})	0.708	1.584	4.008	1.732×10^{-3}

Which material is a liquid at 25°C that will float on water?

(A) Compound W
(B) Compound X
(C) Compound Y
(D) Compound Z

Question 15
Which one of the following lists contains only non-metallic elements?

(A) hydrogen, helium, lithium, beryllium
(B) oxygen, chlorine, sulfur, arsenic
(C) lithium, sodium, magnesium, aluminium
(D) iron, sulfur, carbon, phosphorus

The following information refers to Questions 16 to 18.

The properties of six elements are given in the table below.

Element	Melting temperature (°C)	Boiling temperature (°C)	Electrical conductivity (MS m^{-1})	Thermal conductivity (J s^{-1} m^{-1} K^{-1})	Density (g mL^{-1})
I	1535	2750	10.3	80	7.86
II	−39	357	1.0	8.3	13.53
III	44	280	10^{-15}	0.24	1.82
IV	113	445	10^{-21}	0.27	2.07
V	842	1484	29	200	1.55
VI	−7	59	10^{-16}	0.12	3.12

Question 16
Which of the elements would be liquids at room temperature?

(A) II and III
(B) IV and VI
(C) II and VI
(D) III and IV

Question 17
Mercury is most likely to be element

(A) II (B) III (C) IV (D) V

Question 18
The element with the greatest tensile strength is likely to be

(A) I (B) III (C) IV (D) V

Question 19
Some of the physical properties of four metals, I, II, III and IV are shown in the table below.

Property	I	II	III	IV
melting point (°C)	769	30	1085	232
boiling point (°C)	1384	2403	2572	2602
electrical conductivity (MS m^{-1})	4.3	3.9	58.4	8.7
thermal conductivity (J s^{-1} m^{-1} K^{-1})	35.3	41	401	67
density (g mL^{-1})	2.60	5.91	8.96	7.30

Which metal is most likely to form coloured compounds?

(A) I (B) II (C) III (D) IV

Question 20
Many elements are found on Earth in an uncombined state, i.e. as the free element, whereas others are only found as part of compounds. Which one of the following lists contains *only* elements that occur uncombined on Earth?

(A) aluminium, calcium, chlorine, nitrogen, silver
(B) argon, gold, oxygen, silver, sulfur
(C) bromine, magnesium, silicon, sodium, zinc
(D) fluorine, copper, iron, neon, potassium

Question 21
When compared with non-metals, metals are more likely to

(A) conduct electricity and heat well but be brittle.
(B) have lower densities and melting temperatures.
(C) be malleable, ductile and have high melting temperatures.
(D) appear dull and be poor conductors of heat and electricity.

Question 22
A diagram of the Periodic Table is shown below. The positions of six elements are shown using the labels I, II, III, IV, V and VI.

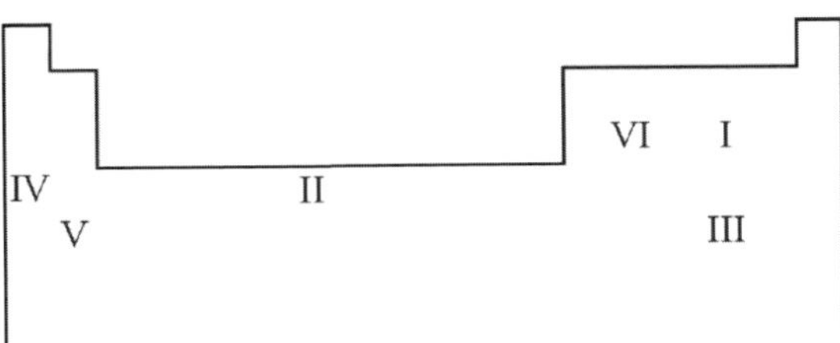

Which elements would be expected to have similar chemical properties?

(A) I and VI (B) I and III (C) III and V (D) II and IV

Question 23
Four elements labelled L, M, Q and R have similar chemical properties. The relative atomic masses of L, M and Q increase in the order L < M < Q. The melting temperatures of L, M and Q are given below.

Element	Melting temperature (°C)
L	–220
M	–101
Q	–7

Which one of the following statements concerning the relative atomic mass and the melting temperature of element R is most likely to be correct?

	Relative Atomic Mass of R	Melting temperature of R
(A)	Is greater than that of Q	Is approximately +100°C
(B)	Is less than that of L	Is approximately –50°C
(C)	Is between that of M and Q	Is approximately +50°C
(D)	Is between that of L and M	Is approximately –250°C

Question 24
In which one of the following sets are all the compounds most likely to be coloured?

(A) $KMnO_4$, $CaCl_2$, NH_4NO_3
(B) Ag_3PO_4, $(NH_4)_2SO_4$, $BaBr_2$
(C) $Cu(OH)_2$, $Fe(NO_3)_3$, $K_2Cr_2O_7$
(D) NaCl, $MgBr_2$, AlI_3

(2) Atomic Structure and Atomic Mass

Question 25
Which one of the following statements about atoms is correct?

(A) Atoms are hard impenetrable spheres.
(B) Most of an atom is empty space.
(C) There are no smaller particles than atoms.
(D) In chemical reactions some atoms are destroyed and new ones are formed.

Question 26
Which one of the following statements about the nucleus of an atom is correct?

(A) The diameter of the nucleus is about half that of the atom.
(B) The nucleus comprises 99.9% of the mass and 99.9% of the space of an atom.
(C) The mass of an atom is evenly spread between the nucleus and the other parts.
(D) Most of the mass of an atom is in a very small nucleus.

Question 27
The neutral species ${}^{40}_{20}Ca$ would contain

(A) 20 neutrons, 40 protons and 40 electrons.
(B) 40 neutrons, 20 protons and 20 electrons.
(C) 20 neutrons, 20 protons and 20 electrons.
(D) 40 neutrons, 20 protons and 40 electrons.

Question 28
A very dangerous radioactive isotope of strontium produced during nuclear explosions is ${}^{90}_{38}Sr$. When this isotope decays a stable isotope of zirconium, ${}^{90}_{40}Zr$ is eventually formed. Compared with the isotope of Sr, the isotope of Zr has

(A) two more protons and two less neutrons.
(B) two more neutrons and two less protons.
(C) one more proton and one more neutron.
(D) two more protons and the same number of neutrons.

Question 29
In which one of the following lists are the species isotopes?

(A) ${}^{31}_{15}P^{3-}$, ${}^{32}_{16}S^{2-}$, ${}^{35}_{17}Cl^{-}$
(B) ${}^{14}_{6}C$, ${}^{14}_{7}N$, ${}^{14}_{8}O$
(C) ${}^{54}_{24}Cr$, ${}^{55}_{25}Mn$, ${}^{56}_{26}Fe$
(D) ${}^{20}_{10}Ne$, ${}^{21}_{10}Ne$, ${}^{22}_{10}Ne$

Question 30
In which one of the following lists do the species have the same number of neutrons?

(A) ${}^{40}_{18}Ar$, ${}^{40}_{19}K$, ${}^{40}_{20}Ca$
(B) ${}^{22}_{10}Ne$, ${}^{23}_{11}Na$, ${}^{24}_{12}Mg$
(C) ${}^{28}_{14}Si$, ${}^{29}_{14}Si$, ${}^{30}_{14}Si$
(D) ${}^{35}_{17}Cl^{-}$, ${}^{37}_{18}Ar$, ${}^{39}_{19}K^{+}$

Question 31
The atomic structures of three particles (X, Y, Z) are given in the table below.

Particle	No. of protons	No. of electrons	No. of neutrons
X	13	10	14
Y	12	10	13
Z	11	10	12

These particles are
(A) isotopes. (B) anions. (C) non-metals. (D) cations.

Question 32
A particle has 27 protons, 28 neutrons and 25 electrons. If the element has the symbol X, then this particle may be represented by the symbol

(A) ${}^{55}_{27}X^{2+}$ (B) ${}^{53}_{25}X^{2+}$ (C) ${}^{55}_{27}X^{2-}$ (D) ${}^{53}_{25}X^{2-}$

Question 33
Four particles, I, II, III and IV are described in the table below.

	Mass number	Atomic number	Number of electrons
I	127	53	54
II	127	53	53
III	129	53	53
IV	127	52	54

Which of the following pairs of particles are isotopes?

(A) I and II (B) II and III (C) I and IV (D) II and IV

Question 34

The number of neutrons in an atom of $^{197}_{79}Au$ is

(A) 79 (B) 118 (C) 197 (D) 276

Question 35

^{12}C, ^{13}C and ^{14}C are isotopes of carbon. Atoms of these isotopes will differ in

(A) the number of protons in their nuclei.
(B) their electron configurations.
(C) their chemical properties.
(D) their physical properties.

Question 36

The electron configuration of an element in Group 3 of the periodic table would be

(A) $1s^22s^22p^63s^2$
(B) $1s^22s^22p^63s^23p^1$
(C) $1s^22s^22p^63s^23p^2$
(D) $1s^22s^22p^63s^23p^3$

Question 37

Which one of the following electron configurations is least likely to be that of a metallic element?

(A) $1s^22s^22p^63s^23p^5$
(B) $1s^22s^22p^63s^23p^63d^94s^2$
(C) $1s^22s^22p^63s^23p^64s^2$
(D) $1s^22s^22p^63s^1$

Question 38

The maximum number of electrons that can occupy the third shell is

(A) 10 (B) 14 (C) 16 (D) 18

Question 39

Four elements W, X, Y and Z have the electron configurations shown below.

Element	Electron configuration
W	$1s^22s^22p^6$
X	$1s^22s^22p^63s^1$
Y	$1s^22s^22p^63s^23p^2$
Z	$1s^22s^22p^63s^23p^5$

Which element is expected to be the least reactive?

(A) W (B) X (C) Y (D) Z

Question 40

Which one of the following statements about the ions $^{31}_{15}P^{3-}$ and $^{24}_{12}Mg^{2+}$ is correct?

(A) Their electron configurations are the same as that of an atom of neon.
(B) These ions have the same number of electrons.

(C) Their electron configurations are the same as that of an inert gas.
(D) They have the same number of electron shells.

Question 41
Isoelectronic species have the same electron configuration and the same structure (same number of atoms and the same connectivity). Which one of the following lists contains isoelectronic species?

(A) $^{24}_{12}Mg$, $^{40}_{20}Ca$, $^{88}_{38}Sr$
(B) $^{37}_{17}Cl$, $^{38}_{18}Ar$, $^{39}_{19}K$
(C) $^{56}_{26}Fe$, $^{56}_{26}Fe^{2+}$, $^{56}_{26}Fe^{3+}$
(D) $^{19}_{9}F^-$, $^{22}_{10}Ne$, $^{23}_{11}Na^+$

Question 42
The 3d subshell can take a maximum of

(A) 2 electrons.
(B) 5 electrons.
(C) 10 electrons.
(D) 14 electrons.

Question 43
An ion which has the same electron configuration as a magnesium ion and has a charge of negative two is the

(A) oxide ion.
(B) sulfide ion.
(C) sodium ion.
(D) aluminium ion.

Question 44
The transition metal titanium forms the ion Ti^{3+} in water. The electronic configuration of Ti^{3+} ion is most likely to be

(A) $1s^2 2s^2 2p^6 3s^2 3p^6 3d^5 4s^2$
(B) $1s^2 2s^2 2p^6 3s^2 3p^6 3d^2 4s^2$
(C) $1s^2 2s^2 2p^6 3s^2 3p^5 4s^2$
(D) $1s^2 2s^2 2p^6 3s^2 3p^6 3d^1$

Question 45
Naturally occurring iridium has a relative atomic mass of 192.2 and consists of two isotopes, $^{191}_{77}Ir$ and $^{193}_{77}Ir$. The percentage of the lighter isotope is

(A) 20%
(B) 40%
(C) 60%
(D) 80%

Question 46
Copper obtained from naturally occurring deposits contains two isotopes, ^{63}Cu and ^{65}Cu. The relative atomic mass of copper is 63.6. From this information it can be deduced that the ratio of ^{63}Cu : ^{65}Cu in the natural deposits of copper is approximately

(A) 7 : 3
(B) 3 : 1
(C) 0.6 : 2
(D) 1 : 3

Question 47
Naturally occurring magnesium consists of more than one isotope. The most common isotope is ^{24}Mg with an abundance of 79.0%. If the relative atomic mass of

magnesium is 24.31, then the other isotope (or isotopes) of naturally occurring magnesium is (are) most likely to be

(A) 21.0% of ^{26}Mg.
(B) 21.0% of ^{25}Mg
(C) approximately equal amounts of ^{25}Mg and ^{26}Mg.
(D) approximately equal amounts of ^{23}Mg and ^{26}Mg.

Question 48
In which one of the following cases is the species in an excited state?

(A) A sodium atom with the electron configuration $1s^22s^22p^63s^1$
(B) A fluoride ion with the electron configuration $1s^22s^22p^6$
(C) A calcium atom with the electron configuration $1s^22s^22p^63s^23p^63d^2$
(D) A magnesium ion with the electron configuration $1s^22s^22p^6$

Question 49
When a flame test is carried out using a solution of sodium chloride an intense yellow colour is seen. When the light is examined in more detail the yellow light has the lowest energy in this part of the sodium spectrum. Which one of the following changes in electron configuration is most likely to produce the yellow light?

(A) $1s^22s^22p^63s^1$ to $1s^22s^22p^63p^1$
(B) $1s^22s^22p^63p^1$ to $1s^22s^22p^63s^1$
(C) $1s^22s^22p^64p^1$ to $1s^22s^22p^63s^1$
(D) $1s^22s^22p^63s^1$ to $1s^22s^22p^64p^1$

Question 50
The metal ion present in an ionic solution can often be identified by means of a flame test. Flame tests are one example of emission spectra. Emission spectra arise from an atom or ion

(A) gaining an electron.
(B) losing an electron.
(C) gaining energy so that an electron moves to a higher energy level.
(D) losing energy so that an electron moves to a lower energy level.

Question 51
Below are four statements concerning electrons in atoms.

I Electrons move in orbits around the nucleus.
II An electron behaves like a cloud of negative charge.
III When an electron is in an orbit it has a defined energy.
IV Energy is emitted or absorbed if an electron changes orbit.

Which of these statements did Bohr use to explain the emission spectra of elements?

(A) I, II, III and IV
(B) I, III and IV
(C) II, III and IV
(D) I, II and IV

Question 52
Which one of the following ideas is **not** common to the theories of both Bohr and Schrödinger?

(A) Atoms have a central nucleus surrounded by orbiting electrons.
(B) Electrons exist in energy levels called shells.
(C) Each shell can hold a certain maximum number of electrons.
(D) Shells are subdivided into energy levels called subshells.

Question 53
Which one of the following was **not** part of Bohr's model of the atom?

(A) Electrons move in regions of space called orbitals.
(B) Electrons move in energy levels called shells.
(C) Electrons closer to the nucleus have lower energy.
(D) Orbiting electrons do not lose energy.

Question 54
The electron configuration of a neutral atom with its electrons in an excited state is

(A) $1s^22s^22p^2$ (atomic number = 6).
(B) $1s^22s^22p^33s^1$ (atomic number = 8).
(C) $1s^22s^22p^53s^1$ (atomic number = 9).
(D) $1s^22s^22p^5$ (atomic number = 10).

Question 55
The emission of a β–particle from an unstable atom is most likely to occur when the

(A) atomic number is greater than 83.
(B) n : p ratio is greater than 1 : 1.
(C) n : p ratio is less than 1 : 1.
(D) atom is radioactive.

Question 56
When a radioactive atom decays, one or more types of radiation (α–particles, β–particles, γ–rays) may be emitted. Which of these types of radiation will be deflected by an electric field?

(A) α–particles only
(B) α and β–particles
(C) β–particles only
(D) γ–rays only

Question 57
A radioactive isotope used in some industries to measure the thickness of materials is $^{90}_{38}Sr$. When this isotope decays, the following reactions occur to produce a stable isotope of zirconium.

$^{90}_{38}Sr \rightarrow ^{90}_{39}Y + x$; followed by $^{90}_{39}Y \rightarrow ^{90}_{40}Zr + x$

The particle x is

(A) a neutron.
(B) a proton.
(C) an electron.
(D) a positron.

Question 58

Which one of the following atoms is likely to be stable?

(A) $^{3}_{1}H$ (B) $^{14}_{6}C$ (C) $^{20}_{10}Ne$ (D) $^{238}_{92}U$

Question 59

When atoms of uranium–235 undergo fission a number of different reactions are possible. One such reaction is represented by the nuclear equation shown below.

$$^{235}_{92}U + ^{1}_{0}n \rightarrow Q + 3^{1}_{0}n + R$$

The identities of the atoms Q and R are

	Q	R
(A)	$^{131}_{53}I$	$^{104}_{39}Y$
(B)	$^{102}_{43}Tc$	$^{134}_{46}Pd$
(C)	$^{143}_{56}Ba$	$^{93}_{36}Kr$
(D)	$^{90}_{38}Sr$	$^{143}_{54}Xe$

Question 60

An isotope of thorium, Th, has a n : p ratio of 1.56 : 1. It is likely that this isotope will

(A) be stable.
(B) emit an alpha particle.
(C) emit a beta particle.
(D) emit a positron.

Question 61

The isotope ^{11}C is produced in cyclotrons for use in medical diagnoses. It has a half-life of 20 minutes. If 1.0×10^{-4} g of this isotope remains one hour after production, how much ^{11}C was initially produced?

(A) 1.0×10^{-4} g
(B) 3.0×10^{-4} g
(C) 4.0×10^{-4} g
(D) 8.0×10^{-4} g

Question 62

A radioactive isotope is most likely to be produced when there are

(A) more protons than neutrons in the atom.
(B) more protons than electrons in the atom.
(C) when the outer shell of the atom has eight electrons.
(D) when the number of protons and neutrons are equal.

Question 63

Each of the following lists contains three isotopes. Which one is most likely to contain only unstable isotopes?

(A) $^{214}_{82}Pb$, $^{99}_{43}Tc$, $^{14}_{7}N$
(B) $^{232}_{90}Th$, $^{40}_{20}Ca$, $^{147}_{61}Pm$
(C) $^{226}_{88}Ra$, $^{40}_{20}Ca$, $^{16}_{8}O$
(D) $^{238}_{92}U$, $^{46}_{20}Ca$, $^{99}_{43}Tc$

Question 64

The isotope $^{35}_{16}S$ is produced according to the equation

$^{34}_{16}S + ^{1}_{0}n \rightarrow ^{35}_{16}S$

Where would you expect a commercial quantity of $^{35}_{16}S$ to be produced?

(A) A synchrotron
(B) A mass spectrometer
(C) A particle accelerator
(D) A nuclear reactor

Question 65

The following equation shows how the radio-isotope $^{24}_{11}Na$ is produced in a nuclear reactor:

$^{27}_{13}Al + X \rightarrow ^{24}_{11}Na + Z$

Which one of the following correctly identifies X and Z?

	X	Z
(A)	Electron	Proton
(B)	Neutron	α–particle
(C)	Neutron	Proton
(D)	Proton	α–particle

(3) Periodicity

Question 66

Which one of the following statements about an atom of sodium (Z = 11) and an atom of potassium (Z = 19) is correct?

(A) For both elements three electron shells are used to place all their electrons.
(B) Both sodium and potassium atoms have one electron in their outer electron shells.
(C) Sodium atoms have two completely filled electron shells whereas potassium atoms have three completely filled shells.
(D) The first electron shell of potassium contains more electrons than the first electron shell of sodium.

Question 67

Which of the following pairs of atoms both have three completely filled electron shells?

(A) Ar and K
(B) Na and K
(C) Zn and Kr
(D) Ar and Kr

Question 68

The chemical reactivity of metals according to their positions in the Periodic Table

(A) decreases from left to right across a period and from top to bottom of a group.
(B) increases from left to right across a period and from top to bottom of a group.
(C) decreases from left to right across a period and from bottom to top of a group.
(D) increases from left to right across a period and from bottom to top of a group.

Question 69
The properties of the elements used to produce the modern form of the Periodic Table are their

(A) atomic number and ionisation energy.
(B) atomic mass and chemical properties.
(C) chemical properties and ionisation energy.
(D) atomic number and electron configuration.

Question 70
Which one of the following will have the largest radius?

(A) Be atom (B) Mg atom (C) Ca atom (D) Sr atom

Question 71
When going down Group 1, from lithium to caesium, which one of the following statements is correct?

(A) The first ionisation energy increases.
(B) The atoms are more likely to react to form 2+ cations.
(C) The elements become more reactive.
(D) The electronegativity increases.

Question 72
When going *down* a group in the periodic table the properties of the elements, such as electronegativity, atomic radius, first ionisation energy and metallic character all change. Which one of the following correctly states these changes?

	Electronegativity	Atomic radius	Ionisation energy	Metallic character
(A)	increases	increases	increases	increases
(B)	increases	decreases	increases	decreases
(C)	decreases	increases	decreases	increases
(D)	decreases	decreases	decreases	decreases

Question 73
Of the following elements, which one is most likely to have similar chemical properties to the element with atomic number 16?

(A) Phosphorus (B) Chlorine
(C) Argon (D) Selenium

Question 74
Which of the following elements would be expected to have the lowest first ionisation energy?

(A) Potassium
(B) Magnesium
(C) Silver
(D) Gold

Question 75

The first ionisation energies, in kJ mol^{-1}, of four metallic elements, I, II, III and IV are given in the table below.

Element	Ionisation Energy (kJ mol^{-1})
I	502
II	744
III	425
IV	752

The most reactive element is most likely to be

(A) Element I.
(B) Element II.
(C) Element III.
(D) Element IV.

Question 76

The properties of the elements of the third period vary as one goes across the period from sodium to chlorine. Which one of the following shows how the atomic radius, the first ionisation energy and electronegativity vary from sodium to chlorine?

	Atomic radius	First ionisation energy	Electronegativity
(A)	increases	increases	decreases
(B)	increases	decreases	increases
(C)	decreases	increases	increases
(D)	decreases	decreases	decreases

Question 77

The elements chlorine (a gas), bromine (a liquid) and iodine (a solid) are placed in the same group in the Periodic Table because they

(A) have the same chemical properties.
(B) have the same number of outer shell electrons.
(C) are all non-metals.
(D) show a gradation in physical properties.

Question 78

In going down Group 1 of the Periodic Table, i.e. from Li to Na to K, the first ionisation energy

(A) decreases and the atomic radius decreases.
(B) decreases and the atomic radius increases.
(C) increases and the atomic radius decreases.
(D) increases and the atomic radius increases.

Question 79
Which one of the following properties shows a general increase across the Periodic Table from sodium to chlorine?

(A) Metallic character
(B) Atomic radius
(C) First ionisation energy
(D) Reactivity with water

Question 80
The first eight ionisation energies of an element are shown in the graph below.

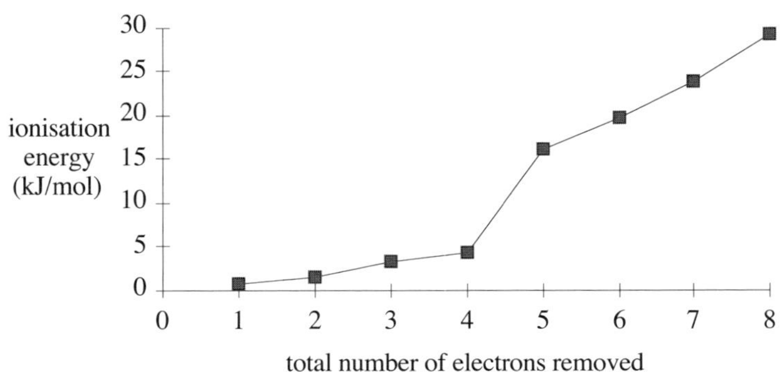

The element is most likely to be

(A) carbon. (B) oxygen. (C) neon. (D) silicon.

Question 81
Which one of the following species would have the smallest radius?

(A) Na^+ (B) K^+ (C) Cl^- (D) F^-

Question 82
Which one of the following species will have the largest radius?

(A) Na atom (B) Na^+ ion (C) K atom (D) K^+ ion

Question 83
The metallic character of the elements in Group 4 of the periodic table increases going down this group. The best explanation for this trend is that there is

(A) an increase in electronegativity from C to Pb.
(B) a decrease in the first ionisation energy from C to Pb.
(C) a decrease in the size of the atoms from C to Pb.
(D) an increase in the number of outer shell electrons from C to Pb.

Question 84
The first five electrons are removed from an atom of element Z. At each step the energy (in kJ mol^{-1}) required is measured and the values are shown in the table on the next page.

Electron removed	1st	2nd	3rd	4th	5th
Energy required (kJ mol^{-1})	744	1457	7739	10 547	13 636

It is most likely that element Z is located in the Periodic Table in group

(A) 2. (B) 3. (C) 4. (D) 5.

Question 85
Element X has an atomic radius that is larger than that of magnesium. When element X undergoes a chemical reaction the ion formed has the same electron configuration as the F^- ion. Element X is most likely to be

(A) beryllium.
(B) lithium.
(C) neon.
(D) sodium.

Question 86
Two of the elements in Period 3 are sodium and chlorine. It is expected that chlorine would have the

(A) lower electronegativity and a smaller atomic radius.
(B) lower electronegativity and a larger atomic radius
(C) higher electronegativity and a smaller atomic radius.
(D) higher electronegativity and a larger atomic radius.

Question 87
An inert (noble) gas is most likely to have an outer shell electron configuration of

(A) d^{10} (B) s^2p^6 (C) $s^2p^4d^6$ (D) $s^2p^6d^{10}$

Question 88
Which one of the following statements about transition metals is *incorrect*?

(A) Most transition metals have a partly filled d-subshell.
(B) Many compounds of transition metals are coloured.
(C) Transition metals have high melting temperatures, are hard and dense and are highly reactive.
(D) Most transition metals can form more than one oxidation state.

Question 89
When main group metals, such as potassium and calcium, are compared with transition metals in the same period, such as iron and copper, which of the following is correct?

	Main Group metals	**Transition metals**
(A)	form coloured compounds	are usually hard
(B)	are highly reactive	are usually soft
(C)	have lower ionisation energy	have higher melting temperatures
(D)	display one oxidation state	have larger atomic radius

Question 90
The most chemically reactive metals occur in Groups 1 and 2 of the Periodic Table. The reactivity of these metals with water

(A) increases down a group.
(B) decreases down a group.
(C) is approximately the same within a group.
(D) is not related to the position within a group.

Question 91
The chemical reactivity of a metal is often related to the historical period of its discovery. Metals with low reactivity are most likely to have been known

(A) since earliest times.
(B) since the discovery of chemical reduction reactions.
(C) since the discovery of electrolytic processes.
(D) since the discovery of nuclear reactions.

(4) **Bonding**

Question 92
Two elements, X and M react to form a covalently bonded molecule. It is most likely that

(A) the electronegativity of element X is much greater than that of element M.
(B) the electronegativity of element M is much greater than that of element X.
(C) both elements have high electronegativity, i.e. greater than 2.5.
(D) both elements have low electronegativity, i.e. less than 2.0.

Question 93
The electronegativities (on the Pauling scale) of four elements, Q, R, X and Z are given in the table below.

Element	Electronegativity
Q	2.58
R	2.20
X	3.98
Z	3.44

Which two covalent bonds will be the most polar?

(A) Q — R and X — Z
(B) Q — X and R — X
(C) Q — Z and R — Z
(D) X — X and Z — Z

Question 94
The bonding in ionic compounds is best explained as

(A) the sharing of two or more pairs of electrons.
(B) the attraction between oppositely charged ions.
(C) the formation of inert gas configuration by atoms.
(D) the attraction between two nuclei and a pair of electrons.

Question 95

An element has the electron configuration $1s^2 2s^2 2p^6 3s^2 3p^4$. When it reacts to form an ionic compound it is most likely that it will

(A) lose two electrons and form a 2+ cation.
(B) gain one electron and form a 1– anion.
(C) lose six electrons and form a 6+ cation.
(D) gain two electrons and form a 2– anion.

Question 96

The elements carbon, nitrogen, chlorine and manganese all form more than one oxide. For each element two of the oxides have the formulae XO and XO_2. These oxides are most likely to be *ionic* for

(A) carbon.
(B) nitrogen.
(C) chlorine.
(D) manganese.

Question 97

The best description of covalent bonding is that it results from

(A) complete transfer of one or more electrons from one atom to another.
(B) sharing of electrons by two atoms.
(C) the attraction between a cation and an anion.
(D) the reaction of a non-metal atom with a metal atom.

Question 98

The molecular formulae of four substances are given below. For which one would the structure contain only single bonds?

(A) CH_3PH_2 (B) C_2H_3N (C) CH_2O (D) N_2O_3

Question 99

Aluminium reacts with oxygen to form aluminium oxide. The electron configurations of the *ions* formed will be

	aluminium	oxide
(A)	$1s^2 2s^2 2p^6 3s^2 3p^6$	$1s^2 2s^2 2p^6$
(B)	$1s^2 2s^2 2p^6$	$1s^2 2s^2 2p^6$
(C)	$1s^2 2s^2 2p^6 3s^2 3p^1$	$1s^2 2s^2 2p^4$
(D)	$1s^2 2s^2 2p^6$	$1s^2 2s^2 2p^6 3s^2 3p^6$

Question 100

An ionic compound has the empirical formula MX_2. The elements that reacted to form this compound are most likely to be

(A) M = sodium and X = sulfur.
(B) M = calcium and X = fluorine.
(C) M = magnesium and X = oxygen.
(D) M = carbon and X = oxygen.

Question 101
The shape of a molecule is mostly determined by

(A) the size of the atoms attached to the central atom.
(B) the number of bonding pairs of electrons around the atom.
(C) the number of pairs of electrons in the valence shell.
(D) the difference in electronegativity between the atoms in the moleule.

Question 102
Which one of the following molecules has a triangular pyramid shape?

(A) CH_4 (B) NH_3 (C) CO_2 (D) H_2S

Question 103
Of the four molecules, C_2H_2, HCl, PCl_3 and N_2, the one with a different shape to the other three is

(A) C_2H_2 (B) HCl (C) PCl_3 (D) N_2

Question 104
Which of the covalent bonds shown below is the most polar?

(A) C–H (B) N–H (C) O–H (D) F–H

Question 105
Of the molecules CO_2, CH_4, CF_4 and PH_3 the polar molecule is

(A) CO_2 (B) CH_4 (C) CF_4 (D) PH_3

Question 106
A metal M has the electron configuration $1s^2 2s^2 2p^6 3s^2$ and reacts with a non-metal X with the electron configuration $1s^2 2s^2 2p^5$. The formula of the ionic compound formed in this reaction is

(A) MX (B) M_2X (C) MX_2 (D) M_2X_5

Question 107
A metal J has the electron configuration $1s^2 2s^2 2p^6 3s^2 3p^1$. The formulae of its oxide and chloride will be

(A) JO and JCl
(B) J_2O and JCl_2
(C) J_2O_3 and JCl_3
(D) J_3O_2 and J_3Cl

Question 108
The electron configuration of phosphorus is $1s^2 2s^2 2p^6 3s^2 3p^3$ and that of fluorine is $1s^2 2s^2 2p^5$. The formula of the compound that forms when phosphorus reacts with fluorine is expected to be

(A) PF_3 (B) P_3F (C) P_5F (D) P_3F_5

Question 109
The formulae of four substances are given below. For which one would the structure **not** contain a double covalent bond?

(A) CO_2 (B) SO_2 (C) CH_2O (D) CH_4O

Question 110
Which one of the following elements does **not** form double bonds?

(A) carbon
(B) nitrogen
(C) oxygen
(D) fluorine

Question 111
"Diamond, graphite and buckminsterfullerenes (buckyballs) are all ___________ of carbon?" The word or words missing from this sentence is/are

(A) allotropes
(B) giant structures
(C) isomers
(D) isotopes

Question 112
Graphite, carbon nanotubes and graphene are all forms of carbon. Which one of the following statements about their structures is correct?

(A) Only graphite is able to conduct electricity.
(B) All of the carbon atoms are in flat layers, i.e. flat planes.
(C) In these materials each carbon atom forms a covalent bond to three other carbon atoms.
(D) Some of the carbon atoms form double bonds to other carbon atoms.

Question 113
Diamond, graphite, and buckyballs are all forms of carbon. For these materials the number of carbon atoms each carbon atom is bonded to is

	Diamond	Graphite	Buckyballs
(A)	3	3	3
(B)	4	3	3
(C)	4	3	4
(D)	4	4	4

Question 114
Graphite is a good conductor of electricity and is used in electric motors. The conduction of electricity by graphite results from

(A) strong bonding between carbon atoms in only two dimensions.
(B) a mobile "sea of electrons" surrounding carbon ions.
(C) one electron from each carbon atom moving freely along layers.
(D) the ability of sheets of carbon atoms to slide over one another.

Question 115

A type of carbon molecule known as a buckyball is a sphere made up of carbon atoms chemically bonded together in hexagons and pentagons so its appearance resembles that of a soccer ball.

Which one of the following diagrams demonstrates the most likely chemical bonding in the buckyball.

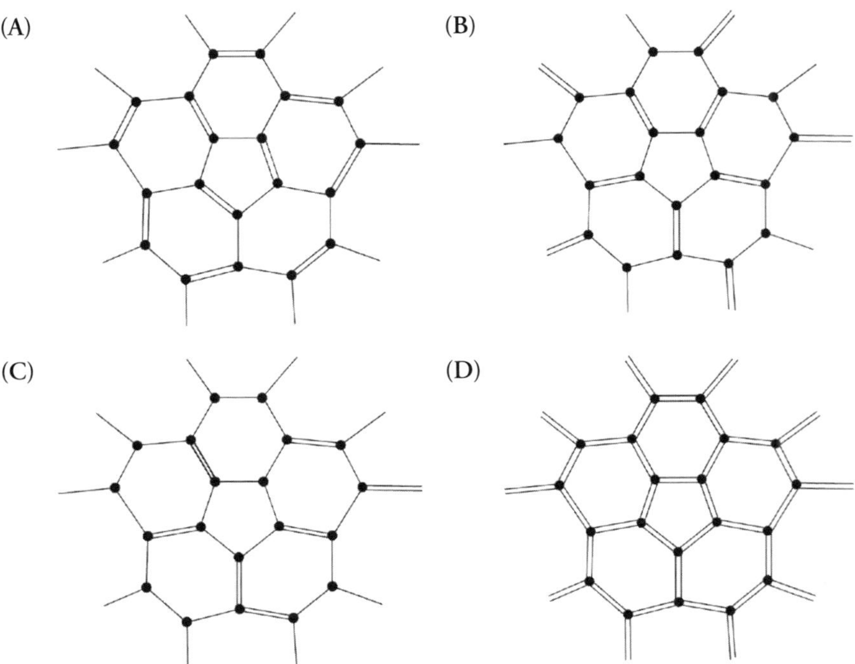

The following information refers to Questions 116 to 119.

Four statements about the structural features of metals are given below.

I In metals the particles are strongly attracted to one another.
II The particles are tightly packed together in a metal.
III Charged particles that are free to move are present in metals.
IV In metals the attractive forces between the particles are able to adjust when the particles are moved.

Question 116
Which one of the above statements is best able to explain why metals are malleable and ductile?

(A) I (B) II (C) III (D) IV

Question 117
Which one of the statements on the previous page is best able to explain why metals are good conductors of electricity?

(A) I (B) II (C) III (D) IV

Question 118
Which one of the statements on the previous page is best able to explain why most metals have high melting and boiling temperatures?

(A) I (B) II (C) III (D) IV

Question 119
Which one of the statements on the previous page is best able to explain why many metals have high densities?

(A) I (B) II (C) III (D) IV

Question 120
Which one of the substances below does not form a covalent network lattice?

(A) Na_2CO_3 (B) Si
(C) C(diamond) (D) CSi

Question 121
The molecules CH_3F, CH_3Cl, CH_3Br and CH_3I have similar dipoles. Which one of these molecules is expected to have the lowest boiling temperature?

(A) CH_3F (B) CH_3Cl (C) CH_3Br (D) CH_3I

Question 122
Which one of the following statements best describes molecular substances?

(A) They are always compounds.
(B) Molecular substances have low melting points.
(C) All molecular substances are gases at room temperature.
(D) Some molecular substances conduct electricity.

Question 123
Four molecular substances are oxygen, O_2, propane, C_3H_8, hydrogen fluoride, HF and butan-1-ol, $CH_3CH_2CH_2CH_2OH$. The most likely order of **decreasing** solubility in water of the compounds listed above is

(A) butan-1-ol, hydrogen fluoride, propane, oxygen.
(B) hydrogen fluoride, butan-1-ol, propane, oxygen.
(C) propane, oxygen, butan-1-ol, hydrogen fluoride.
(D) oxygen, hydrogen fluoride, butan-1-ol, propane.

Question 124
The boiling temperature of methanol, CH_3OH, is 65°C, whereas that of ethanol, CH_3CH_2OH, is 78°C. The reason for the higher boiling temperature of ethanol is an increase in the strength of

(A) the dispersion forces in ethanol.
(B) the hydrogen bonding in ethanol.
(C) the dipole–dipole attractions in ethanol.
(D) the dispersion forces and the hydrogen bonding in ethanol.

Question 125
The structural formulae of four substances are shown below. Which one would be expected to have hydrogen bonding between its molecules?

(A) $H_2C{=}O$ (H, H, C=O)

(B) H—C(H)(H)—O—C(H)(H)—H

(C) H—C(H)(H)—N(H)—H

(D) H_2CF_2 (H, H, C, F, F)

Question 126
Some of the properties of ionic compounds are given below.

I Ionic compounds are usually hard and brittle.
II Ionic compounds have high melting and boiling temperatures.
III When solid, ionic compounds do not conduct electricity.
IV When molten or in aqueous solution, ionic compounds will conduct electricity.

Which of the above properties of ionic compounds can be explained by strong attractive forces between particles?

(A) I and II
(B) II and III
(C) III and IV
(D) I and IV

Question 127
Ionic salts at room temperature are

(A) liquids with positively and negatively charged ions free to move.
(B) solids in which the positively and negatively charged ions are grouped together in pairs.
(C) liquids in which the positively and negatively charged ions are randomly arranged.
(D) solids with alternate positively and negatively charged ions fixed in place in a giant lattice.

Question 128
Molecular substances have atoms joined together by covalent bonding and might be expected to

(A) conduct electricity in the liquid state but not when solid.
(B) be malleable and ductile.
(C) sometimes have low melting and boiling temperatures.
(D) be good thermal conductors.

Question 129
Which one of the following processes will require the most energy?

(A) $2H_2O(l) \rightarrow 2H_2O(g)$
(B) $2H_2O(s) \rightarrow 2H_2O(g)$
(C) $2H_2O(s) \rightarrow 2H_2O(l)$
(D) $2H_2O(l) \rightarrow 2H_2(g) + O_2(g)$

Extended Response Questions

(1) Properties of Matter

Question 1
Some of the properties of zinc, iodine and zinc iodide are given in the table below.

Property	Zinc	Iodine	Zinc iodide
State at 25°C	solid	solid	solid
colour	grey	violet	white
melting temperature (°C)	420	114	446
boiling temperature (°C)	907	184	624
density (g mL^{-1})	7.14	4.9	4.7

Use this information to explain why zinc iodide is said to be a compound and not a mixture of zinc and iodine. (Total = 3 marks)

Question 2
The boiling temperatures of five liquids are given in the table below.

methanol	ethanol	propanol	butanol	pentanol
64.7°C	78.3°C	97.2°C	117.7°C	138.0°C

A mixture consisting of *three* of these liquids is placed in a flask and heated until it boils. The mixture is separated by fractional distillation and two fractions are collected. The boiling temperature when the second fraction is collected is 117.7°C.

(a) Describe the principles of fractional distillation. (2 marks)

(b) Identify the liquid remaining in the flask. Give an explanation of your answer. (2 marks)

(c) What comment can be made about the nature of the first fraction? (1 mark)

(Total = 5 marks)

Question 3
Table salt (sodium chloride, NaCl) and sugar (sucrose, $C_{12}H_{22}O_{11}$) are both soluble in water. The solubility of each material at different temperatures is given in the table

below. The values are grams of solute that dissolve in 100 g of water at the specified temperature.

Temperature (°C)	**0**	**20**	**40**	**60**	**80**
mass of table salt (g)	35.7	36.0	36.5	37.3	38.1
mass of sugar (g)	179	204	238	287	362

A mixture consists of 50.0 g of table salt and 50.0 g of sugar. Water is added to the mixture and is heated to 80°C.

(a) Calculate the mass of water at 80°C that would just dissolve all of the sugar from this mixture? (1 mark)

(b) Using your answer from part (a) calculate the mass of table salt that also dissolves at this temperature. (1 mark)

(c) Calculate the mass of table salt is **not** dissolved at 80°C? (1 mark)

The mixture is filtered at 80°C to remove the undissolved table salt and the solution is cooled to 0°C.

(d) Calculate the mass of sugar will crystallize from the solution at 0°C? (1 mark)

(e) Calculate the mass of table salt will remain in the solution at 0°C? (1 mark)

(Total = 5 marks)

Question 4

A student determines the percentage of water in hydrated sodium carbonate, $Na_2CO_3.10H_2O$, in the following manner. He weighs an empty crucible and weighs it again with some of the sodium carbonate. He heats the crucible and contents strongly for 10 minutes, allows it to cool and reweighs the crucible and contents. He then repeats this procedure three more times. His results are tabulated below.

mass of crucible	56.38 g
mass of crucible + sodium carbonate before heating	65.00 g
mass of crucible + sodium carbonate after 1st heating	60.66 g
mass of crucible + sodium carbonate after 2nd heating	59.84 g
mass of crucible + sodium carbonate after 3rd heating	59.57 g
mass of crucible + sodium carbonate after 4th heating	59.57 g

(a) Deduce why the student repeated the procedure four times (1 mark)

(b) Calculate the percentage of water in the hydrated sodium carbonate. (3 marks)

(c) Describe what safety precautions the student should take before carrying out the experiment (2 marks)

(Total = 6 marks)

Question 5

Hydrated copper sulfate, $CuSO_4.5H_2O$ contains 36.1% water. 6.04 g of a mixture of hydrated copper sulfate and sodium chloride, NaCl, is heated so that all of the water is removed. The final mass of the solid is 4.77 g. Calculate the masses of the two materials in the original mixture. (Total = 3 marks)

Question 6

Define the terms (i) element, (ii) compound and (iii) mixture. (Total = 3 marks)

Question 7

Use the physical separation techniques in the following list to identify a method which could be used to separate each of the mixtures in the table.

Centrifuging, Cryogenics, Crystallisation, Distillation, Evaporation, Filtration, Froth Flotation, Magnetism, Sedimentation, Separating funnel, Sieving

Mixture	Separation Method
Liquid Air	
Coffee grounds in water	
Blood cells in plasma	
Gold particles in crushed rock	
Lumps in flour	
Useful metal ores from worthless rock	
Dissolved salts from water	
Liquids with different boiling points	
Vegetable oil and water	
Magnetic and non magnetic substances	

(Total = 5 marks)

Question 8

Describe as a series of steps how a mixture of iron filings, gold particles, salt and naphthalene ("moth balls") could be treated to obtain a separate sample of each. Justify each step in your method. (Total = 8 marks)

Question 9

Identify the correct formulae for the following compounds.

(a) chromium(III) oxide
(b) potassium nitrate
(c) magnesium carbonate
(d) mercury(II) chloride
(e) aluminium hydroxide
(f) lithium phosphate
(g) sodium hydrogen carbonate
(h) calcium fluoride
(i) barium nitride
(j) iron(II) sulfate

(Total = 5 marks)

Question 10

For the following formulae give the correct name.

(a) $LiBr$
(b) $Al_2(SO_4)_3$
(c) PbS
(d) $CrBr_3$
(e) $Zn(NO_3)_2$
(f) K_2O
(g) $Ni(OH)_2$
(h) $Cu_3(PO_4)_2$
(i) $FeCl_3$
(j) AgI

(Total = 5 marks)

Question 11

Three elements, X, Y and Z have the following physical properties.

Property	Element X	Element Y	Element Z
melting temperature (°C)	2300	39	1495
boiling temperature (°C)	3660	686	2870
electrical conductivity ($MS\ m^{-1}$)	10^{-10}	7.6	16
thermal conductivity ($J\ s^{-1}\ m^{-1}\ K^{-1}$)	27	58	100
density ($g\ mL^{-1}$)	2.34	1.53	8.90

Classify these elements as either a main group metal or a transition metal or a non-metal. Give reasons for your answers. (5 marks)

Question 12

(a) Give three properties of non-metals that distinguish them from metals. (3 marks)

(b) Identify an example of a non-metal that is

(i) a gas (ii) a liquid (iii) a solid

at room temperature and pressure. (3 marks)

(Total = 3 + 3 = 6 marks)

Question 13

The thermal and electrical conductivities of some elements are given in the table below. Use this information to distinguish the elements as either a metal, a semi-metal or a non-metal.

Element	Thermal conductivity ($J\ s^{-1}\ m^{-1}\ K^{-1}$)	Electrical conductivity ($MS\ m^{-1}$)	Metal, semi-metal, non-metal
bromine	0.12	10^{-16}	
chromium	94	7.9	
germanium	60	10^{-4}	
iodine	0.45	10^{-13}	
indium	82	12	
nickel	91	14	
osmium	88	11	
phosphorus	0.24	10^{-15}	
tellurium	3	10^{-4}	
titanium	22	2.3	

(Total = 5 marks)

Question 14

(a) In the second period of the Periodic Table identify those elements that are solids at room temperature and good conductors of heat and electricity. (3 marks)

(b) In the third period of the table identify an element that is

(i) a solid at room temperature and a non-metal (1 mark)

(ii) a gas at room temperature and a non-metal (1 mark)

(c) In the group of elements known as the 'alkali metals' identify the element that is the most reactive and the one that is the least reactive. (2 marks)
(Total = 7 marks)

(2) Atomic Structure and Atomic Mass

Question 15
Define the following terms.

(a) atomic number
(b) mass number
(c) isotopes (Total = 2 + 2 + 2 = 6 marks)

Question 16
(a) The number of protons, neutrons and electrons for six species, I, II, III, IV, V and VI are given in the table below. For each species identify whether it is a neutral atom, a cation or an anion.

Species	Protons	Neutrons	Electrons	Neutral atom, cation, anion
I	12	12	12	
II	10	12	10	
III	9	10	10	
IV	12	14	10	
V	14	14	14	
VI	13	14	10	

(3 marks)

(b) Which species from part (a) are isotopes? (1 mark)
(c) Give the correct symbol for species VI. (1 mark)
(Total = 5 marks)

Question 17
For the following atoms, write their electron configurations and also identify how many neutrons are present.

(a) $^{21}_{10}Ne$ (b) $^{17}_{8}O$ (c) $^{27}_{12}Mg$ (d) $^{30}_{14}Si$ (e) $^{40}_{19}K$
(Total = 5 marks)

Question 18
(a) Complete the following table.

	Number of protons	Number of neutrons	Electron configuration
$^{7}_{4}Be$			
$^{14}_{7}N$			
$^{37}_{17}Cl$			
$^{33}_{15}P$			

(8 marks)

Question 19

When an electrical discharge is passed through a sample of hydrogen a pink glow is produced. If this light is passed through a prism, the light is separated into four lines of different colours. The wavelength of each line and its associated energy are shown in the diagram below and in Table 1.

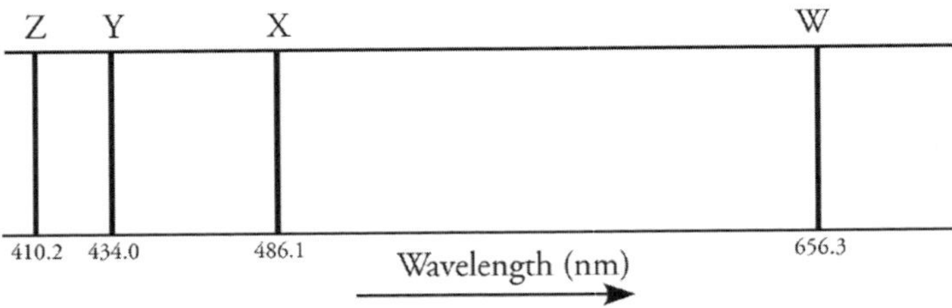

Table 1

Line	Wavelength (nm)	Energy (kJ mol^{-1})
W	656.3	182.4
X	486.1	246.1
Y	434.0	276.0
Z	410.2	291.4

(a) What name is given to this type of spectrum? (1 mark)

The first six energy levels available to an electron on a hydrogen atom are shown on the diagram at the right. The energy of each of these levels is shown in Table 2 below.

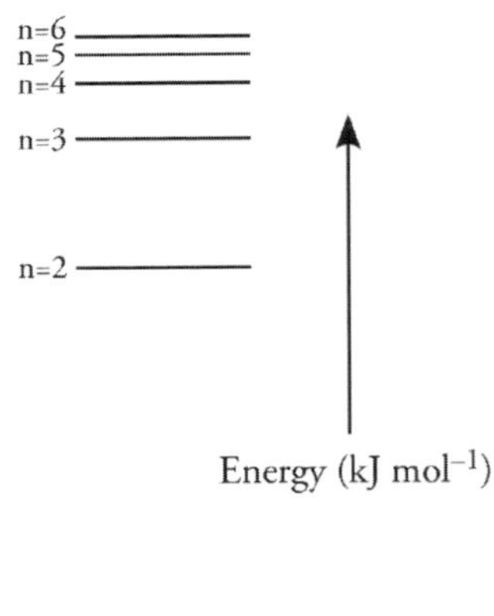

Table 2

Energy level (n)	Energy (kJ mol^{-1})
1	–1313.2
2	–328.1
3	–145.7
4	–82.0
5	–52.1
6	–36.7

(b) When a hydrogen atom is in its ground state, which energy level does the electron occupy? (1 mark)

(c) Assuming that the hydrogen electrons start in the ground state, explain what happens to the electrons to produce the above spectrum. (2 marks)

(d) Use the information in Tables 1 and 2 to decide the electron movements (jumps) that have occurred to produce each line in the spectrum. (3 marks)

(e) Which electron movement (jump) will produce a line of highest energy? (1 mark)

(Total = 8 marks)

Question 20

Lithium, sodium and potassium have similar outer shell electron configuration yet produce different colours in a flame test. Lithium gives a red colour, sodium produces a yellow flame and potassium produces a lilac (pale violet) colour.

(a) State the outer shell electron configuration for each of these elements. (3 marks)

(b) Explain why these elements produce different colours in a flame test. (3 marks)

(Total = 6 marks)

Question 21

The relative atomic mass of lead can vary depending on the source of the element. This occurs because the three heavier stable isotopes of lead are the end products from the decay of radioactive materials, for example ^{238}U eventually decays to ^{206}Pb, ^{235}U decays to ^{207}Pb and ^{232}Th decays to ^{208}Pb. A sample of lead from a particular source was analysed using a mass spectrometer and the results are given in the table below.

Isotope	Relative Isotopic Mass	% Abundance
^{204}Pb	203.973	1.4
^{206}Pb	205.975	28.3
^{207}Pb	206.976	26.3
^{208}Pb	207.977	44.0

(a) Calculate the relative atomic mass of the lead from this particular source. (2 marks)

(b) The accepted value for the relative atomic mass of lead is 207.2. Comment on the difference between this value and your answer from part (a). (2 marks)

(Total = 4 marks)

Question 22

For each of the scientists named below, briefly describe their contribution, if any, to the development of atomic theory in the areas shown.

	Rutherford	**Bohr**	**Schrödinger**	**Chadwick**
Nucleus				
Electron Shells				
Subshells				
Orbitals				

(Total = 16 x ½ = 8 marks)

Question 23

When high-energy sparks are passed through a sample of hydrogen, hydrogen atoms in an excited state are produced. The sample of hydrogen then emits light. If this light is passed through a prism, a series of discrete lines can be seen (an emission spectrum).

(a) What is meant by 'an excited state'? (1 mark)

(b) How does the electron configuration of an excited state differ from that of the ground state? (1 mark)

(c) How are the lines in the spectrum produced? (2 marks)

Use the first four shells of hydrogen (that is n = 1, 2, 3 and 4) to answer parts (d) and (e).

(d) How many lines would be expected in the emission spectrum of hydrogen? (2 marks)

(e) Which line would be expected to have the highest energy? (1 mark)

(Total = 7 marks)

Question 24

A sample of element X is placed in a tube and high energy sparks are passed through the tube. Some of the atoms in the sample now have the electron configuration $1s^2 2s^2 2p^3 4s^1$.

(a) What is the name and the chemical symbol of element X? (1 mark)

(b) If the electron configuration of the atoms mentioned above changed from $1s^2 2s^2 2p^3 4s^1$ to $1s^2 2s^2 2p^3 3s^1$, would the process release energy or absorb energy? Explain your reasoning. (2 marks)

(c) What is the electron configuration of the atoms of element X in their ground state? (1 mark)

(Total = 4 marks)

Question 25

Most common household smoke detectors contain very small amounts of the synthetic element americium, Am. Isotopes of this element were first produced in 1944. An equation for the production of americium–241 is shown below.

$$^{239}_{94}\text{Pu} + \text{X} \rightarrow \,^{240}_{94}\text{Pu} + \text{Y} \rightarrow \,^{241}_{94}\text{Pu} \rightarrow \,^{241}_{95}\text{Am} + \text{Z}$$

(a) Identify the particles represented by X, Y and Z (3 marks)

(b) In a smoke detector americium–241 slowly changes into neptunium–237. Write a balanced nuclear equation for this transformation. (2 marks)

(Total = 5 marks)

Question 26

The rarest naturally occurring element is astatine (At) with very small traces of ^{219}At being found in ores of uranium.

(a) Why are atoms of ^{219}At expected to be unstable? (1 mark)

(b) ^{219}At is thought to occur in the radioactive decay series starting with ^{235}U. Four alpha emissions and one beta emission are required to change ^{235}U into ^{219}At. If the isotope ^{227}Ac also occurs in this part of the decay series, suggest which other atoms might be present between ^{235}U and ^{219}At. (3 marks)

(Total = 4 marks)

Question 27

Naturally occurring thorium, ^{232}Th, is radioactive and decays to ^{208}Pb, which is stable, by six alpha emissions and four beta emissions.

(a) What types of nuclei are unstable? (2 marks)

(b) Write the nuclear equation that converts ^{232}Th into ^{228}Ra. (1 mark)

(c) ^{224}Ra is also part of the sequence mentioned above. Suggest the reactions that would convert ^{228}Ra into ^{224}Ra. (2 marks)

(d) Describe the process by which an unstable isotope such as ^{214}Pb undergoes radioactive decay to form ^{214}Bi. (1 mark)

(Total = 6 marks)

Question 28

^{15}O and ^{19}O are two radioactive isotopes of oxygen that decay by different processes.

(a) By what type of reaction will these two isotopes decay? (2 marks)

(b) Write the nuclear equations for the decay of these isotopes. (2 marks)

(Total = 4 marks)

Question 29

Radioisotopes are used extensively in medicine and industry. Write balanced nuclear equations for each of the following decay processes.

(a) β-Emission from $^{24}_{11}Na$

(b) Positron emission from $^{39}_{20}Ca$

(c) Electron capture from $^{103}_{46}Pd$

(d) β-Emission from $^{131}_{53}I$

(Total = 4 marks)

Question 30

An isotope of the element curium, $^{242}_{96}Cm$, can be produced in two ways. One method involves a two-step process starting from $^{241}_{95}Am$. The second process is a single step reaction starting from $^{239}_{94}Pu$. Write balanced nuclear equations for these two processes. (Total = 2 + 2 = 4 marks)

(3) Periodicity

Question 31

The elements of Group 17 (Group VII) are fluorine, chlorine, bromine and iodine. For each of the properties below, state how the property varies going down the group from F to I and give a reason for your answer.

(a) atomic radius (2 marks)

(b) reactivity (2 marks)

(c) electronegativity (2 marks)

(Total = 6 marks)

Question 32

Barium and calcium are in the same vertical group of the periodic table as magnesium.

(a) Explain why these three elements are in the same group. (1 mark)

(b) The electronegativity of barium (0.89) is lower than that of magnesium (1.31). Give an explanation for this difference. (2 marks)

(c) In terms of shells and subshells, give the electron configuration for a calcium atom. (1 mark)

(d) In terms of shells and subshells, describe how the electron configuration of a calcium ion, Ca^{2+}, will differ from that of a calcium atom. (1 mark)

(e) The radius of a magnesium atom is 160 pm (1.60×10^{-10} m) and the radius of a magnesium ion, Mg^{2+}, is 72 pm (0.72×10^{-10} m). Explain why the magnesium atom is significantly larger than the Mg^{2+} ion. (1 mark)

(Total = 6 marks)

Question 33

(a) Write the correct chemical symbols for the following elements by using the Periodic Table.

(i) The element that forms a –1 ion with the electron configuration $1s^22s^22p^6$. (1 mark)

(ii) the element from the second period that has the smallest atomic radius. (1 mark)

(iii) the element from Group 17 that has the largest electronegativity. (1 mark)

(iv) the element from the first transition series that has 7 electrons in the 3d subshell. (1 mark)

(v) the element whose excited state has the electron configuration $1s^22s^22p^53s^23p^43d^1$. (1 mark)

(b) Across the third period, from sodium to chlorine the electronegativity of the elements increases. Give an explanation of this observation. (2 marks)

(Total = 7 marks)

Question 34

(a) Two of the properties of elements are atomic radius and electronegativity. In the table below state how these two properties change when moving from sodium to chlorine across the third period. Give an explanation for your prediction.

Property	**Increases or decreases**	**Explanation for predicted trend**
Atomic radius		
Electronegativity		

(4 marks)

(b) Another property that changes across the third period is the first ionisation energy. This property also changes going down groups in the periodic table.

(i) Explain what is meant by the expression 'ionisation energy'?

(ii) The atomic radius of lithium is 152 pm while that of sodium is 186 pm. However the first ionisation of lithium is 526 kJ mol^{-1} and that of sodium is 502 kJ mol^{-1}. Give explanations for these observations.

(1 + 2 = 3 marks)

(Total = 7 marks)

(4) Bonding

Question 35

The electronegativities (Pauling scale) of four elements, J, L, M and Q, are given below.

J = 0.93 L = 3.16 M = 2.55 Q = 1.00

Which combination of elements is most likely result in the following types of bonding? Give an explanation for your answers.

(i) metallic bonding (ii) ionic bonding
(iii) polar covalent bonding (iv) pure covalent bonding (Total = 8 marks)

Question 36

The formulae of some oxides and fluorides of the elements of the third period are given in the table below.

Element	Na	Mg	Al	Si	P	S	Cl
oxide					P_2O_5		Cl_2O_7
fluoride	NaF			SiF_4		SF_6	ClF_5

(a) Use this information to deduce the formulae of the missing compounds. (4 marks)

(b) For each compound identify the type of bonding present. (2 marks)

(c) Using the electron configurations of the elements, explain the trend in these formulae. (2 marks)

(Total = 8 marks)

Question 37

When the following pairs of elements react together an ionic compound is formed. In each case give the balanced formula of the product and the electron configurations of the ions that are formed.

	Elements	Formula	Electron Configurations of the Ions Formed
(a)	lithium and phosphorus		
(b)	sodium and sulfur		
(c)	potassium and oxygen		
(d)	calcium and fluorine		
(e)	aluminium and chlorine		
(f)	magnesium and nitrogen		

(Total = 12 marks)

Question 38

For each of the compounds below determine the electrovalency of the cation.

(a) TiO_2 (b) $V(OH)_2$
(c) AuI (d) $Co(NO_3)_3$
(e) $InCl_3$ (f) $PdBr_2$
(g) $Ga_2(SO_4)_3$ (h) $SrCO_3$

(Total = 8 marks)

Question 39

Determine the covalency for each of the elements in the molecular compounds given below.

(a) SF_4 (b) NH_3 (c) PCl_5 (d) H_2SO_4

(Total = 4 marks)

Question 40

(a) Give the electron configuration for each of the following atoms

(i) aluminium (ii) calcium (iii) fluorine (iv) sulfur

(4 marks)

(b) Use electron dot (Lewis dot) diagrams to demonstrate how the electron configurations of the atoms change when the following reactions take place.

(i) aluminium + fluorine → aluminium fluoride
(ii) aluminium + sulfur → aluminium sulfide
(iii) calcium + fluorine → calcium fluoride
(iv) calcium + sulfur → calcium sulfide

(4 marks)
(Total = 8 marks)

Question 41

Draw valence structures for the following substances.

(a) HCN (b) H_2S (c) HNO_2
(d) CH_2O (e) SiF_4 (f) HCO_2H

(Total = 6 × 1 = 6 marks)

Question 42

For each of the following molecules describe its shape and decide whether it is polar or non-polar.

	Molecule	Shape	Polar/non-polar
(a)	F_2		
(b)	CH_2O		
(c)	CCl_4		
(d)	HCN		
(e)	BF_3		

(Total = 5 × 2 = 10 marks)

Question 43

Using only the elements hydrogen, carbon, nitrogen, oxygen and fluorine draw valence structures for the following types of molecules.

(a) A linear molecule containing four atoms (1 mark)
(b) A planar molecule containing six atoms (1 mark)
(c) A pyramidal molecule (1 mark)
(d) A tetrahedral molecule (1 mark)

(Total = 4 marks)

Question 44

Draw the structural formula for each of the substances on the next page. Show any electron pairs (lone pairs) that **are** not used to form covalent bonds.

(a)	HCN	(b)	H_2S	(c)	HNO_2
(d)	CH_2O	(e)	SiF_4	(f)	HCO_2H

(Total = 6 marks)

Question 45

(a) In its compounds, nitrogen shows a wide range of covalencies. Complete the table below by giving the formula of the oxide of nitrogen corresponding to the covalency in the first column. (5 marks)

Nitrogen covalency	Formula of oxide
1	
2	
3	
4	
5	

(b) Which of the oxides in part (a) contain an unpaired electron?

(2 marks)
(Total = 7 marks)

Question 46

(a) Diamond and graphite are allotropes of carbon. Explain the meaning of the term 'allotrope'. (1 mark)

(b) Briefly describe the chemical bonding and structure in each of diamond and graphite. (2 marks)

(c) Explain how the chemical bonding in each substance accounts for the **properties** listed below.
   (i) Diamond is much harder than graphite.
   (ii) Graphite is a good conductor of electricity but diamond is not.
   (iii) Diamond has a higher density than graphite.

(3 marks)

(d) Explain how the properties of each substance accounts for the **uses** listed below.

Diamonds are used for	(i)	cutting and drilling tools to drill, e.g. rock.
	(ii)	jewellery.
Graphite is used	(iii)	for 'grey lead' pencils.
	(iv)	as containers for high temperature work.
	(v)	as electrodes

(5 marks)
(Total = 11 marks)

Question 47

Carbon nanotubes are a recently discovered form of carbon. These materials are stiff and strong. They are good conductors of heat and electricity. How does the bonding in a carbon nanotube account for the observed properties? (3 marks)

Question 48

In 1985, the fullerene C_{60} was isolated for the first time. When the mass spectrum was measured the result shown on the next page was obtained.

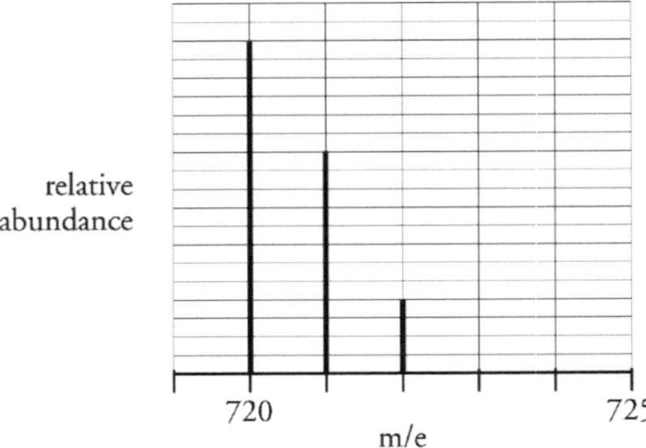

(a) If naturally occurring carbon consists only of ^{12}C and ^{13}C isotopes, account for the peaks in the spectrum. (3 marks)

(b) The areas of the three peaks are in the ratio 18:12:4, respectively. Use this information to calculate the percentage of ^{13}C in naturally occurring carbon. (3 marks)

(c) From other information the accepted value for the percentage of ^{13}C in naturally occurring carbon is 1.11%. Suggest a reason why your answer to part (b) differs from this value. (2 marks)

(Total = 8 marks)

Question 49

Four substances, A, B, C and D have the properties given in the table below. Identify them as either covalent network, ionic, metallic or covalent molecular materials.

A	Hard, high melting temperature, brittle, crystalline, only conducts electricity when in solution or molten.
B	Solid which sublimes at a moderate temperature, non conductor of electricity, insoluble in water.
C	Hard, very high melting temperature, crystalline, non conductor, insoluble in water.
D	Fairly hard, high melting temperature, malleable, solid conducts electricity, insoluble in water.

(Total = 4 marks)

Question 50

The melting and boiling temperatures of sodium, chlorine and sodium chloride are given in the table below.

	Melting temperature (°C)	Boiling temperature (°C)
sodium	98	883
chlorine (Cl_2)	–101	–34
sodium chloride	801	1465

(a) Describe the nature of the bonding in solid sodium, solid chlorine and solid sodium chloride. (2 marks)

(b) In terms of the bonding described in part (a), explain the difference between the melting temperatures of chlorine and sodium chloride. (2 marks)

(Total = 4 marks)

Question 51

The melting temperature of sodium fluoride, NaF is 992°C, while that of magnesium oxide, MgO is 2800°C.

(a) Write the formulae of the ions present in
 (i) sodium fluoride
 (ii) magnesium oxide. (2 marks)

(b) Write the electron configuration for the ions in part (a). (1 mark)

(c) Explain why the melting temperature of magnesium oxide is so much higher than that of sodium fluoride. (2 marks)

(Total = 5 marks)

Question 52

Potassium (K) has an atomic number of 19. It is a solid at room temperature and is easily cut with a knife. Chromium (Cr) has an atomic number of 24, is also a solid at room temperature but is a hard substance.

(a) Give the electron configuration of potassium and of chromium. (2 marks)

(b) Describe the bonding expected in potassium and chromium. (2 marks)

(c) Compare the properties of potassium and chromium. Propose
 (i) two properties that they have in common (2 marks)
 (ii) two ways in which potassium and chromium will be different. (2 marks)

(Total = 8 marks)

Question 53

Methyl chloride, methyl bromide and methyl iodide are polar molecules with approximately the same dipole. The boiling temperatures of the three halomethanes are given below.

Compound	Boiling temperature (°C)
methyl chloride, CH_3Cl	–24.2
methyl bromide, CH_3Br	3.6
methyl iodide, CH_3I	42.4

(a) Calculate the number of electrons in each molecule. (3 marks)

(b) Give an explanation for the variation in the boiling temperatures of the three compounds. (2 marks)

(Total = 5 marks)

Question 54

The table below contains the boiling temperatures and relative masses of three compounds, propane, C_3H_8, dimethyl ether, CH_3OCH_3, and ethanol, CH_3CH_2OH.

Compound	Boiling temperature (°C)	Relative mass
propane	–42	44.1
dimethyl ether	–23	46.1
ethanol	+78	46.1

(a) Draw the structural formulae of the three compounds. (3 marks)

(b) How are dimethyl ether and ethanol related? (1 mark)

(c) How many electrons are present in a molecule of each compound? (1 mark)

(d) How would you expect the size of the dispersion forces to vary between the three compounds? (2 marks)

(e) Why is the boiling temperature of dimethyl ether higher than that of propane but lower than that of ethanol? (3 marks)

(Total = 10 marks)

Question 55

Magnesium chloride, $MgCl_2$, conducts electricity when in an aqueous solution or when molten but does not conduct when it is solid. Use your knowledge of ionic bonding to explain these observations. (3 marks)

Question 56

When water is converted into steam a physical change occurs. However, when an electric current is passed through water hydrogen and oxygen are formed and a chemical change occurs. Describe what happens to the intermolecular and intramolecular bonding of water when these two changes take place and thus explain the difference between physical and chemical change. (4 marks)

Test: Properties of Matter and Atomic Structure

Multiple Choice Items

Question 1

A mixture of petrol and water could be separated by

(A) distillation.
(B) using a separating funnel.
(C) igniting the petrol.
(D) sedimentation.

Question 2

Some of the properties of four elements, L, M, Q and R are shown in the table below.

Property	L	M	Q	R
melting point (°C)	44	217	232	450
boiling point (°C)	280	685	2602	990
electrical conductivity ($MS\ m^{-1}$)	10^{-15}	10^{-4}	8.7	10^{-4}
thermal conductivity ($J\ s^{-1}\ m^{-1}\ K^{-1}$)	0.24	3	67	3
density ($g\ mL^{-1}$)	1.82	4.80	7.30	6.24

Which element is most likely to be malleable and ductile?

(A) Element L
(B) Element M
(C) Element Q
(D) Element R

Question 3
A student wishes to determine the percentage of water in a sample of hydrated nickel sulfate, $NiSO_4.6H_2O$. He heats 5.34 g of the hydrated salt to remove all of the water. 3.14 g of $NiSO_4$ remains. From these results he calculates the percentage of water in the hydrated nickel sulfate to be

(A) 2.20% (B) 41.2% (C) 58.8% (D) 70.1%

Question 4
Which one of the following lists contains only correct formulae?

(A) $Li(NO_3)_2$, $MgBr_2$, Al_2O_3, $PbSO_4$
(B) $Ca(NO_3)_2$, $Zn_3(PO_4)_2$, $FeCl_3$, AgO
(C) $BaSO_4$, K_2O, $AlCl_3$, $(NH_4)_3PO_4$
(D) SnS, $Cr_2(SO_4)_3$, $CuBr_3$, $NaCO_3$

Question 5
The mass number of an atom is defined as the

(A) total number of neutrons and protons in an atom.
(B) number of protons in an atom.
(C) total mass of the neutrons and protons in the atom.
(D) number of neutrons in an atom.

Question 6
An atom of copper has 29 protons and 35 neutrons. The correct symbol for this atom is

(A) $^{35}_{29}Cu$ (B) $^{64}_{29}Cu$ (C) $^{29}_{64}Cu$ (D) $^{64}_{35}Cu$

Question 7
Which one of the following species has a different number of electrons from the other three?

(A) $_{12}Mg^{2+}$ (B) $_{16}S^{2-}$ (C) $_{21}Sc^{3+}$ (D) $_{19}K^{+}$

Question 8
Which one of the following species has the largest number of neutrons?

(A) $^{55}_{25}Mn$ (B) $^{58}_{26}Fe$ (C) $^{58}_{27}Co$ (D) $^{59}_{28}Ni$

Question 9
The metal calcium forms the Ca^{2+} ion. The electron configuration of this ion is

(A) $1s^22s^22p^6$
(B) $1s^22s^22p^63s^23p^64s^2$
(C) $1s^22s^22p^63s^23p^63d^2$
(D) $1s^22s^22p^63s^23p^6$

Question 10
In which one of the sets on the next page will all of the nuclei be radioactive?

(A) $^{3}_{1}H$ $^{12}_{6}C$ $^{238}_{92}U$
(B) $^{16}_{8}O$ $^{40}_{19}K$ $^{11}_{6}C$
(C) $^{65}_{30}Zn$ $^{18}_{8}O$ $^{24}_{12}Mg$
(D) $^{14}_{6}C$ $^{239}_{94}Pu$ $^{60}_{27}Co$

Question 11
Which one of the species given below is not iso-electronic with the others?

(A) $^{32}S^{2-}$ (B) ^{40}Ar (C) ^{40}K (D) $^{40}Ca^{2+}$

Question 12
Which one of the following transitions could **not** contribute to the emission spectrum of an excited magnesium atom?

(A) An electron in a 4s orbital moves to a 3p orbital.
(B) An electron in a 3s orbital moves to a 4p orbital.
(C) An electron in a 5p orbital moves to a 4s orbital.
(D) An electron in a 5d orbital moves to a 3p orbital.

Extended Response Questions

Question 1
The atomic number of iron is 26.

(a) Using the s, p, d notation give the electron configuration of an iron atom in its ground state. (1 mark)

(b) Explain why iron is classified as a transition metal. (1 mark)

(c) In many compounds iron is often present as a 3+ cation. Give the electron configuration of Fe^{3+}. (1 mark)

(Total = 3 marks)

Question 2
When an electric discharge (electrical energy) is passed through a sample of hydrogen atoms light is emitted. When this light is passed through a prism, a series of lines of different energies is observed as shown below.

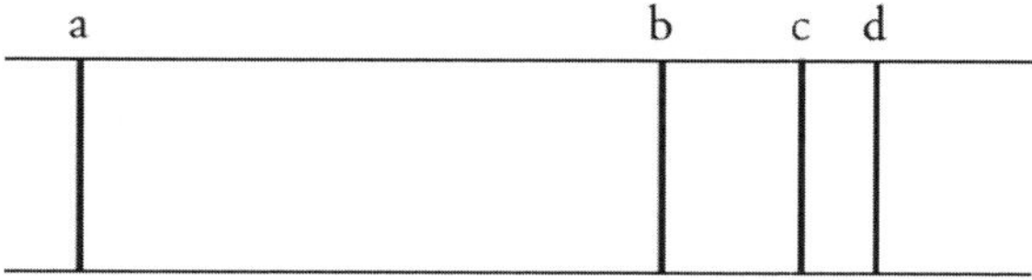

(a) Which of the lines has the highest energy? (1 mark)

(b) The diagram on the next page represents energy levels of the hydrogen atom. Select the most likely electron movement to explain each of the lines **a**, **b**, **c** and **d**. (4 marks)

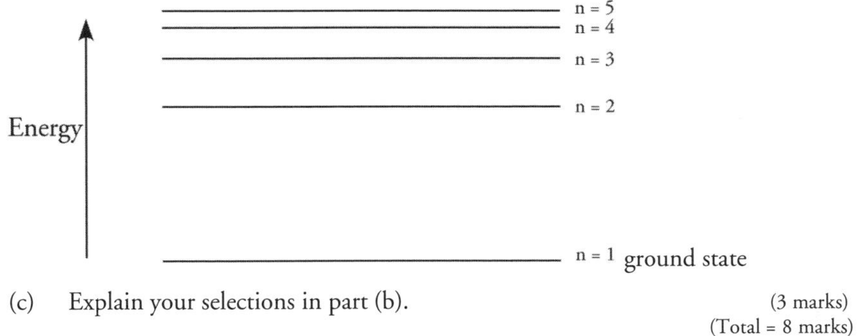

(c) Explain your selections in part (b). (3 marks)

(Total = 8 marks)

Question 3

Naturally occurring thallium consists of two isotopes, ^{203}Tl and ^{205}Tl. If the relative isotopic masses are 202.97 and 204.97, respectively, and the relative atomic mass of thallium is 204.38, calculate the percentage of each isotope present in naturally occurring thallium. (Total = 4 marks)

Question 4

Give the correct name for the following formulae.

(a) Cr_2O_3 (b) K_2SO_4 (c) CuCl (d) $BaCO_3$

(Total = 4 marks)

Question 5

Write balanced nuclear equations for the processes below.

(a) Electron capture by ^{18}F (b) Beta emission by ^{31}Si

(c) Positron emission by ^{26}Al (d) Alpha emission by ^{213}Bi

(Total = 4 marks)

(Total = 35 marks)

Test: Periodicity and Bonding

Multiple Choice Items

Question 1

Lithium and fluorine are both in Period 2. It is expected that fluorine would have the

(A) smaller radius and lower electronegativity.
(B) smaller radius and higher electronegativity.
(C) larger radius and lower electronegativity.
(D) larger radius and higher electronegativity.

Question 2
When a metal reacts with a non-metal to produce an ionic compound the atoms of the metal

(A) lose electrons to form positively charged cations.
(B) gain electrons to form positively charged cations.
(C) lose electrons to form negatively charged anions.
(D) gain electrons to form negatively charged anions.

The following information refers to Questions 3 and 4.

The graphs below show the first six ionisation energies for four *different* elements.

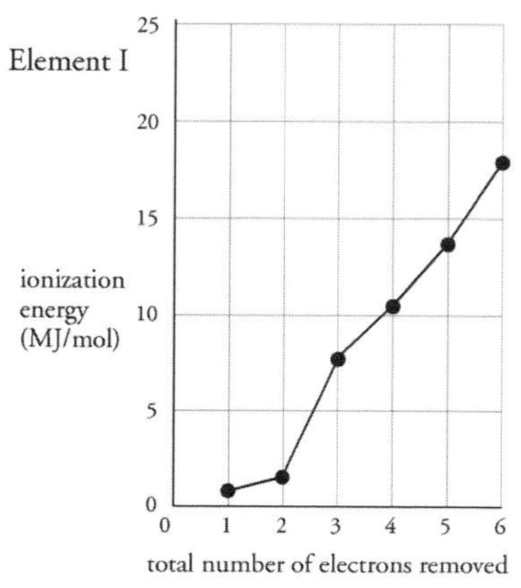

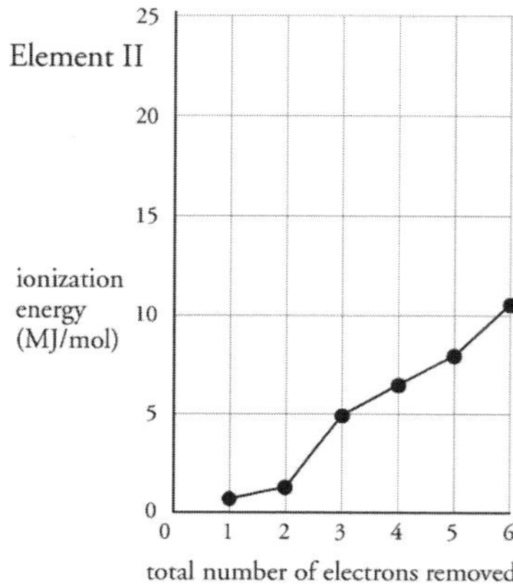

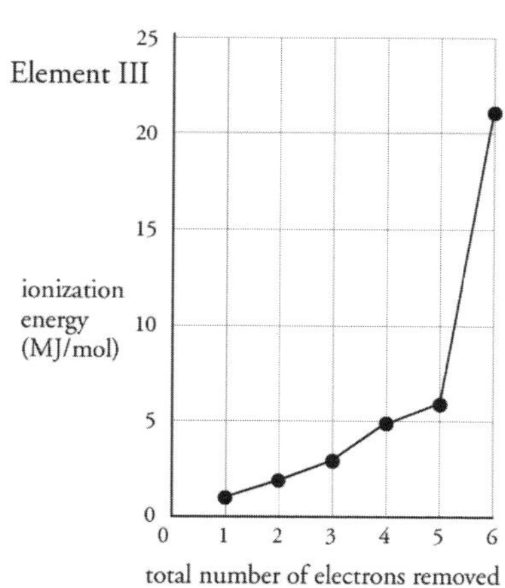

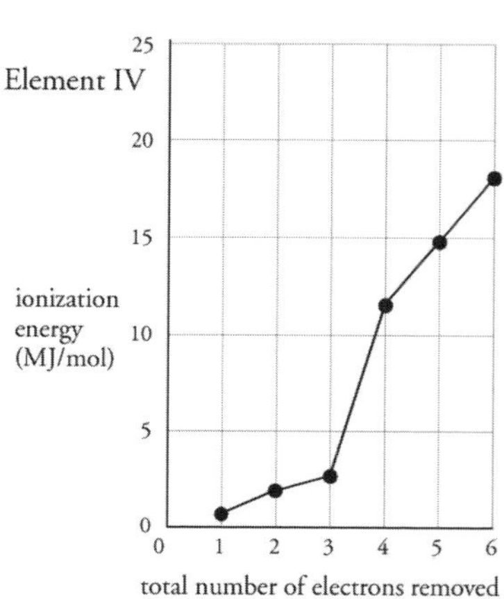

Question 3
Which of these elements is from Group 3 of the Periodic Table?

(A) Element I
(B) Element II
(C) Element III
(D) Element IV

Question 4
Which two elements are in the same Group in the Periodic Table?

(A) I and II
(B) I and IV
(C) II and III
(D) III and IV

Question 5
Which of the species below has the largest radius?

A. K^+ B. Cl^- C. S^{2-} D. Ca^{2+}

Question 6
The electron configurations of four elements are given below.

I $1s^2 2s^2 2p^4$
II $1s^2 2s^2 2p^5$
III $1s^2 2s^2 2p^6 3s^1$
IV $1s^2 2s^2 2p^6 3s^2$

Which element is most likely to react with chlorine to form an ionic compound with the formula XCl_2 (X = element I, II, III or IV)?

(A) I (B) II (C) III (D) IV

Question 7
The number of covalent bonds formed by a nitrogen atom, which has the electron configuration $1s^2 2s^2 2p^3$, is usually

(A) 2 (B) 3 (C) 4 (D) 5

Question 8
Of the molecules CO_2, CH_4, NH_3, H_2O, BF_3 and H_2S, the two with the same shape are

(A) CO_2 and H_2O (B) H_2O and H_2S
(C) CH_4, and NH_3 (D) BF_3 and NH_3

Question 9
The bonding in metals is best explained as attraction between

(A) oppositely charged ions.
(B) a proton and an electron.
(C) two nuclei and a pair of electrons.
(D) positive ions in a sea (cloud) of electrons.

Question 10
Diamond has very high melting and boiling temperatures, whereas methane, CH_4, has very low melting and boiling temperatures. This difference is best explained because

(A) there are more bonds to each carbon atom in diamond.
(B) the bonds to each carbon atom are much stronger in diamond.
(C) methane exists as small molecules and there is only weak bonding between the molecules.
(D) the bonding between the molecules in diamond is strong.

Question 11
Carbon dioxide is a non-polar molecule. The reason for this is that

(A) carbon and oxygen have the same electronegativity.
(B) bonding electrons are equally shared between carbon and oxygen atoms.
(C) the covalent bonds between carbon and oxygen atoms are double bonds.
(D) the carbon dioxide molecule is linear.

Question 12
Ionic compounds do not conduct electricity in the solid state but are good conductors when molten. Which one of the following statements best explains these observations?

(A) There are no charged particles in the solid ionic compounds but heating produces ions.
(B) Charged particles are present but are only free to move in the melt.
(C) Heating produces electrons which can move through the melt.
(D) Heating makes electrons more mobile.

Question 13
Which one of the compounds below is expected to have the highest boiling temperature?

(A) $CH_3CH_2CH_2CH_3$
(B) $CH_3CH_2CH_2NH_2$
(C) $CH_3CH_2NHCH_3$
(D) $(CH_3)_3N$

Question 14
Two elements, X and Z have the following electronegativities, X = 3.16 and Z = 2.05. The bond formed between atoms of X and Z is most likely to be

(A) a polar covalent bond.
(B) a pure covalent bond.
(C) a metallic bond.
(D) an ionic bond.

Question 15
Which one of the molecules below is expected to be the least polar?

(A) CH_3F (B) CH_3Cl (C) CH_3Br (D) CH_3I

Extended Response Questions

Question 1
Explain what is meant by each of the following terms.

(a) electronegativity (2 marks)
(b) core charge (2 marks)
(c) first ionisation energy (2 marks)
(Total = 6 marks)

Question 2

Draw electron dot (Lewis dot) diagrams for the following substances.

(a)	PH_3	(b)	CF_4	(c)	N_2H_4
(d)	Cl_2O	(e)	C_2H_6	(f)	NH_2OH

(Total = 6 marks)

Question 3

Silicon and carbon are both in Group 4 and hence the elements have similar properties. However at room temperature silicon dioxide, SiO_2, is a hard solid whereas carbon dioxide, CO_2, is a gas. Explain these observations by referring to the structures of SiO_2 and CO_2. (4 marks)

Question 4

Carbon and fluorine form the molecule carbon tetrafluoride (tetrafluoromethane), CF_4. There is a large difference in the electronegativity of carbon and fluorine but carbon tetrafluoride is a non-polar molecule. Explain this observation. (2 marks)

Question 5

(a) Methane and water are both small molecules. However at room temperature methane is a gas but water is a liquid. Also methane has very low solubility in water. Suggest reasons for these differences. (2 marks)

(b) Ammonia is also a small molecule but is very soluble in water. Give a reason for this observation. (1 mark)

(c) Iodine, I_2, has low solubility in water but will dissolve in hexane, C_6H_{14}. Give a reason for this observation. (1 mark)

(Total = 4 marks)

(Total = 37 marks)

Chapter 2

Introduction to Quantitative Chemistry

Multiple Choice Items

(1) Chemical Reactions and Stoichiometry

Question 1
Some students determined the mass of copper that could be obtained from a known mass of red copper oxide using the equipment shown below.

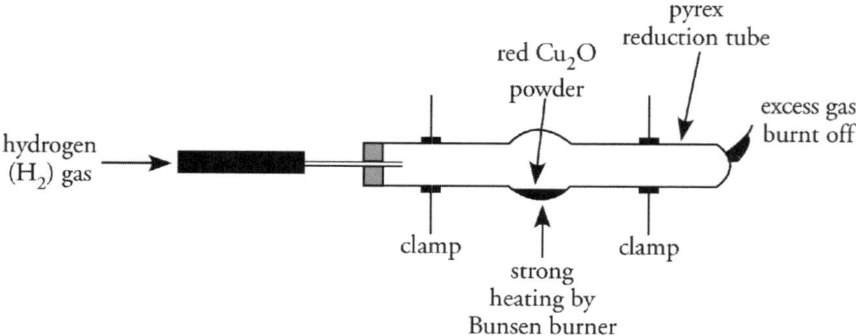

The equation for the reaction is

$Cu_2O(s) + H_2(g) \rightarrow 2Cu(s) + H_2O(g)$

If the mass of copper oxide used was 0.80 g, then it is expected that the mass of copper formed would be

(A) equal to the mass of copper oxide less the mass of water formed.
(B) equal to the mass of copper oxide plus the mass of hydrogen.
(C) less than the mass of copper oxide.
(D) the same as the mass of copper oxide.

Question 2
When methane, CH_4, is burnt the following reaction occurs

$CH_4(g) + 2O_2(g) \rightarrow CO_2(g) + 2H_2O(g)$

If the combustion of 1.6 g of methane produces 4.4 g of carbon dioxide and 3.6 g of water, then the mass of oxygen consumed in the reaction is closest to

(A) 3.2 g (B) 6.4 g (C) 8.0 g (D) 10.0 g

Question 3
Which one of the equations on the next page is **not** balanced?

(A) $C_3H_8(g) + 5O_2(g) \rightarrow 3CO_2(g) + 4H_2O(l)$
(B) $2Fe(s) + 2O_2(g) \rightarrow Fe_2O_3(s)$
(C) $N_2(g) + 3H_2(g) \rightarrow 2NH_3(g)$
(D) $4NH_3(g) + 5O_2(g) \rightarrow 4NO(g) + 6H_2O(l)$

Question 4
When copper reacts with concentrated nitric acid the following reaction occurs

$qCu(s) + wHNO_3(l) \rightarrow xCu(NO_3)_2 + yNO_2(g) + zH_2O(l)$

The coefficients in the balanced equation are

	q	w	x	y	z
(A)	1	2	1	2	1
(B)	1	3	1	1	1
(C)	2	4	2	2	2
(D)	1	4	1	2	2

Question 5
Stoichiometry refers to the relative quantities of reactants and products in chemical reactions. Some students were studying the reaction between hydrogen and oxygen.

$2H_2(g) + O_2(g) \rightarrow 2H_2O(l)$

Below are three comments made by the students about this reaction.

I The mass of hydrogen reacting depends upon the mass of oxygen used.
II The ratio mass of hydrogen : mass of oxygen is constant.
III The molecular ratio is 2 : 1 : 2.

Which of these statements refer to the stoichiometry of the above reaction?

(A) I, II and III (B) I and II (C) I and III (D) II and III

The following information refers to Questions 6 and 7.

A student weighs a test tube, adds some sodium hydrogen carbonate, $NaHCO_3$, and weighs it again. He then heats the test tube to drive off some gaseous substances until no further mass loss occurs. His results are given below.

Mass of test tube	15.16 g
Mass of test tube + $NaHCO_3$	20.79 g
Mass of test tube after heating	18.71 g

Question 6
The percentage mass loss is

(A) 10.0% (B) 11.1% (C) 36.9% (D) 63.1%

Question 7
The balanced equation for the reaction occurring in the heated test tube is most likely to be

(A) $NaHCO_3(s) \rightarrow NaOH(s) + CO_2(g)$
(B) $2NaHCO_3(s) \rightarrow Na_2O(s) + H_2O(l) + 2CO_2(g)$
(C) $2NaHCO_3(s) \rightarrow Na_2C_2O_4(s) + H_2(g) + O_2(g)$
(D) $2NaHCO_3(s) \rightarrow Na_2CO_3(s) + H_2O(l) + CO_2(g)$

(2) The Mole Concept

Question 8

Amounts of substance in chemistry are measured in moles. The mole is a measure of the

(A) concentration of particles.
(B) density of particles.
(C) volume of particles.
(D) number of particles.

Question 9

If the mass of an atom of ^{12}C is taken as 12 units exactly, then the atomic weight (relative atomic mass) of an element is defined as the

(A) mass of one atom of the element relative to an atom of ^{12}C.
(B) weighted mean of the relative masses of the isotopes of the element on the ^{12}C scale.
(C) mass of one mole of the element in grams.
(D) average mass of one mole of the isotopes of the element in grams.

Question 10

One mole is defined as

(A) the number of atoms in 12 g of carbon–12.
(B) 12 g of naturally occurring carbon.
(C) the number of atoms in 1.0 g of hydrogen.
(D) the mass of 6.02×10^{23} atoms of carbon–12.

Question 11

The molar mass of a substance is the

(A) sum of the relative atomic masses of the elements in the formula of the substance.
(B) ratio of the mass of 1 mole of the substance to 12 g of carbon–12.
(C) mass of one mole of the substance.
(D) mass of one molecule of the substance relative to the mass of one atom of ^{12}C take as 12 exactly.

Question 12

The Avogadro Constant is best defined as

(A) the number of atoms in exactly 12 g of carbon.
(B) the number of atoms in exactly 12 g of carbon–12.
(C) one mole of carbon–12.
(D) the mass of carbon–12 that contains one mole of atoms.

Question 13
Considering the following reaction

$$2CuSO_4(aq) + 4KI(aq) \rightarrow 2CuI(s) + I_2(s) + 2K_2SO_4(aq)$$

Which one of the following statements is **incorrect**?

(A) 2 mol of $CuSO_4$ is required to produce 1 mol of I_2.
(B) 0.5 mol of KI is required to produce 0.125 mol of I_2.
(C) 4 mol of $CuSO_4$ is required to produce 4 mol of CuI.
(D) 1 mol of KI is required to produce 1 mol K_2SO_4.

Question 14
The relative formula mass of calcium hydroxide, $Ca(OH)_2$, is

(A) 57 (B) 74 (C) 97 (D) 114

Question 15
The mass of potassium, in grams, in 0.25 mol of potassium chloride, KCl is closest to

(A) 9.78 (B) 18.65 (C) 39.1 (D) 156.4

Question 16
Which one of the following contains the smallest mass of hydrogen?

(A) 20 g of methane, CH_4
(B) 36 g of water, H_2O
(C) 10 g of hydrogen, H_2
(D) 40 g of butane, C_4H_{10}

Question 17
The number of mole of sodium atoms in 16.4 g of sodium phosphate, Na_3PO_4 (formula mass = 164 g mol^{-1}), is closest to

(A) 0.10 (B) 0.30 (C) 10 (D) 30

Question 18
The number of mole of oxygen atoms in 40.0 g of iron(III) sulfate, $Fe_2(SO_4)_3$, (formula mass = 400 g mol^{-1}) is closest to

(A) 0.40 (B) 0.70 (C) 1.20 (D) 120

Question 19
A student weighs a sample of aluminium nitrate, $Al(NO_3)_3$ and then finds that he has taken 0.15 mol of the compound. What mass of nitrogen is present in this sample?

(A) 95.85 g (B) 31.95 g (C) 6.3 g (D) 2.1 g

Question 20
An element forms an oxide with the formula X_2O_5. If the formula mass of the oxide is approximately 182 g mol^{-1}, then the relative atomic mass of the element is closest to

(A) 166 (B) 102 (C) 51 (D) 30

Question 21
The molar mass of chromium(III) oxide, Cr_2O_3, in g mol^{-1} is

(A) 188 (B) 68 (C) 73 (D) 152

Question 22
A student weighs 2.20 g of lithium sulfate, Li_2SO_4. The number of mole of compound present in 2.20 g is

(A) 50 (B) 25 (C) 0.04 (D) 0.02

Question 23
Uranium hexafluoride, UF_6, is used in the production of uranium fuel rods for nuclear power stations. The number of mole of fluorine atoms in 5.84 g of UF_6 is closest to

A. 0.00277 B. 0.0166 C. 0.0995 D. 0.116

Question 24
The mass of oxygen, in grams, that reacts with manganese to form 5.00 g of manganese(III) oxide, Mn_2O_3, is closest to

(A) 0.51 (B) 1.52 (C) 2.54 (D) 48.0

Question 25
Hydrogen sulfide gas, H_2S, burns in oxygen to produce steam and sulfur dioxide according to the equation below.

$$2H_2S(g) + 3O_2(g) \rightarrow 2H_2O(g) + 2SO_2(g)$$

What mass of oxygen gas would be required to produce 9.6 g of sulfur dioxide?

(A) 3.2 g (B) 3.6 g (C) 7.2 g (D) 14.4 g

Question 26
Two reactants, X and Y, react to produce the product XY. If reactant X is in excess, this means that

(A) the reaction will proceed until all of X is used up.
(B) the reaction will proceed until both reactants X and Y are completely used up.
(C) the limiting reactant is X.
(D) the reaction will proceed until all of Y is completely used up.

Question 27
Ammonia will react with oxygen to produce nitrogen and steam.

$$4NH_3(g) + 3O_2(g) \rightarrow 2N_2(g) + 6H_2O(g)$$

If 36 mol of NH_3 and 30 mol of O_2 are mixed and allowed to react, the amount of N_2 formed will be

(A) 18 mol. (B) 20 mol. (C) 27 mol. (D) 66 mol.

Question 28
Sulfur reacts with oxygen according to the following equation

$S(s) + O_2(g) \rightarrow SO_2(g)$

What mass of sulfur will remain when 160 g of sulfur is reacted with 64 g of oxygen?

(A) 0 g (B) 32 g (C) 64 g (D) 96 g

Question 29
The equation for the reaction of methane with oxygen is

$CH_4(g) + 2O_2(g) \rightarrow CO_2(g) + 2H_2O(l)$

What mass of carbon dioxide is produced when 3.2 g of methane and 3.2 g of oxygen are allowed to react?

(A) 2.2 g (B) 4.4 g (C) 6.4 g (D) 8.8 g

Question 30
The amount of chlorine in a pesticide may be determined by precipitation of the chlorine as silver chloride, AgCl. If 1.75 g of pesticide reacts to give 0.177 g of AgCl, then the percentage, by mass, of chlorine in the pesticide is

(A) 0.0705% (B) 2.50% (C) 10.1% (D) 40.9%

Question 31
The percentage of oxygen in potassium sulfate, K_2SO_4, is

(A) 57.14 (B) 36.73 (C) 12.68 (D) 9.19

Question 32
Iodine will react with fluorine to form a compound with the formula IF_5. The percentage by mass of fluorine in this compound is approximately

(A) 42.81 (B) 57.19 (C) 13.02 (D) 83.35

Question 33
Which one of the following compounds contains the greatest percentage of carbon?

(A) $C_2H_4O_2$ (B) CH_5N (C) $C_3H_8O_3$ (D) CH_4O

Question 34
A compound of sodium, chlorine and oxygen contains 18.78% sodium and 28.98% chlorine. What mass of oxygen is present in 6.4 g of the compound?

(A) 1.20 g (B) 1.85 g (C) 3.06 g (D) 3.34 g

Question 35
A compound of tin and chlorine has the formula $SnCl_4$ and contains 45.53% tin. The mass of chlorine, in grams, in 6.25 g of the compound is

(A) 1.25 (B) 2.85 (C) 3.40 (D) 5.00

Question 36
A compound of sodium, sulfur and oxygen was analysed. 5.65 g of the compound contained 1.72 g of oxygen and 1.64 g of sodium. The percentage of sulfur in the compound is closest to

(A) 59.47 (B) 40.53 (C) 30.44 (D) 29.03

Question 37
The mass of 1.5 mol of propanoic acid, CH_3CH_2COOH, is

(A) 111 g (B) 0.0203 g (C) 49.3 g (D) 74 g

Question 38
Ethane, C_2H_6, is one of the compounds found in natural gas. Which of the following statements about ethane is **not** correct?

(A) 0.1 mole of C_2H_6 contains 4.8×10^{23} atoms.
(B) 3.0 g of ethane contains 2.4 g of carbon.
(C) 1.0 g of ethane contains 4.0×10^{22} atoms of carbon.
(D) 1 molecule of ethane has a mass of 30 g.

Question 39
The number of hydrogen atoms present in 4.0 g of methane, CH_4, is

(A) 1.5×10^{23} atoms (B) 6.0×10^{23} atoms
(C) 2.4×10^{24} atoms (D) 9.6×10^{24} atoms

Question 40
Which one of the following has the smallest number of atoms?

(A) 0.10 mol of hydrogen, H_2.
(B) 6×10^{22} molecules of ethyne, C_2H_2
(C) 1.0 g of water, H_2O.
(D) 0.05 mol of butane, C_4H_{10}.

Question 41
A compound of carbon and hydrogen contains 80% carbon. The empirical formula of the compound is most likely to be

(A) C_4H (B) C_3H (C) CH_3 (D) CH_4

Question 42
An oxide of chlorine contains 38.8% chlorine. The empirical formula of the compound is

(A) ClO (B) ClO_3 (C) ClO_4 (D) Cl_2O_7

Question 43

A compound has the empirical formula CH_2O and has a relative molecular mass of 90. The most likely molecular formula of the compound is

(A) CH_2O
(B) $C_3H_6O_3$
(C) $C_4H_{10}O_2$
(D) $C_5H_{14}O$

Question 44

A compound of carbon, hydrogen and oxygen has the empirical formula C_2H_4O. 2.0 mol of the compound weighs 176 g. The molecular formula of the compound is most likely to be

(A) $C_{16}H_{32}O_8$
(B) $C_8H_{16}O_4$
(C) $C_4H_8O_2$
(D) C_2H_4O

Question 45

A student adds 3.561 g of tin to 5.076 g of iodine and allows the reaction to proceed until all of the iodine has been consumed. The student finds that at the end of the reaction 2.374 g of tin remains. From these results the empirical formula of tin iodide is

(A) Sn_3I_4 (B) SnI_2 (C) SnI_4 (D) Sn_4I

Question 46

When 1 mole of a hydrocarbon is burnt in oxygen equal amounts (in mole) of CO_2 and H_2O are formed. The formula of the hydrocarbon is most likely to be

(A) C_5H_6 (B) C_5H_8 (C) C_5H_{10} (D) C_5H_{12}

Question 47

Lactic acid has the molecular formula $C_3H_6O_3$. The percentage of carbon in lactic acid is

(A) 2.5 (B) 25 (C) 36 (D) 40

Question 48

Which one of the following compounds contains the greatest percentage of carbon?

(A) C_2H_5F B. C_3H_7N (C) C_3H_8O (D) C_4H_9Cl

Question 49

Lead nitrate reacts with potassium iodide according to the following equation.

$Pb(NO_3)_2(aq) + 2KI(aq) \rightarrow PbI_2(s) + 2KNO_3(aq)$

The **mass** of lead iodide precipitate formed when 200.0 mL of 1.50 mol L^{-1} potassium iodide solution reacts with 150.0 mL of a 0.500 mol L^{-1} lead nitrate solution is closest to

(A) 138 g (B) 35.0 g (C) 2.80×10^2 g (D) 69.0 g

Question 50
Which of the quantities below has the greatest mass?

(A) 60 g of zinc.
(B) 6.0 moles of copper.
(C) 4.0×10^{22} molecules of oxygen.
(D) 2.4×10^{23} atoms of mercury.

Question 51
A scientist adds 2.540 g of iodine to 2.298 g of indium and heats the mixture in a solvent until all of the iodine has reacted. The remaining indium is washed, dried and weighed. 1.532 g of indium remains. The empirical formula of indium iodide is

(A) InI (B) In_3I_2 (C) In_2I_3 (D) InI_3

(3) Concentration and Molarity

The following information refers to Questions 52 and 53.
Solutions of potassium permanganate solutions can range in colour from pink to purple. Dilute solutions appear pink while more concentrated solutions are dark purple. Crystals of potassium permanganate were added to four test tubes containing varying amounts of distilled water as shown below.

Test tube	1	2	3	4
Volume of distilled water (mL)	1.0	5.0	20.0	50.0
Mass of $KMnO_4$ added	50.0 mg	100 mg	0.10 g	0.50 g

Question 52
Once all of the crystals have dissolved in each test tube the test tube containing the solution that is the palest pink is

(A) test tube 1.
(B) test tube 2.
(C) test tube 3.
(D) test tube 4.

Question 53
The concentration, in g L^{-1}, of the potassium permanganate solution in test tube 2 is

(A) 20. (B) 2.0. (C) 0.20. (D) 0.020.

Question 54
A solution is formed by dissolving 0.30 mol of calcium bromide, $CaBr_2$, in 150 mL of water. The concentration of the solution in g L^{-1} is

(A) 400 (B) 9.0 (C) 2.0 (D) 0.40

Question 55
Different masses of four compounds are added to separate 100 mL samples of water at 25°C, as shown in the table below.

Compound	Mass of solid added to 100 mL of water
Potassium chloride, KCl	20.0
Potassium nitrate, KNO_3	30.0
Sodium bromide, NaBr	40.0
Sodium chloride, NaCl	20.0

Which solution would have the lowest concentration in mol L^{-1}?

(A) Potassium chloride solution
(B) Potassium nitrate solution
(C) Sodium bromide solution
(D) Sodium chloride solution

Question 56
An aqueous solution is labelled "0.75 mol L^{-1} $CaBr_2$". The best explanation of this label is that the solution contains

(A) 0.75 mol of calcium bromide added to 1.0 L of distilled water.
(B) 150 g of calcium bromide added to 1.0 L of distilled water.
(C) 0.15 g of calcium bromide per 1.0 mL of solution.
(D) 0.75 g of calcium bromide per 1.0 mL of solution.

Question 57
When a solution of bleach is diluted, the number of moles of bleach

(A) increases.
(B) decreases.
(C) remains constant.
(D) varies according to the amount of dilution.

Question 58
What volume of water is needed to dissolve 1.00 mole of potassium bromide, KBr, to produce a solution with a concentration of 60 g/100 mL?

(A) 50.4 mL (B) 71.4 mL (C) 160 mL (D) 198 mL

Question 59
The mass of potassium nitrate, KNO_3, in grams, present in 0.750 L of a 2.20 mol L^{-1} potassium nitrate solution is closest to

(A) 34.5 (B) 167 (C) 222 (D) 296

Question 60
Household bleach contains 35.0 g of sodium hypochlorite, NaClO, per litre of bleach. What volume of water must be added to 200 mL of bleach to change the concentration of NaClO to 5.00 g per litre?

(A) 1.20 L (B) 1.40 L (C) 0.280 L (D) 0.080 L

Question 61

The active ingredient in household bleach is sodium hypochlorite, NaClO. If the molarity of a sample of bleach is 0.711 mol L^{-1} and the density of the solution is 1.0 g mL^{-1}, what is the concentration of sodium hypochlorite in this solution expressed as % composition (% m/m)?

(A) 5.30 (B) 53.0 (C) 10.5 (D) 0.0711

Question 62

A lead nitrate solution has a molarity of 0.50 mol L^{-1}. How many moles of lead nitrate are in 500 mL of solution?

(A) 1.0×10^{-3} (B) 0.10 (C) 0.25 (D) 0.50

Question 63

A solution of ammonia, NH_3, contains 6.3 mg of ammonia dissolved in 100 mL of solution. What is the concentration of the solution in g L^{-1}?

(A) 6.3×10^{-4}
(B) 6.3×10^{-2}
(C) 6.3
(D) 63

Question 64

What is the concentration of a solution that contains 2.00 g of silver nitrate, $AgNO_3$, dissolved in 300 mL of solution?

(A) 0.00354 mol L^{-1}
(B) 0.0118 mol L^{-1}
(C) 0.0392 mol L^{-1}
(D) 6.67 mol L^{-1}

Question 65

A solution of copper chloride contains 5.70 g of copper chloride, $CuCl_2$, in 750 mL of solution. What is the concentration of the solution?

(A) 0.0424 mol L^{-1}
(B) 0.0566 mol L^{-1}
(C) 0.0768 mol L^{-1}
(D) 1.02 mol L^{-1}

Question 66

What is the concentration of chloride ions in a 1.2 mol L^{-1} solution of aluminium chloride, $AlCl_3$?

(A) 4.8 mol L^{-1}
(B) 3.6 mol L^{-1}
(C) 2.4 mol L^{-1}
(D) 1.2 mol L^{-1}

Question 67

The amount, in mol, of Cl^- ions in 500 mL of a 0.50 mol L^{-1} $AlCl_3$ solution is

(A) 0.083 (B) 0.25 (C) 0.75 (D) 1.0

Question 68

The mass of solute, in grams, in 200 mL of 2.50 mol L^{-1} $Fe(NO_3)_2(aq)$ is

(A) 14.4 (B) 89.9 (C) 180 (D) 450

Question 69
Which one of the following solutions contains the largest amount of nitrate ion?

(A) 400 mL of 0.45 mol L^{-1} sodium nitrate, $NaNO_3$.
(B) 500 mL of 0.30 mol L^{-1} calcium nitrate, $Ca(NO_3)_2$.
(C) 250 mL of 0.30 mol L^{-1} aluminium nitrate, $Al(NO_3)_3$.
(D) 300 mL of 0.20 mol L^{-1} thorium nitrate, $Th(NO_3)_4$.

Question 70
200 mL of a 2.0 mol L^{-1} solution of sodium nitrate is diluted to 500 mL. The concentration of the diluted solution is

(A) 0.40 mol L^{-1}
(B) 0.80 mol L^{-1}
(C) 2.0 mol L^{-1}
(D) 5.0 mol L^{-1}

Question 71
A glucose solution has a concentration of 1.50 mol L^{-1}. What volume of water must be added to 300 mL of this solution to change the concentration to 0.500 mol L^{-1}?

(A) 100 mL (B) 300 mL (C) 600 mL (D) 900 mL

Question 72
The amount of fluoride in water supplies must be carefully controlled. In which one of the following solutions is the concentration of NaF 500 ppm? (Assume the density of the solutions is 1.0 g mL^{-1}.)

(A) 5.00 mL of a solution that contains 5.00 mg of NaF.
(B) 0.500 g of NaF in 500 mL of solution.
(C) A solution with a NaF concentration of 0.100 g L^{-1}.
(D) 50.0 mg of NaF in 100 mL of solution.

Question 73
Sulfur dioxide, SO_2, is used in small quantities as an antibiotic and antioxidant to maintain the quality of wines. In many countries the maximum amount of SO_2 permitted in wine is 210 ppm. What mass of SO_2 must be added to a 750 mL bottle of wine to reach this concentration? (Assume the density of wine = 1.0 g mL^{-1}.)

(A) 0.210 g (B) 0.280 g (C) 0.158 mg (D) 158 mg

Question 74
The amount of ethanol in alcoholic drinks is often expressed as %(v/v), i.e. the volume of ethanol in 100 mL of the solution. Which one of the following contains the largest amount of alcohol?

(A) 350 mL of beer containing 5.3% alcohol
(B) 150 mL of champagne containing 12.5% alcohol
(C) 200 mL of wine containing 12.0% alcohol
(D) 50 mL of brandy containing 40.0% alcohol

Question 75

260 mL of 0.500 mol L^{-1} potassium sulfate solution are added to 430 mL of 1.70 mol L^{-1} aluminium sulfate solution. What is the **concentration** of sulfate ions in the final solution?

(A) 3.37 mol L^{-1}
(B) 1.25 mol L^{-1}
(C) 1.52 mol L^{-1}
(D) 3.56 mol L^{-1}

Question 76

A solution contains 7.70 g of potassium iodide. What is the **least** volume of 2.00 mol L^{-1} lead nitrate solution that would be required to ensure complete precipitation of the iodide ions as lead iodide?

(A) 46.4 mL
(B) 36.55 mL
(C) 23.2 mL
(D) 11.6 mL

Question 77

What volume of 0.045 mol L^{-1} aluminium chloride will contain 1.0 mole of chloride ions?

(A) 7.41 L
(B) 741 mL
(C) 2.47 L
(D) 823 mL

Question 78

Lead chloride, $PbCl_2$, has a solubility of 1.08 g in 100 mL of H_2O at 25°C. This corresponds to a concentration of

(A) 0.388 mol L^{-1}.
(B) 108 g L^{-1}.
(C) 1080 mg L^{-1}.
(D) 10800 ppm.

Question 79

Which of the following sodium chloride (NaCl) solutions contains the largest number of moles of sodium chloride?

(A) 400 mL of a 3.0 mol L^{-1} solution
(B) 300 mL of a 40.0 g L^{-1} solution
(C) 300 mL of a 0.4 mol L^{-1} solution
(D) 400 mL of a 0.25 g mL^{-1}solution

Question 80

Sodium carbonate is reacted with silver nitrate according to the following equation

$Na_2CO_3(aq) + 2AgNO_3(aq) \rightarrow Ag_2CO_3(s) + 2NaNO_3(aq)$

If 20.0 mL of 0.150 mol L^{-1} sodium carbonate solution is added to 30.00 mL of 0.250 mol L^{-1} silver nitrate solution, the maximum mass of silver carbonate, in grams, that would be precipitated is

A. 0.414.
B. 0.827.
C. 1.65.
D. 2.07.

(4) Gas Laws

Question 81
The scientist who first researched the relationship between the reacting volumes and product volumes in gaseous chemical reactions was

(A) Amedeo Avogadro.
(B) Joseph Gay-Lussac.
(C) John Dalton.
(D) Robert Boyle.

Question 82
Which one of the graphs below best represents Boyle's Law?

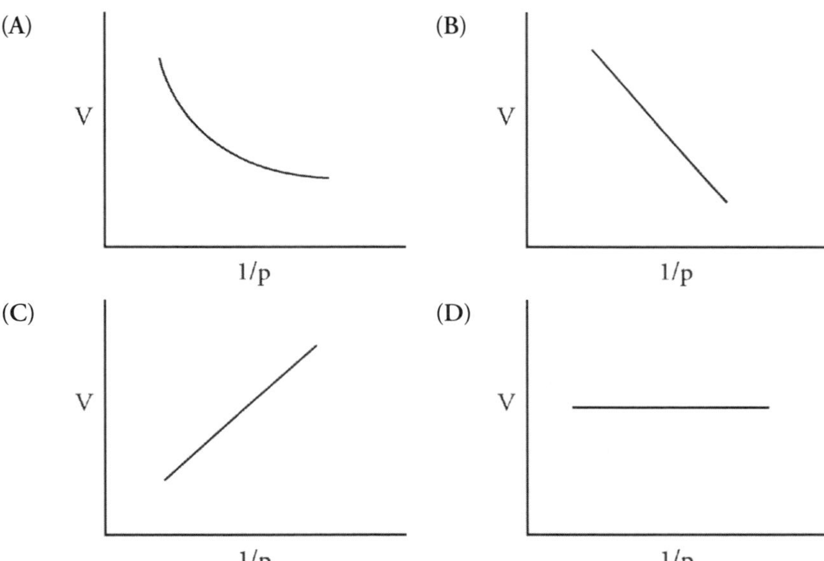

Question 83
Which one of the following best represents Charles' Law?

(A) At constant pressure the volume of a fixed mass of gas varies directly with the absolute temperature.
(B) At constant temperature the volume of a fixed mass of gas varies inversely with the pressure.
(C) At constant temperature and constant volume the pressure of a gas varies directly with the mass of the gas.
(D) At constant pressure the volume of a fixed mass of a gas varies directly with the centigrade temperature.

Question 84
Which scientist made the following statement?

"At the same temperature and the same pressure equal volumes of all gases contain the same number of particles."

(A) Robert Boyle
(B) Joseph Gay-Lussac
(C) Jacques Charles
(D) Amadeo Avogadro

Question 85
Neon gas at 20°C and standard atmospheric pressure is placed in a 1.00 L closed container. Under these conditions

(A) all neon atoms have the same kinetic energy.
(B) the average kinetic energy of neon atoms is different from that of other gases under the same conditions.
(C) the average kinetic energy of neon atoms is proportional to the temperature.
(D) the percentage of atoms with high kinetic energy is higher than it would be at the same pressure and volume and a temperature of 40°C.

Question 86
Assuming that other conditions remain constant, which one of the following will **not** increase the pressure of a gas in a closed container?

(A) Increasing the volume of the container
(B) Increasing the temperature of the gas
(C) Introducing a second inert gas
(D) Increasing the amount of gas in the container

Question 87
If a mixture of nitrogen and helium is placed in a closed container:

(A) a chemical reaction will occur between the two gases and the gas pressure will change.
(B) forces of attraction between the gas particles will decrease the number of collisions with the walls of the container.
(C) there are more collisions with the container walls than if the same total number of particles were of only one element.
(D) each gas collides with the container walls as if it were the only gas occupying the container.

Question 88
A balloon has a volume of 1.50 L at 25°C and 101.3 kPa. What will be the new volume if the pressure decreases to 95.3 kPa and the temperature remains constant?

(A) 1.41 L. (B) 1.51 L. (C) 1.59 L. (D) 0.94 L.

Question 89
The volume of a gas syringe is 500 mL and the gas pressure is 99.5 kPa. What will be the new pressure if the volume is decreased to 125 mL and the temperature remains constant?

(A) 398 kPa. (B) 24.9 kPa. (C) 6.22 kPa. (D) 49.8 kPa.

Question 90
Which one of the following corresponds to a temperature of –139°C?

(A) –134 K (B) 134 K (C) –412 K (D) 412 K

Question 91

Four gas syringes, W, X, Y and Z are all at the same temperature and pressure and contain equal masses of a different gas as shown in the table below.

Syringe	W	X	Y	Z
Gas	Oxygen, O_2	Sulfur dioxide, SO_2	Sulfur trioxide, SO_3	Methane, CH_4

Which one of the following statements is correct?

(A) W and Z contain equal volumes of gas.
(B) The volume of sulfur dioxide is twice the volume of oxygen.
(C) The volume of methane is five times greater than the volume of sulfur trioxide.
(D) Y contains the largest number of atoms.

Question 92

A weather balloon with a volume of 500 L at 25°C and 1.00 atm pressure is carried to Antarctica where the temperature is –33°C. If the pressure is unchanged, what will be the new volume of the weather balloon?

(A) 621 L. (B) 1.65 L. (C) 402 L. (D) 0.606 L.

Question 93

A sample of 0.35 mol of fluorine has a volume of 5.9 L. At constant temperature and pressure, what will be the volume occupied by 2.3 mol of fluorine?

(A) 3.9×10^4 L. (B) 0.90 L. (C) 0.14 L. (D) 39 L.

Question 94

Under standard laboratory conditions, SLC,

(A) the volume occupied by one mole of chlorine gas, Cl_2, is approximately double the volume occupied by one mole of argon, Ar.
(B) the volume occupied by 39.95 g of argon is approximately the same as the volume occupied by 4.00 g of helium.
(C) the volume occupied by one mole of ammonia is exactly the same as the volume occupied by one mole of helium.
(D) the volume occupied by one mole of all real gases is exactly the same as there are no interparticle forces of attraction.

Question 95

The behaviour of air is closer to that of an ideal gas at

(A) sea level.
(B) the absolute zero of temperature.
(C) inside a car tyre.
(D) high altitudes.

Question 96

The molar volume of a gas at 75.0 kPa and –40°C is closest to

(A) 25.8 L. (B) 24.5 L. (C) 34.7 L. (D) 22.4 L.

Question 97

An air bubble trapped in ice at –18°C and 2.00 atm pressure has a volume of 1.50 mL. What will be the increase in volume of the air bubble when the ice melts to water at 0°C and the pressure is 1.00 atm?

(A) 0.50 mL. (B) 1.70 mL. (C) 3.20 mL. (D) 4.70 mL.

Question 98

Assuming that all real gases deviate from ideal gas behaviour, one mole of which of the following gases might be expected to occupy the smallest volume at SLC?

(A) ammonia.
(B) oxygen.
(C) argon.
(D) methane.

Question 99

A sealed 5.00 L flask contains a gas at 35°C and 156 kPa pressure. If 0.083 mol of gas is removed from the flask, the amount of gas remaining is

(A) 0.025 mol. (B) 0.22 mol. (C) 0.31 mol. (D) 0.39 mol.

Question 100

A syringe contains 75.0 mL of nitrogen at 20°C and a pressure of 101.3 kPa. The plunger of the syringe is pushed down until the volume of the nitrogen is reduced to 57.3 mL. What is the new pressure of the nitrogen if the temperature has increased to 23°C?

(A) 4.99 kPa. (B) 43.1 kPa. (C) 130 kPa. (D) 135 kPa.

Question 101

If the pressure, in kPa, and temperature, in K, of 146 mL of hydrogen are doubled, then the new volume of the hydrogen will be

(A) 146 mL. (B) 73 mL. (C) 292 mL. (D) 438 mL.

Question 102

Equal volumes of sulfur dioxide and oxygen are at the same temperature and pressure. Both gas samples

(A) contain equal masses.
(B) have all molecules moving with the same velocity.
(C) contain equal numbers of atoms.
(D) have molecules with the same average kinetic energy.

Question 103

20 mL of a gaseous oxide of nitrogen is completely decomposed to nitrogen and oxygen. 20 mL of nitrogen and 50 mL of oxygen are produced. If all of the volumes are measured at the same temperature and pressure, then the formula of the oxide is most likely to be

(A) N_2O (B) NO_2 (C) N_2O_3 (D) N_2O_5

Question 104

A student collects a sample of gas from an experiment and finds that at 18°C and a pressure of 760 mm Hg it occupies 450 mL. The next day the student finds that the volume of the gas is 475 mL but the pressure is still 760 mm Hg. The new temperature of the gas is closest to

(A) –4°C. (B) 2°C. (C) 19°C. (D) 34°C.

Question 105

The products of a reaction between carbon disulfide gas and oxygen gas are carbon dioxide and sulfur dioxide. The volume of the products is 60 mL.

$CS_2(g) + 3O_2(g) \rightarrow CO_2(g) + 2SO_2(g)$

Assuming complete reaction of both reactants, what are their initial volumes under the same temperature and pressure?

	volume of CS_2 (mL)	volume of O_2 (mL)
(A)	20	40
(B)	60	20
(C)	20	60
(D)	40	20

Question 106

The equation for the reaction of hydrogen chloride with oxygen is

$4HCl(g) + O_2(g) \rightarrow 2H_2O(l) + 2Cl_2(g)$

50 mL of oxygen gas reacts completely with excess hydrogen chloride gas. If the volumes are measured at the same temperatureand pressure, then the volume of hydrogen chloride reacting and the volume of the products will be

	volume of HCl (mL)	volume of products (mL)
(A)	200	100
(B)	50	200
(C)	12.5	25
(D)	100	50

Question 107

Methane reacts with oxygen according to the following equation,

$CH_4(g) + 2O_2(g) \rightarrow CO_2(g) + 2H_2O(g)$

100 mL of methane is completely combusted to carbon dioxide and water vapour with no excess oxygen remaining. Assuming that all reactants and products are in the gaseous state and at the same temperature and pressure, the *change* in total volume during the reaction is

(A) 0.00 mL. (B) 3.00 mL. (C) 100 mL. (D) 300 mL.

Question 108

A sample of air in a 3.0 L container at 2.0 atm is connected to another sample of air in a 2.0 L container at 3.0 atm. The tap between the two containers is opened so that both samples of air have access to both containers. If the temperature remains constant throughout, the final pressure in both containers will be

(A) 2.0 atm (B) 2.4 atm (C) 2.5 atm (D) 3.0 atm

Question 109
11.94 g of a gaseous element has a volume of 7.82 L at a temperature of 27°C and a pressure of 100 kPa. The element is most likely to be

(A) oxygen. (B) chlorine. (C) fluorine. (D) nitrogen.

Question 110
Samples of two different gases, Q and J, have equal masses and volumes and are at the same temperature. Gas Q has a higher molar mass than gas J. Which one of the following statements is correct?

(A) Gas Q will exert a greater pressure.
(B) Gas J will exert a greater pressure.
(C) Both gases will exert the same pressure.
(D) The gas with the higher density will exert a greater pressure.

Extended Response Questions

(1) Chemical Reactions, Stoichiometry and the Mole Concept

Question 1
Write balanced formula equations for the following reactions.

(a) Magnesium reacting with steam. (2 marks)
(b) Calcium reacting with dilute hydrochloric acid. (2 marks)
(c) Sodium reacting with oxygen. (2 marks)
(Total = 6 marks)

Question 2
Write balanced formula equations for the following reactions.

(a) The reaction of chromium with oxygen to form chromium(III) oxide. (2 marks)
(b) The reaction of lead with chlorine to form lead(IV) chloride. (2 marks)
(c) The reaction of potassium with water. (2 marks)
(d) The reaction of aluminium with steam. (2 marks)
(e) The reaction of iron with dilute hydrochloric acid to form iron(III) chloride. (2 marks)
(f) The reaction of aluminium with sulfuric acid to form aluminium sulfate. (2 marks)
(Total = 12 marks)

Question 3
When heated strongly sodium hydrogen carbonate, $NaHCO_3$, decomposes. The products are sodium carbonate, Na_2CO_3, water and carbon dioxide. In a typical experiment, 5.163 g of a pure sample of $NaHCO_3$ after heating to drive off all of the water and CO_2 gave 3.258 g of Na_2CO_3. In a second experiment 4.687 g of an impure sample of $NaHCO_3$ was heated in a similar way. 3.207 g of solid remained.

(a) Write a balanced symbol equation for the reaction. (2 marks)

(b) Calculate the percentage loss of mass that occurred when the pure $NaHCO_3$ was heated. (2 marks)

(c) What was the percentage purity of the $NaHCO_3$ used in the second experiment? (2 marks)

(Total = 6 marks)

Question 4

A scientist determines a value for the Avogadro Constant by the following method. Using a Geiger counter the scientist measures the number of particles emitted by a sample of radium in one second and obtains a value of 6.2×10^{10}. Each particle is converted into an atom of helium. The helium is collected and after 10 days the mass of helium is 3.68×10^{-7} g. Use the scientist's results to calculate a value for the Avogadro Constant. (Total = 4 marks)

Question 5

Write balanced symbol equations for the following reactions.

(a) Copper(s) reacts with nitric acid, HNO_3(aq), to give copper nitrate(aq), water and nitrogen dioxide. (2 marks)

(b) Ethane gas (C_2H_6) burns in oxygen to give carbon dioxide and water. (2 marks)

(c) Phosphorus (P_4) reacts with fluorine (F_2) to form phosphorus pentafluoride. (2 marks)

(d) Aluminium sulfate solution reacts with barium chloride solution to give aluminium chloride solution and a precipitate of barium sulfate. (3 marks)

(e) Heating lead nitrate(s) produces lead oxide(s), oxygen and nitrogen dioxide. (3 marks)

(Total = 12 marks)

Question 6

Calculate the molar mass of the following substances

(a) $(NH_2)_2CO$ (b) $Na_2SO_4.10H_2O$ (c) $K_3Fe(CN)_6$

(Total = 3 marks)

Question 7

For a 3.60 g sample of ethanoic acid (CH_3COOH) calculate

(a) the number of mole of ethanoic acid. (1 mark)

(b) the number of molecules of ethanoic acid. (1 mark)

(c) the number of mole of oxygen atoms (1 mark)

(d) the total number of atoms. (1 mark)

(Total = 4 marks)

Question 8

In the nineteenth century, scientists calculated the relative atomic mass (atomic weight) of an element by measuring the mass of oxygen that reacted with a known mass of the element. With this method the scientists had to make an assumption about the formula of the oxide. Before 1869, scientists had calculated that the element indium, In, had a relative atomic mass (atomic weight) of 75. This value of the relative atomic mass was incorrect since the scientists had assumed an incorrect formula for the oxide. In a typical experiment, 5.00 g of indium was converted into 6.06 g of indium oxide.

(a) Deduce the formula the scientists had assumed for indium oxide. (3 marks)

(b) Later scientists assumed that the formula of indium oxide was In_2O_3. What value did they calculate for the relative mass (atomic weight) of indium? (3 marks)

(Total = 6 marks)

Question 9

Bornite is an ore of copper and has the formula Cu_5FeS_4.

(a) Calculate the relative formula mass of bornite. (1 mark)
(b) Calculate the percentage composition of bornite. (3 marks)
(c) What mass of copper could be obtained from 1.0 kg of bornite? (2 marks)

(Total = 6 marks)

Question 10

All plants need a source of nitrogen in order to grow. Urea, $CO(NH_2)_2$, ammonium sulfate, $(NH_4)_2SO_4$, and ammonium nitrate, NH_4NO_3 have all been used as nitrogen fertilisers.

(a) For each compound calculate the percentage of nitrogen present. (3 marks)
(b) Calculate the number of moles of nitrogen that are present in 100 g of ammonium nitrate. (2 marks)
(c) Calculate the mass of nitrogen that could be obtained from 500 g of ammonium sulfate. (2 marks)

(Total = 7 marks)

Question 11

Describe what is meant by

(a) relative molecular mass. (2 marks)
(b) molar mass. (2 marks)

(Total = 4 marks)

Question 12

One of the components of natural gas is propane, C_3H_8. For an 11.0 g sample of propane, calculate the following:

(a) the molar mass of propane. (1 mark)
(b) the number of mole of molecules present. (1 mark)
(c) the number of molecules present. (1 mark)
(d) the number of mole of hydrogen atoms present. (1 mark)
(e) the total number of atoms present. (1 mark)

(Total = 5 marks)

Question 13

A sample of ethane, C_2H_6, contains 1.20×10^{23} atoms of carbon.

(a) Calculate the number of mole of carbon present. (1 mark)
(b) Calculate the mass of carbon that this represents. (1 mark)
(c) Calculate the number of molecules of ethane that are present. (1 mark)
(d) Calculate the number of atoms of hydrogen that are combined with this number of carbon atoms. (1 mark)
(e) Calculate the total mass of ethane. (2 marks)

(Total = 6 marks)

Question 14

Sodium carbonate, Na_2CO_3, is a base often used in acid-base reactions. For a 0.250 mol sample of sodium carbonate, calculate the following:

(a) the relative formula mass. (1 mark)
(b) the mass of sodium carbonate in this sample. (1 mark)
(c) the number of mole of sodium present. (1 mark)
(d) the mass of oxygen atoms present in this sample. (2 marks)
(Total = 5 marks)

Question 15

A 15.00 g sample of an oxide of nitrogen is heated and decomposes to nitrogen and oxygen. All of the oxygen is removed and 3.89 g of nitrogen remains.

(a) What mass of oxygen was also formed when the sample decomposed? (1 mark)
(b) Calculate the number of mole of nitrogen and the number of mole of oxygen that were combined in the compound. (2 marks)
(c) Deduce the empirical formula of this oxide of nitrogen. (2 marks)
(Total = 5 marks)

Question 16

A hydrocarbon (a compound that contains only carbon and hydrogen atoms) contains 0.48 g of carbon chemically combined with 0.12 g of hydrogen.

(a) Calculate the number of mole of hydrogen and the number of mole of carbon in this compound. (2 marks)
(b) What is the empirical formula of the compound? (2 marks)
(c) If the molar mass of the compound is 30.0 g mol^{-1}, deduce the molecular formula of the compound. (2 marks)
(Total = 6 marks)

Question 17

A compound of carbon and hydrogen is burnt in air to give carbon dioxide, CO_2, and water. In a typical experiment 1.00 g of the compound gave 3.14 g of carbon dioxide on combustion.

(a) Calculate the number of mole of carbon dioxide produced. (1 mark)
(b) Calculate the number mole of carbon present in the carbon dioxide and thus in the original compound. (1 mark)
(c) Calculate the mass of carbon present in 1.00 g of the compound. (1 mark)
(d) Calculate the mass of hydrogen present in 1.00 g of the compound. (1 mark)
(e) Deduce the empirical formula of the compound. (2 marks)
(f) If 0.250 mole of the compound weighs 14.0 g, calculate the molecular formula of the compound. (2 marks)
(Total = 8 marks)

Question 18

A compound contains 0.15 mole of carbon combined with 0.40 g of hydrogen and 9.0×10^{22} atoms of oxygen. What is the empirical formula of the compound?
(3 marks)

Question 19

A compound of carbon, hydrogen, nitrogen and oxygen has the following percentage composition:

% carbon = 50.00; % hydrogen = 8.33; % nitrogen = 19.44

(a) Calculate the percentage of oxygen in the compound. (1 mark)

(b) Deduce the empirical formula of the compound. (3 marks)

21.6 g is found to represent 0.150 mol of the compound.

(c) Calculate the molar mass of the compound. (1 mark)

(d) Deduce the molecular formula of the compound. (2 marks)

(Total = 7 marks)

Question 20

(a) A compound commonly found in anti–freeze has the following compostion, 38.71% carbon, 9.68% hydrogen and the remainder being oxygen. Calculate the empirical formula of the compound. (3 marks)

(b) If the molar mass of the compound is 62 g mol^{-1}, what is the molecular formula of the compound? (2 marks)

(Total = 5 marks)

Question 21

A student placed 5.21 g of lead nitrate, $Pb(NO_3)_2$ in a test tube and heated the test tube strongly. Nitrogen dioxide and oxygen were driven from the test tube. When no more gas was evolved the test tube was cooled and reweighed. 3.51 g of lead(II) oxide remained. 1.45 g of nitrogen dioxide was also produced in the reaction.

(a) Calculate the mass of oxygen was produced by this reaction. (1 mark)

(b) Calculate the amounts, in mole, of each of the following:

(i) lead nitrate (1 mark)

(ii) lead(II) oxide (1 mark)

(iii) nitrogen dioxide (1 mark)

(iv) oxygen (1 mark)

(c) Using the amounts of substances calculated in part (b), write a balanced equation for the decomposition of lead nitrate. (2 marks)

(Total = 7 marks)

Question 22

Sodium carbonate is reacted with 1.62 g of silver nitrate according to the following equation,

$$Na_2CO_3(aq) + 2AgNO_3(aq) \rightarrow Ag_2CO_3(s) + 2NaNO_3(aq)$$

(a) Calculate the mass of sodium carbonate needed to react with the silver nitrate. (3 marks)

(b) Calculate the mass of silver carbonate formed. (2 marks)

(Total = 5 marks)

Question 23

Waste water from electroplating processes often contains chromium(III) chloride, $CrCl_3$. It can be removed by reacting it with sodium hydroxide according to the equation shown on the next page.

$CrCl_3(aq) + 3NaOH(aq) \rightarrow Cr(OH)_3(s) + 3NaCl(aq)$

(a) If a sample of water contains 2.35 kg of chromium chloride, what mass of sodium hydroxide is required to react with it? (2 marks)

(b) Calculate the masses of chromium(III) hydroxide and sodium chloride formed by the reaction in part (a). (4 marks)

(Total = 6 marks)

Question 24

100 g of sulfur dioxide is mixed with 100 g of oxygen and allowed to react to form sulfur trioxide according to the equation,

$2SO_2(g) + O_2(g) \rightarrow 2SO_3(g)$

(a) Determine which reactant is in excess and calculate the mass remaining at the completion of the reaction. (3 marks)

(b) Calculate the mass of sulfur trioxide formed. (2 marks)

(Total = 5 marks)

Question 25

The following method was used to determine the empirical formula of magnesium oxide. A crucible and lid was weighed then a small piece of magnesium ribbon was added and the crucible and lid reweighed. The crucible and lid was then strongly heated. Occasionally the lid was raised for a few moments and then lowered again. Heating was continued until no more reaction occurred. After cooling the crucible, lid and contents were then weighed again.

Results:	mass of crucible and lid	= 15.67 g
	mass of crucible, lid and magnesium	= 15.86 g
	mass of crucible, lid and magnesium oxide	= 15.96 g

(a) Why was the lid raised for a few moments? (1 mark)

(b) Use the above results to calculate the empirical formula of magnesium oxide. (3 marks)

(c) The accepted empirical formula of magnesium oxide is MgO. Suggest two reasons why it differs from the answer calculated in part (b). (2 marks)

(Total = 6 marks)

Question 26

A student determines the formula of zinc iodide by the following method. The student weighs a conical flask adds a small amount of zinc and weighs the flask again. A similar amount of iodine was then added and the flask weighed for a third time. Aproximately 5 mL of water and a few drops of ethanoic acid were added to the flask. The flask was warmed slightly until the colour of iodine had completely disappeared. Some zinc remained unreacted. The liquid was decanted from the remaining zinc. The remaining zinc was washed and then dried.

Results:	mass of flask	= 24.62 g
	mass of flask and zinc	= 26.58 g
	mass of flask, zinc and iodine	= 28.66 g
	mass of flask and remaining zinc	= 26.04 g

(a) Why was the remaining zinc washed? (1 mark)

(b) Use the above results to calculate the empirical formula of zinc iodide. (3 marks)

(Total = 4 marks)

Question 27

(a) Determine the relative formula mass of the mineral malachite, $Cu_2CO_3(OH)_2$ (1 mark)

(b) What is the percentage composition of copper (Cu) in malachite? (2 marks)

(c) What mass of copper could be obtained from 500 kg of malachite? (3 marks)

(Total 6 marks)

Question 28

A student determines the formula of copper oxide by the following method. 0.256 g of copper oxide was dissolved in 50 mL of dilute sulfuric acid. Small amounts of zinc were added until the blue colour of copper sulfate completely disappeared and all of the copper had been formed. The copper solid was collected washed and dried. The mass of copper was 0.203 g. Use these results to determine the empirical formula of copper oxide. (Total = 3 marks)

Question 29

Calculate the percentage composition of methyl butanoate, $CH_3CH_2CH_2COOCH_3$. (3 marks)

Question 30

2.167 g of a compound of carbon, hydrogen and oxygen is completely burnt in oxygen. 4.761 g of carbon dioxide and 2.605 g of water are formed.

(a) Calculate the percentage composition of the compound. (3 marks)

(b) Calculate the empirical formula of the compound. (2 marks)

(c) The molecular formula of this compound must be the same as its empirical formula. Suggest a reason for this. (1 mark)

(d) Draw the structural formulae for two isomers with this formula. (2 marks)

(Total = 8 marks)

Question 31

Hydrazine, N_2H_4, and hydrogen peroxide, H_2O_2, are both liquids at room temperature and react according to the following equation,

$$2H_2O_2(l) + N_2H_4(l) \rightarrow N_2(g) + 4H_2O(g)$$

The reaction occurs easily at room temperature and also produces a large amount of heat energy. This pair of compounds has been used as the propellant system for some rockets.

(a) Give two reasons why these materials be suitable as propellants. (2 marks)

(b) If the maximum load of the propellant liquids for a rocket is 2500 kg, calculate the separate masses of hydrazine and hydrogen peroxide that need to be loaded onto the rocket. (3 marks)

(Total = 5 marks)

Question 32

The element silicon is produced by heating silica (SiO_2) to approximately 2000°C with carbon. The equation of the reaction is

$$2C(s) + SiO_2(l) \rightarrow Si(l) + 2CO(g)$$

In one experiment, 800 kg of silica is heated with 250 kg of carbon.

(a) Determine which reactant is in excess and calculate the mass of this reactant remaining. (3 marks)

(b) Calculate the mass of silicon (Si) formed in this experiment. (2 marks)

(Total = 5 marks)

Question 33

Sodium penicillin has the formula, $C_{16}H_{17}N_2NaO_4S$ (molar mass = 356.4 g mol^{-1}). It is administered in units where 1.00 unit is equivalent to 6.00 μg. A dose of 50 000 units is administered to a patient. For this dose calculate

(a) the number of mole of sodium. (2 marks)
(b) the mass of nitrogen. (2 marks)
(c) the number of carbon atoms. (2 marks)

(Total = 6 marks)

(3) Concentration and Molarity

Question 34

A chemist prepares 250 mL of 0.0500 mol L^{-1} magnesium chloride ($MgCl_2$) solution.

(a) Calculate the amount, in mol, of magnesium chloride in the solution. (1 mark)
(b) Calculate the amount, in mol, of chloride ions in solution. (1 mark)
(c) Calculate the number of ions in the solution. (1 mark)
(d) Calculate the mass of magnesium chloride needed to make the solution. (1 mark)

(Total = 4 marks)

Question 35

A 1.20 g antacid tablet contains 80.0% magnesium hydroxide ($Mg(OH)_2$ as the active ingredient.

(a) Write an equation for the reaction of solid magnesium hydroxide and hydrochloric acid (HCl) if magnesium chloride and water are the only products. (2 marks)
(b) Calculate the number of mole of $Mg(OH)_2$ in the tablet. (2 marks)
(c) Calculate the number of mole of HCl needed to react with the $Mg(OH)_2$. (1 mark)
(d) What volume of 0.250 M hydrochloric acid could the antacid tablet neutralise? (2 marks)

(Total = 7 marks)

Question 36

An outdoor spa holds 5000 L of water. 40.0 kg of salt, NaCl, is dissolved in the spa.

(a) Determine the concentration in mol L^{-1} of the salt solution. (2 marks)
(b) After a spell of hot weather the volume of water in the spa is reduced to 4500 L. Calculate the new concentration of this salt solution. (2 marks)

(Total = 4 marks)

Question 37

100 mL of 0.25 mol L^{-1} chromium(III) nitrate, $Cr(NO_3)_3$ solution is mixed with 0.600 L of 0.10 mol L^{-1} sodium hydroxide solution, NaOH. A precipitate of chromium(III) hydroxide, $Cr(OH)_3$, is formed.

(a) Give the overall equation for this reaction if the only other product is sodium nitrate. (1 mark)
(b) Which is the excess reactant and by how many mol? (3 marks)
(c) What mass of chromium(III) hydroxide would be formed? (2 marks)
(d) Calculate the concentration of nitrate ions in the final liquid. (2 marks)
(Total = 8 marks)

Question 38

Hydrochloric acid is often sold as a solution with a concentration of 10.0 mol L^{-1}.

(a) Calculate the mass of HCl present in 25.0 L of this solution. (2 marks)
(b) If the density of this acid is 1.16 g mL^{-1}, calculate the % composition (% m/m) of this solution. (2 marks)
(c) A class needs a dilute solution of hydrochloric acid for an experiment. If the required concentration of the dilute solution is 0.125 mol L^{-1}, calculate the volume of the concentrated acid needed to make 2.50 L of the dilute solution. (2 marks)
(d) Calculate the volume of water needed to dilute 50.0 mL of the concentrated acid to a concentration of 0.500 mol L^{-1}. (2 marks)
(e) Calculate the final molarity of a hydrochloric acid solution when 200 mL of 0.600 mol L^{-1} HCl is mixed with 300 mL of 1.60 mol L^{-1} HCl. (2 marks)
(Total = 10 marks)

Question 39

A student dissolves 12.83 g of aluminium sulfate in enough water to make 250 mL of solution.

(a) Calculate the concentration of aluminium sulfate in
(i) mol L^{-1} (ii) g L^{-1} (3 marks)

50.0 mL of this solution is diluted so that the new concentration is 0.100 mol L^{-1}.

(b) Calculate the volume of water added to the 50.0 mL of solution to achieve the new concentration. (2 marks)
(c) Calculate the concentration of sulfate ions, in g L^{-1}, in the diluted solution. (2 marks)
(Total = 7 marks)

Question 40

A solution of ethanol in water is made by dissolving 15.3 g of ethanol in 120 mL of water. The density of ethanol is 0.785 g mL^{-1}.

(a) Calculate the volume of the ethanol before it is dissolved. (1 mark)
(b) Calculate the expected volume of the ethanol solution. (1 mark)
(c) The volume of the ethanol solution is found to be only 135 mL. Give a possible explanation for this observation. (1 mark)
(d) Calculate the concentration of the ethanol solution in the following units:
(i) mol L^{-1} (ii) g L^{-1} (iii) % m/m
(iv) % m/v (v) ppm (5 marks)
(Total = 8 marks)

Question 41

(a) Calculate the molarity of OH^- ions in a solution of calcium hydroxide made by completely dissolving 4.50 g of calcium hydroxide in water to make 500 mL of solution. (3 marks)

(b) Calculate the volume of the solution from part (a) that is needed to completely react with 100 mL of 0.150 mol L^{-1} hydrochloric acid. (3 marks)

(c) If 25.0 mL of the solution from part (a) is added to a 1.00 L volumetric flask and water is added to the mark, calculate the concentration of calcium hydroxide in the new solution in ppm. (2 marks)

(Total = 8 marks)

Question 42

50.0 mL of 0.250 mol L^{-1} zinc chloride is added to 50.0 mL of 0.500 mol L^{-1} potassium carbonate solution.

(a) Write the equation for the reaction. (1 mark)
(b) Calculate the mass of precipitate produced. (2 marks)
(c) Calculate the concentration of the potassium ions in the final solution. (2 marks)

(Total = 5 marks)

Question 43

200 mL of a 3.00 mol L^{-1} solution of iron(III) sulfate is mixed with 120 mL of a 5.00 mol L^{-1} solution of sodium hydroxide. A precipitate of iron(III) hydroxide forms.

(a) Write a balanced equation for the reaction. (1 mark)
(b) Determine which reactant is in excess. (3 marks)
(c) Calculate the final concentration of the reactant in excess. (2 marks)
(d) Calculate the mass of the precipitate formed. (2 marks)

(Total 8 marks)

Question 44

50.0 mL of 1.20 mol L^{-1} silver nitrate solution is reacted with 75.0 mL of 0.800 mol L^{-1} potassium chloride solution.

(a) Write a balanced equation for the reaction. (1 mark)
(b) Which reagent is in excess, and by how many moles? (2 marks)
(c) Name the insoluble product and calculate the mass produced. (2 marks)
(d) Write the ionic equation for the reaction and give the formulae of the spectator ions. (2 marks)

(Total = 7 marks)

(4) Gas Laws

Question 45

10.0 L of argon exerts a pressure of 1.05×10^5 Pa at 27°C.

(a) Calculate the mass of argon present. (2 marks)

The gas is allowed to expand to 20.0 L and the pressure falls to 6.00×10^4 Pa.

(b) Calculate the new temperature of the gas. (2 marks)

A further 10.0 g of argon is added to the gas from part (b).

(c) Calculate the new pressure of the gas if the other conditions from part (b) are unchanged. (2 marks)

(Total = 6 marks)

Question 46
Nitrogen(II) oxide, NO, can be prepared by reacting copper with 7.0 mol L^{-1} nitric acid.

$3Cu(s) + 8HNO_3(aq) \rightarrow 3Cu(NO_3)_2(aq) + 2NO(g) + 4H_2O(l)$

(a) What volume of NO at 18.0°C and 99.85 kPa pressure will be produced if 2.20 g of copper are reacted with an excess of nitric acid? (2 marks)

If copper is reacted with concentrated nitric acid a different reaction occurs and nitrogen(IV) oxide, NO_2, is produced.

$Cu(s) + 4HNO_3(aq) \rightarrow Cu(NO_3)_2(aq) + 2NO_2(g) + 2H_2O(l)$

(b) Calculate the volume of NO_2 produced at 25°C and a pressure of 102.0 kPa if 2.20 g of copper is reacted with an excess of concentrated nitric acid.
(2 marks)
(Total = 4 marks)

Question 47
A helium balloon is to be used to carry scientific instruments into the upper atmosphere. At ground level the balloon has a volume of 15.0 L at a temperature of 20.0°C and a pressure of 752 mm Hg. What will be the volume of the balloon when the temperature is –25.0°C and the pressure is 100 mm Hg? (Total = 3 marks)

Question 48
(a) Use the expression $pV = nRT$ to calculate the molar volume of an ideal gas at 20°C and a pressure of 101.3 kPa. (2 marks)

(b) Use the value from part (a) to calculate the densities, in g L^{-1}, of
(i) nitrogen. (ii) ammonia. (iii) nitrogen(II) oxide.
(3 marks)

The actual densities of these three gases at 20°C and a pressure of 101.3 kPa are given in the table below.

Gas	Density (g L^{-1})
Nitrogen, N_2	1.165
Ammonia, NH_3	0.717
Nitrogen(II) oxide, NO	1.249

(c) For each gas calculate the actual molar volume of the gas. (3 marks)
(d) Comment on any differences between the values in part (a) and those in part (c).
(1 mark)
(Total = 9 marks)

Question 49
An important step in the industrial production of nitric acid involves the oxidation of ammonia at 900°C and 10 atmospheres pressure.

$4NH_3(g) + 5O_2(g) \rightarrow 4NO(g) + 6H_2O(g)$

If 6.00 L of ammonia is mixed with 10.00 L of oxygen and allowed to react under these conditions, calculate the

(a) volumes of ammonia and oxygen that react. (2 marks)

(b) volumes of nitric oxide and steam produced. (2 marks)
(c) final total volume of gases. (1 mark)
(Total = 5 marks)

Question 50

Under certain conditions atmospheric nitrogen and oxygen combine to form nitrogen(II) oxide. This is then further oxidised to nitrogen(IV) oxide.

(a) Write balanced formula equations for the above reactions. (2 marks)
(b) Calculate the total volume of oxygen required to convert 1.50 L of nitrogen to nitrogen(IV) oxide. (2 marks)
(c) If temperature and pressure conditions remain constant and air contains 20% oxygen by volume, what is the minimum volume of air needed to carry out the reactions in part (b)? (2 marks)
(Total = 6 marks)

Question 51

A student heats 0.980 g of cobalt(III) nitrate. He collects from the reaction 0.332 g of solid cobalt(III) oxide and 360 mL of a dark brown gas, which he suspects contains some nitrogen dioxide, NO_2. He then shakes the gas with sodium hydroxide solution and all of the nitrogen dioxide dissolves. 72 mL of a colourless gas, which reignited a glowing splint, remained.
All gas volumes were measured at 20°C and a pressure of 101.3 kPa when the molar volume of gases is 24.05 L mol^{-1}. The molar masses of cobalt(III) nitrate and cobalt(III) oxide are 245 g mol^{-1} and 166 g mol^{-1}, respectively.

(a) Identify the colourless gas. (1 mark)
(b) Calculate the number of mole of cobalt(III) nitrate used. (1 mark)
(c) Calculate the number of mole of cobalt(III) oxide used. (1 mark)
(d) Calculate the number of moles of the two gases formed. (2 marks)
(e) Deduce the equation for the reaction. (2 marks)
(Total = 7 marks)

Question 52

The equation for the reaction between potassium permanganate, sulfuric acid and hydrogen peroxide is given below.

$$2KMnO_4(aq) + 5H_2O_2(aq) + 3H_2SO_4(aq) \rightarrow K_2SO_4(aq) + 2MnSO_4(aq) + 5O_2(g) + 8H_2O(l)$$

(a) Calculate the volume of oxygen, at 20°C and a pressure of 101.3 kPa (molar volume = 24.05 L mol^{-1}), released when 25.0 mL of 0.0200 mol L^{-1} potassium permanganate solution is reacted with an excess of the other two reagents.
(3 marks)

(b) Calculate the volume of 0.0200 mol L^{-1} $KMnO_4$ solution must be used to produce 0.100 g of oxygen assuming that there is an excess of the other reactants. (2 marks)

(c) If 40.0 mL of 0.0200 M $KMnO_4$ solution, 20.0 mL of 0.100 M H_2O_2 solution and 20.0 mL of 1.0 M H_2SO_4 are mixed together, what volume of oxygen at 20°C and a pressure of 101.3 kPa would be released? (3 marks)
(Total = 8 marks)

Question 53

A scientist isolates a gaseous hydrocarbon of unknown formula (i.e. C_xH_y) and determines its formula as follows. 20 mL of the hydrocarbon is mixed with 250 mL of oxygen at 20°C and 1.0 atm. The mixture is ignited and the hydrocarbon is burnt to produce carbon dioxide and water. The temperature and pressure of the gases are returned to 20°C and 1.0 atm and it is found that 80 mL of CO_2 and 130 mL O_2 are present. The equation for the combustion reaction is

$$C_xH_y(g) + (x + 0.25y)O_2(g) \rightarrow xCO_2(g) + 0.5yH_2O(g)$$

(a) From the experimental results, deduce the ratio $n(CO_2) : n(C_xH_y)$ and hence determine the value of x in the equation. (2 marks)

(b) Use the experimental results to deduce the ratio of $n(O_2) : n(C_xH_y)$ and hence determine the value of y in the equation. (2 marks)

(c) What is the molecular formula of the hydrocarbon? (1 mark)

(Total = 5 marks)

Question 54

It has been found that the radioactive element, radium, emits alpha particles (helium nuclei). The number of particles emitted can be counted with a Geiger counter. Each alpha particle is converted into a helium atom by gaining electrons from the surroundings. A certain quantity of radium emits 3.2×10^{17} alpha particles in one day. At the end of 10 days the total volume of helium gas produced, at 20°C and 101.3 kPa pressure, is 0.135 mL. Calculate a value for the Avogadro Constant.

(Total = 3 marks)

Question 55

A flask containing 1.08 g of a gaseous compound, X, at 120°C is evacuated and filled with nitrogen, N_2, at the same temperature and pressure. The mass of nitrogen in the flask is 0.42 g.

(a) Calculate the molar mass of the gas X. (2 marks)

(b) If the compound contains only carbon and hydrogen, deduce the molecular formula of X. (1 mark)

(Total = 3 marks)

Test: Quantitative Chemistry

Multiple Choice Items

Question 1

Which one of the following equations is NOT balanced?

(A) $2H_2S(g) + 3O_2(g) \rightarrow 2H_2O(g) + 2SO_2(g)$

(B) $2C_2H_6(g) + 7O_2(g) \rightarrow 4CO_2(g) + 6H_2O(g)$

(C) $HCl(aq) + NaOH(aq) \rightarrow H_2O(l) + NaCl(aq)$

(D) $3NO(g) + 2O_2(g) \rightarrow 3NO_2(g)$

Question 2
Which one of the following quantities would have the greatest mass?

(A) 1.0 mol of butane, $CH_3CH_2CH_2CH_3$
(B) 1.0 mol of 1–propylamine, $CH_3CH_2CH_2NH_2$
(C) 1.0 mol of propanal, CH_3CH_2CHO
(D) 1.0 mol of ethanoic acid, CH_3COOH

Question 3
Which one of the following contains the largest amount of hydrogen chloride, HCl?

(A) 8.0 L of 0.175 mol L^{-1} hydrochloric acid
(B) 8.0 L of HCl gas at 25°C and 100 kPa pressure
(C) 8.0×10^{23} molecules of HCl
(D) 8.0 g of HCl

Question 4
When 8.8 g of an oxide of nitrogen are decomposed 3.2 g of oxygen are formed. The empirical formula of the oxide is most likely to be

(A) N_2O (B) N_3O (C) N_4O_2 (D) NO_2

Question 5
An important reaction in the production of sulfuric acid is conversion of sulfur dioxide into sulfur trioxide.

$$2SO_2(g) + O_2(g) \rightarrow 2SO_3(g)$$

The mass of sulfur trioxide produced when 60.0 g of sulfur dioxide is reacted with 10.0 g of oxygen is

(A) 25.0 g (B) 50.0 g (C) 75.0 g (D) 100.0 g

Question 6
Four compounds of carbon, hydrogen and oxygen have the molecular formulae CH_4O, $C_2H_4O_2$, $C_3H_8O_3$ and $C_4H_8O_3$. When placed in order of increasing percentage of oxygen the order is (smallest first)

(A) $CH_4O < C_2H_4O_2 < C_3H_8O_3 < C_4H_8O_3$.
(B) $C_4H_8O_3 < C_3H_8O_3 < C_2H_4O_2. < CH_4O$
(C) $C_4H_8O_3 < CH_4O < C_3H_8O_3 < C_2H_4O_2$.
(D) $C_2H_4O_2. < C_3H_8O_3 < CH_4O < C_4H_8O_3$.

Question 7
32.0 g of a compound of carbon and hydrogen contains 2.18 mol of carbon. The molecular formula of the compound is most likely to be

(A) C_2H_5 (B) C_2H_6 (C) C_3H_8 (D) C_8H_3

Question 8
What volume of water must be added to 20.0 mL of 9.0 mol L^{-1} hydrochloric acid to produce a concentration of 1.5 mol L^{-1}?

(A) 100 mL (B) 120 mL (C) 140 mL (D) 160 mL

Question 9
Under suitable conditions oxygen and carbon monoxide will react according the equation shown below.

$2CO(g) + O_2(g) \rightarrow 2CO_2(g)$

A mixture of carbon monoxide and oxygen had a volume of 1.00 L at 60°C and 101.3 kPa. The mixture is allowed to react until one of the reactants is completely consumed. The final volume at this temperature and pressure was 800 mL. The most likely composition of the mixture after reaction is

(A) 500 mL of CO_2 and 300 mL of O_2.
(B) 400 mL of CO and 400 mL of CO_2.
(C) 600 mL of CO and 200 mL of CO_2.
(D) 300 mL of CO_2 and 500 mL of O_2.

Question 10
A solution of ammonia, NH_3, contains 3.70×10^{-4} mole of ammonia dissolved in 100 mL of solution. What is the concentration of the solution in g L^{-1}?

(A) 6.29×10^{-4} (B) 6.29×10^{-2} (C) 6.29 (D) 62.9

Question 11
250 mL of an aqueous solution contains 0.900 mole of ethanol. If the density of the solution is 0.932 g mL^{-1}, then the concentration expressed as % composition is

(A) 15.4 (B) 16.6 (C) 17.8 (D) 41.5

Question 12
Which one of the following solutions has the lowest concentration of chloride ions?

(A) 100 mL of a solution containing 0.05 mol of potassium chloride.
(B) 100 mL of a solution containing 0.03 mol calcium chloride.
(C) 100 mL of a solution containing 0.04 mol aluminium chloride.
(D) 100 mL of a solution containing 0.02 mol tin(IV) chloride.

Question 13
80 mL of ammonia are mixed with 80 mL of oxygen and caused to react according to the following equation,

$4NH_3(g) + 3O_2(g) \rightarrow 2N_2(g) + 6H_2O(g)$

After the reaction the temperature and pressure are returned to the same values as at the beginning of the experiment. The total gas volume will be

(A) 20 mL. (B) 140 mL. (C) 160 mL. (D) 180 mL.

Question 14
When a sample of a hydrocarbon is completely burnt in air 1.76 g of carbon dioxide and 0.90 g of water are formed. The empirical formula of the hydrocarbon is

(A) CH (B) C_2H (C) C_2H_5 (D) C_4H_5

Question 15
40.0 mL of oxygen is reacted with 32.0 mL of carbon monoxide to produce carbon dioxide gas, as in the equation below. If all gas volumes are measured at the same temperature and pressure, what would be the final composition of gases when the reaction is complete?

$$2CO(g) + O_2(g) \rightarrow 2CO_2(g)$$

(A) 72 mL of CO_2
(B) 24 mL of O_2 and 32 mL of CO_2
(C) 8 mL of O_2 and 32 mL of CO_2
(D) 12 mL of CO and 20 mL of CO_2

Extended Response Questions

Question 1
A student obtains the following results for a block of tungsten:

Mass = 154.4 g
Volume = 8.0 mL

He finds the following information in a data book:

Molar mass of tungsten, W = 183.85 g mol^{-1}
Atomic radius of tungsten = 137 pm
1 pm = 1×10^{-10} cm and 1.0 $cm^3 \cong$ 1.0 mL

(a) Calculate the number of mole of tungsten in the block. (1 mark)
(b) Calculate the volume of one atom of tungsten using volume, $V_s = (4/3)\pi(r)^3$. (1 mark)
(c) Calculate the number of tungsten atoms in the block, assuming that there is no space between the atoms. (1 mark)
(d) Calculate Avogadro's constant (number) based on these results. (1 mark)
(e) How does this value compare with the 'expected' value for Avogadro's constant? Suggest a reason for the difference. (1 mark)

(Total = 5 marks)

Question 2
Calculate the percentage composition of iron(III) sulfate. (3 marks)

Question 3
A balloon containing chlorine gas (Cl_2) at 1.23 atm pressure and 50°C has a volume of 6.55 L.

(a) Calculate the mass of chlorine gas in the balloon. (2 marks)

In the presence of sunlight this amount of chlorine is bubbled through 650 mL of water and the following reaction occurs.

$2Cl_2(g) + 2H_2O(l) \rightarrow 4HCl(aq) + O_2(g)$

(b) What volume of oxygen gas will be evolved at 25°C and a pressure of 101.3 kPa? (2 marks)

(c) After the reaction, what will be the concentration of HCl, in mol L^{-1}, in the solution? (2 marks)

(d) After the reaction, what will be the concentration of HCl in the solution, as % m/v, i.e. the mass in 100 mL of solution? (2 marks)

(Total = 8 marks)

Question 4

0.1377 g of nitrogen, N_2, is placed in a flask and exerts a pressure of 1.03 atm. When 0.2038 g of gas X is placed in the same flask at the same temperature it exerts a pressure of 0.97 atm.

(a) Calculate the molar mass of gas X. (3 marks)

(b) Suggest a possible formula for the gas. (1 mark)

(Total = 4 marks)

Question 5

1.25 g of a compound of carbon, hydrogen and oxygen contains 0.763 g of carbon and 0.148 g of hydrogen.

(a) Calculate the empirical formula of the compound. (3 marks)

(b) If the molar mass of the compound is 118 g mol^{-1}, calculate the molecular formula of the compound. (2 marks)

(Total = 5 marks)

(Total = 40 marks)

Chapter 3

Reactive Chemistry

Multiple Choice Items

(1) Chemical Reactions

Question 1
Sodium chloride undergoes a chemical change when

(A) crystals of the salt dissolve in water.
(B) crystals of the salt are broken into smaller fragments.
(C) a solution of sodium chloride is added to a solution of silver nitrate.
(D) crystals are heated until they melt.

Question 2
Which one of the following is **only** a physical change?

(A) Hard boiling an egg.
(B) Liquefying oxygen.
(C) The corrosion of iron.
(D) Combustion of a fuel.

Question 3
Carbon dioxide sublimes from a solid to a gas at -80°C. This process is

(A) A chemical change because it absorbs heat.
(B) A chemical change because a new product forms.
(C) Neither a physical nor a chemical change because it remains as CO_2 molecules.
(D) A physical change because it is reversed by cooling.

Question 4
Solid sulfur may be extracted from the earth by melting using superheated steam under pressure. It is then possible to solidify it in a different crystalline form to the original deposit. This process involves

(A) physical changes only.
(B) chemical changes only.
(C) neither physical nor chemical changes.
(D) both physical and chemical changes.

Question 5
When blue crystals of hydrated copper sulfate are heated, steam is evolved and white anhydrous copper sulfate remains. This change is

(A) physical, because there are changes of state and colour only.
(B) both physical and chemical, because there are changes of state and colour and weak chemical bonds are overcome.

(C) chemical, because weak chemical bonds are overcome and a new substance forms.
(D) chemical, because strong chemical bonds are overcome and a new substance forms.

Question 6
Which of the following is **least** likely to occur in a chemical change?

(A) The change is easily reversible.
(B) Strong chemical bonds are broken.
(C) Energy is absorbed or evolved.
(D) A new substance forms.

The information below refers to Questions 7 to 11.

The formulae of nine chemicals, I, II, III, IV, V, VI, VII, VIII and IX, are given below.

I	$NaOH$	II	$NaCl$	III	$AgNO_3$
IV	C_3H_8	V	O_2	VI	H_2SO_4
VII	H_2	VIII	$MgCO_3$	IX	N_2

Question 7
Which two chemicals would take part in a precipitation reaction?

(A) IV and V
(B) I and VI
(C) II and III
(D) VII and IX

Question 8
The two chemicals that could be used in a synthesis reaction are

(A) IV and V
(B) I and VI
(C) II and III
(D) VII and IX

Question 9
An acid base reaction will occur between

(A) IV and V
(B) I and VI
(C) II and III
(D) VII and IX

Question 10
A combustion reaction is most likely to occur between

(A) IV and V
(B) I and VI
(C) VI and VIII
(D) VII and IX

Question 11
Which chemical is most likely to undergo a decomposition reaction when heated?

(A) I (B) II (C) VI (D) VIII

Question 12

The correct balanced formula equation for the reaction of calcium with water is

(A) $Ca(s) + 2H_2O(aq) \rightarrow Ca(OH)_2(l) + H_2(g)$
(B) $Ca(s) + 2H_2O(l) \rightarrow Ca(OH)_2(aq) + H_2(g)$
(C) $Ca(s) + H_2O(l) \rightarrow CaOH(aq) + H_2(g)$
(D) $Ca(s) + 2H_2O(aq) \rightarrow Ca(OH)_3(l) + H_2(g)$

Question 13

Which one of the following correctly identifies the gas or gases produced when hydrochloric acid is reacted with either zinc, or sodium hydroxide, or sodium carbonate or sodium hydrogen carbonate?

	Zinc	**Sodium hydroxide**	**Sodium carbonate**	**Sodium hydrogen carbonate**
(A)	No gas produced	Hydrogen	Carbon dioxide	Carbon dioxide
(B)	Hydrogen	No gas produced	Carbon dioxide	Carbon dioxide and hydrogen
(C)	Carbon dioxide	Carbon dioxide	Hydrogen	No gas produced
(D)	Hydrogen	No gas produced	Carbon dioxide	Carbon dioxide

(2) Predicting Reactions of Metals

Question 14

A student determines part of the activity series of metals by adding the metals J, Q, M and R, separately to 1.0 mol L^{-1} solutions of the nitrate salts of the same metals. The results from the experiments are shown in the table below. "Y" indicates that a reaction occurred and "N" shows that no reaction occurred.

	$J^{2+}(aq)$	$Q^{2+}(aq)$	$M^{2+}(aq)$	$R^{2+}(aq)$
J(s)		N	Y	N
Q(s)	Y		Y	Y
M(s)	N	N		N
R(s)	Y	N	Y	

From these results this part of the activity series is

(A) J > Q > M > R
(B) Q > R > J > M
(C) Q > J > R > M
(D) R > M > Q > J

Question 15

A student strongly heats a metal carbonate. The colour changes from yellow to black and a gas is evolved. The gas reignites a glowing splint and also gives a positive limewater test. The formula of the metal carbonate is most likely to be

(A) $CuCO_3$ (B) $FeCO_3$ (C) Ag_2CO_3 (D) $NiCO_3$

Question 16
A highly reactive metal is most likely to

(A) have been discovered in Ancient Times.
(B) be used as a structural material.
(C) have not been discovered until electrolysis was in use.
(D) be a transition metal.

Question 17
Which of the following pairs of reactants is least likely to react spontaneously when mixed?

(A) Tin and dilute hydrochloric acid.
(B) Magnesium and water when heated.
(C) Mercury and dilute hydrochloric acid.
(D) Sodium and oxygen.

Question 18
Which one of the following is not a reason why a metal is unreactive when exposed to the air.

(A) The metal forms a protective surface layer of its oxide.
(B) The metal is very low in the activity series.
(C) A protective surface layer of eg. paint or oil can be applied.
(D) Metals do not corrode unless water and oxygen are present.

Question 19
Small pieces of the metals calcium, iron, magnesium and zinc are added to separate test tubes containing dilute hydrochloric acid. The expected order of reactivity of the metals (from highest to lowest) is

(A) iron > zinc > magnesium > calcium.
(B) calcium > magnesium > zinc > iron.
(C) zinc > iron > calcium > magnesium.
(D) magnesium > calcium > iron > zinc.

Question 20
Of the metals given below, which one is likely to be the most difficult to extract from its ores?

(A) Copper (B) Iron (C) Sodium (D) Zinc

Question 21
Several metal production processes have been developed over time. The most recent process is

(A) electrolysis. (B) smelting.
(C) mining. (D) nuclear.

Question 22
When a metal is extracted from its ore by a chemical process

(A) energy is required to break chemical bonds.
(B) there is no overall energy change as chemical bonds break and reform.
(C) energy is evolved when chemical bonds are broken.
(D) energy is neither required nor evolved.

Question 23
In the 21st century more than sixty metals are used by human societies. By contrast 2000 years ago only seven metals were in use. These metals were copper, gold, iron, lead, mercury, silver and tin. The best explanation for the use of metals being limited to these seven metals is that they

(A) are malleable, ductile and most easily worked.
(B) are shiny and attractive for making ornaments.
(C) can be found in the uncombined state or are easily extracted from their ores.
(D) can easily be turned into weapons.

Question 24
Which of the following metals is never found in an uncombined (elemental) form on Earth?
(A) copper (B) silver (C) magnesium (D) iron

Question 25
A metal, M, reacts with dilute hydrochloric acid to release hydrogen gas. Which one of the following statements about M is incorrect?

(A) M displaces silver from a solution of silver nitrate.
(B) M displaces iron from a solution of iron(II) sulfate.
(C) M is a more reactive metal than copper.
(D) M will react with oxygen from the air when heated strongly.

Question 26
Three metals, R, S and T, have the following properties:

- Metal R does not react with 1.0 mol L^{-1} H_2SO_4.
- Metal S will react with 1.0 mol L^{-1} H_2SO_4 to produce H_2, and also reacts with 1.0 mol L^{-1} RCl_2 solution to produce R.
- Metal T will react with 1.0 mol L^{-1} H_2SO_4 to produce H_2 but does not react with 1.0 mol L^{-1} SCl_2 solution.

From this information, the order of reactivity of the metals and H_2, from the highest to the lowest, is

(A) $R > H_2 > T > S$ (B) $H_2 > R > T > S$
(C) $S > H_2 > T > R$ (D) $S > T > H_2 > R$

Question 27
A piece of steel plate is placed in each of four separate containers, each containing a different 0.25 mol L^{-1} aqueous solution. The four solutions are $Pb(NO_3)_2(aq)$, $Zn(NO_3)_2(aq)$, $AgNO_3(aq)$ and $Cu(NO_3)_2(aq)$. It is expected that the piece of steel will be coated with another metal in the solutions of

(A) $Pb(NO_3)_2$, $AgNO_3$ and $Cu(NO_3)_2$.
(B) $Pb(NO_3)_2$ and $AgNO_3$.
(C) $AgNO_3$ and $Cu(NO_3)_2$.
(D) $Zn(NO_3)_2$ only.

Question 28
A student investigated the relative activity of the metals *Q*, *R* and *T* by performing three experiments. In each experiment a piece of metal was placed in a solution containing the ions of one of the other metals. The diagrams below show the results of the experiments.

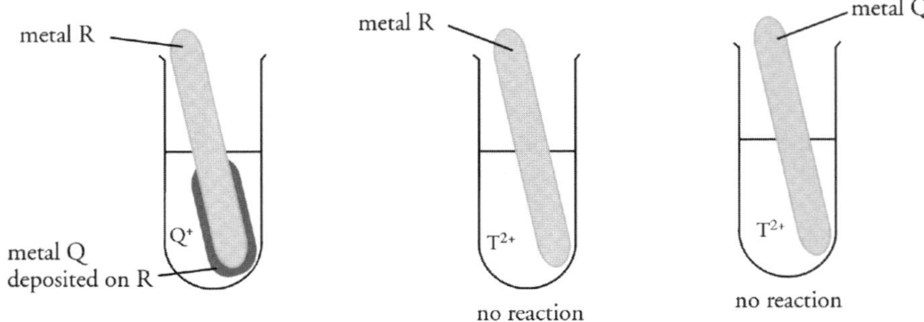

From these results the student determined that the relative activity of the metals was

(A) $Q > T > R$
(B) $R > Q > T$
(C) $T > Q > R$
(D) $T > R > Q$

Question 29
In which of the following lists are the metals placed in order of decreasing reactivity.

(A) Na, Mg, Fe, Cu, Ag.
(B) Mg, Na, Cu, Fe, Ag.
(C) Na, Mg, Fe, Ag, Cu.
(D) Na, Mg, Cu, Fe, Ag.

Question 30
In the equation $Zn(s) + S(s) \rightarrow ZnS(s)$

(A) Zinc is oxidised and is the reductant (reducing agent).
(B) Zinc is oxidised and is the oxidant (oxidising agent).
(C) Zinc is reduced and is the reductant (reducing agent).
(D) Zinc is reduced and is the oxidant (oxidising agent).

Question 31
For which of the following species is the oxidation number of oxygen the lowest?

(A) Na_2O_2
(B) H_2O_2
(C) O_2
(D) H_2SO_4

Question 32

Iodate ion, IO_3^-, is as an oxidising agent. The half-equation for the reaction is

$IO_3^-(aq) + 6H^+(aq) + ne^- \rightarrow I^+(aq) + 3H_2O(l)$

The value of n in this equation is

(A) 3 (B) 4 (C) 5 (D) 6

Question 33

In which one of the following reactions does sulfur have the largest change in oxidation number?

(A) $2S_2O_3^{2-}(aq) + I_2(aq) \rightarrow S_4O_6^{2-}(aq) + 2I^-(aq)$
(B) $2SO_2(g) + O_2(g) \rightarrow 2SO_3(g)$
(C) $H_2SO_4(l) + 8HI(g) \rightarrow H_2S(g) + 4H_2O(l) + 4I_2(s)$
(D) $S(l) + O_2(g) \rightarrow SO_2(g)$

Question 34

There are a number of compounds of sodium, oxygen and sulfur. For which one of the following compounds does sulfur have the lowest oxidation number?

(A) $Na_2S_2O_8$ (B) Na_2SO_4 (C) Na_2SO_3 (D) $Na_2S_2O_4$

Question 35

The following galvanic cell is set up.

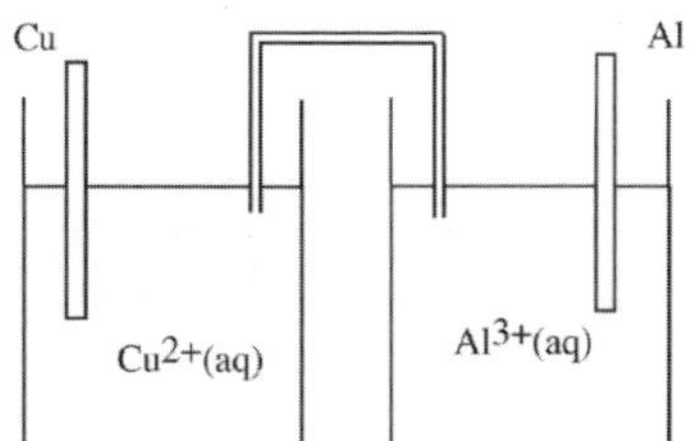

In this cell the aluminium electrode will be the

(A) anode and negatively charged.
(B) anode and positively charged.
(C) cathode and negatively charged.
(D) cathode and positively charged.

Question 36

Silver oxide and zinc are used in some galvanic cells. When these cells produce an electric current, the following reaction occurs:

$Ag_2O(s) + Zn(s) + H_2O(l) \rightarrow 2Ag(s) + Zn(OH)_2(s)$

The reaction occurring at the positive electrode when cells of this type produce a current is

(A) $Zn(s) + 2OH^-(aq) \rightarrow Zn(OH)_2(s) + 2e^-$
(B) $Zn(OH)_2(s) + 2e^- \rightarrow Zn(s) + 2OH^-(aq)$
(C) $Ag_2O(s) + H_2O(l) + 2e^- \rightarrow 2Ag(s) + 2OH^-(aq)$
(D) $2Ag(s) + 2OH^-(aq) \rightarrow Ag_2O(s) + H_2O(l) + 2e^-$

The following information refers to Questions 37 and 38.

Two galvanic cells are set up as shown in the diagram below.

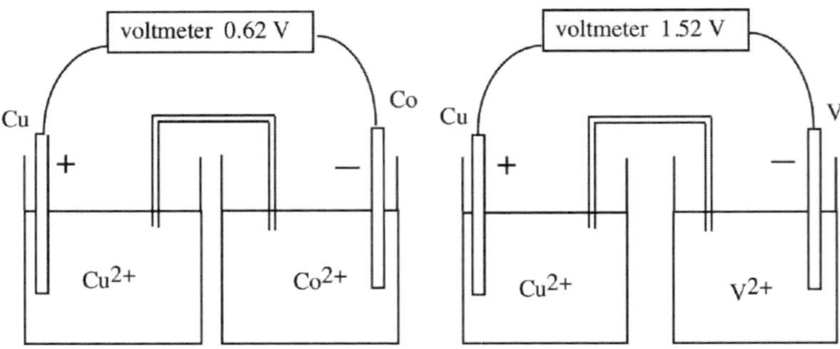

Question 37
The strongest reductant present is

(A) Co (B) Cu (C) V (D) Cu^{2+}

Question 38
The voltage of a cell using the Co/Co^{2+} and V/V^{2+} half-cells would be

(A) 0.90 V with the V electrode negative.
(B) 0.90 V with the Co electrode negative.
(C) 2.14 V with the V electrode negative.
(D) 2.14 V with the Co electrode negative.

The following information refers to Questions 39 and 40.

Four metals, Cu, p, q and r, were each placed in a solution of their metal ions. The electrodes and solutions were then connected in pairs as shown in the diagram below and the voltage of each cell was recorded.

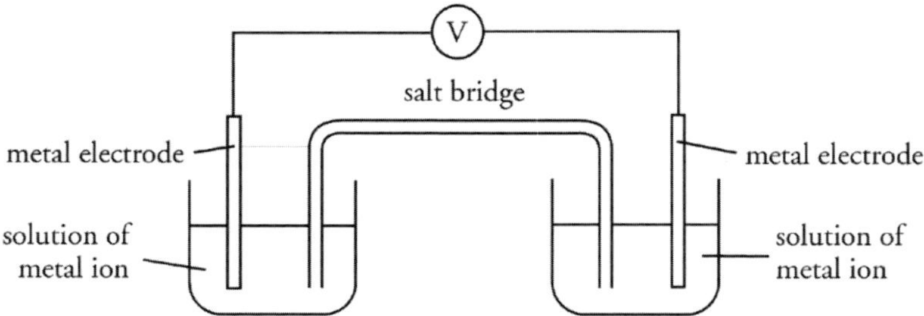

The table below shows the results obtained.

Negative terminal	Positive terminal	Voltage (V)
Cu	p	0.45
Cu	q	1.29
r	Cu	0.75

Question 39
From this information, place the metals in order showing the increasing ease of oxidation (easiest to oxidise last).

(A) $p < q < r <$ Cu
(B) Cu $< r < q < p$
(C) $q < p <$ Cu $< r$
(D) $r <$ Cu $< p < q$

Question 40
If the metals p and q were connected, then the results expected would be

	Negative terminal	Voltage (V)
(A)	p	0.84
(B)	p	1.74
(C)	q	0.84
(D)	q	1.74

Question 41
Galvanised iron consists of a piece of iron covered with a thin layer of zinc. A piece of galvanised iron has been scratched and corrosion has started to occur.

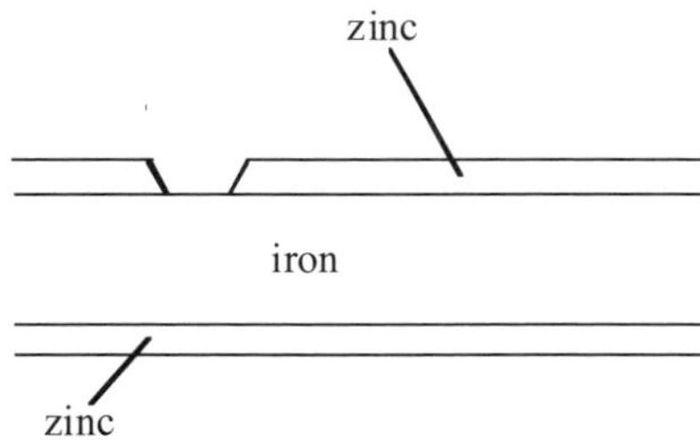

During this corrosion process

(A) the zinc acts as the negative electrode and the iron is oxidised.
(B) the zinc acts as the negative electrode and the zinc is oxidised.
(C) the iron acts as the negative electrode and the iron is oxidised.
(D) the iron acts as the negative electrode and the zinc is oxidised.

Question 42
A Cu/Cu^{2+} half-cell and a Zn/Zn^{2+} half-cell are connected using a salt bridge and the system is used to produce an electric current. The purpose of the salt bridge is to

(A) allow the reactants to make contact with each other.
(B) allow cations and anions to flow in and out of the two half-cells.
(C) provide essential reactants for the overall reaction.
(D) provide electrons to complete the circuit in the cell.

Question 43
In which one of the reactions below has the metal species been reduced?

(A) $2FeBr_2(aq) + Br_2(g) \rightarrow 2FeBr_3(aq)$
(B) $2Cu(NO_3)_2(aq) + 4KI(aq) \rightarrow 2CuI(s) + I_2(aq) + 4KNO_3(aq)$

(C) $2Cr(OH)_3(aq) \rightarrow Cr_2O_3(s) + 3H_2O(l)$
(D) $Ba(s) + 2HCl(aq) \rightarrow BaCl_2(aq) + H_2(g)$

Question 44
The diagram below shows an electrochemical cell, which has copper and nickel electrodes.

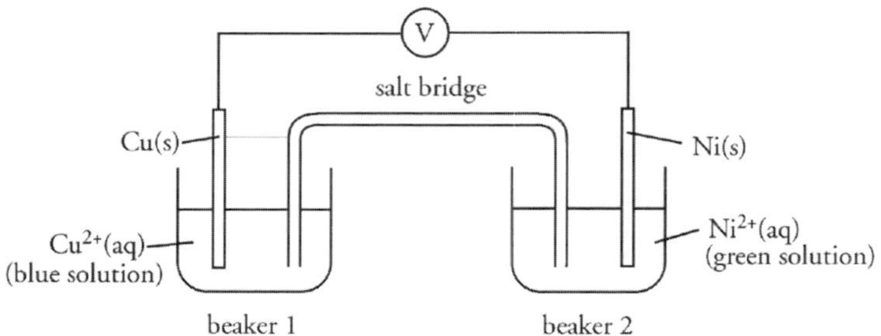

What three observations for this cell are correct?

	Observation 1	Observation 2	Observation 3
(A)	The reading shown on the voltmeter was -0.57 V.	The solution in beaker 1 became a darker blue.	The solution in beaker 2 became a fainter green.
(B)	The reading shown on the voltmeter was -0.11 V.	A red/brown solid formed on the copper electrode.	The solution in beaker 1 became a fainter blue.
(C)	A grey solid formed on the nickel electrode.	In beaker 1 the solution became a darker blue.	The solution in beaker 2 became a darker green.
(D)	The nickel electrode was the negative terminal.	A red/brown solid formed on the copper electrode.	The solution in beaker 2 became a darker green.

Question 45
The greatest change in oxidation number occurs when

(A) CrO_4^{2-} is converted into Cr^{3+}.
(B) PbO_2 is converted into $PbSO_4$.
(C) V^{2+} is converted into VO_2^+.
(D) IO_3^- is converted into I^-.

Question 46
When potassium iodide solution is added to a solution of iron(III) sulfate the following reaction occurs.

$2Fe^{3+}(aq) + 2I^-(aq) \rightarrow 2Fe^{2+}(aq) + I_2(aq)$

For this reaction it is correct to state that the $Fe^{3+}(aq)$ ions have been

(A) oxidised and have lost electrons.
(B) reduced and have lost electrons.
(C) oxidised and have gained electrons.
(D) reduced and have gained electrons.

Question 47

A galvanic cell is set up as shown in the diagram below.

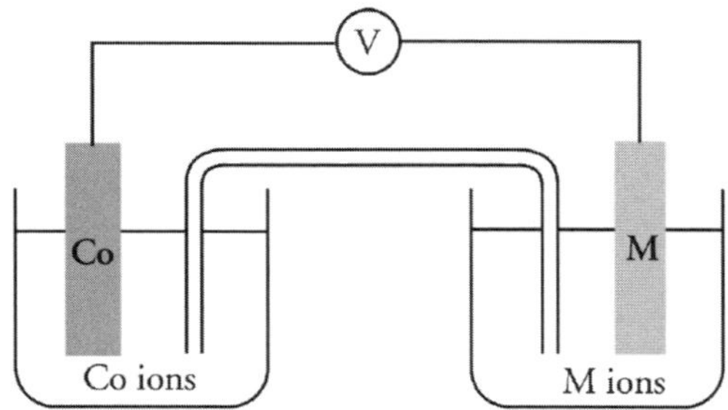

If the metal (M) acts as the cathode, which one of the following would, in theory, produce the lowest cell potential?

(A) Cadmium (B) Copper (C) Iron (D) Tin

Question 48

The following redox couples and their E° values have been taken from a table of standard reduction potentials.

Redox Couple	E°
Co^{2+}/Co	–0.28 V
Cu^{2+}/Cu	0.34 V
Mn^{2+}/Mn	–1.18 V
Ru^{2+}/Ru	0.46 V

If the metals are ranked in order of decreasing electrochemical activity, the order is

(A) Mn > Co > Cu > Ru
(B) Ru > Cu > Co > Mn
(C) Mn > Ru > Cu > Co
(D) Co > Mn > Cu > Ru

Use the information below to answer Questions 49 and 50.

A common redox reaction is represented by the equation below.

$$MnO_4^-(aq) + 8H^+(aq) + 5Fe^{2+}(aq) \rightarrow Mn^{2+}(aq) + 4H_2O(l) + 5Fe^{3+}(aq)$$

Question 49

The oxidising agent in this reaction is

(A) H^+ (B) Mn^{2+} (C) Fe^{2+} (D) MnO_4^-

Question 50

From the table of standard reduction potentials the expected E^{o}_{cell} for this reaction is

(A) 0.74 V (B) 1.07 V (C) 2.28 V (D) 3.11 V

Question 51

Use the table of standard reduction potentials to predict which one of the following reactions would occur spontaneously.

(A) $2Cl^-(aq) + Br_2(aq) \rightarrow Cl_2(aq) + 2Br^-(aq)$
(B) $2Fe^{3+}(aq) + Cu(s) \rightarrow 2Fe^{2+}(aq) + Cu^{2+}(aq)$
(C) $Cu^{2+}(aq) + 2Ag(s) \rightarrow Cu(s) + 2Ag^+(aq)$
(D) $Zn^{2+}(aq) + 2Cr^{2+}(aq) \quad Zn(s) + 2Cr^{3+}(aq)$

(3) Rates of Reactions

Question 52

A student adds 0.250 g of zinc to 100 mL of 1.00 mol L^{-1} hydrochloric acid at 20°C. The hydrogen gas produced by the reaction is collected in a gas syringe and its volume is measured at regular time intervals. The student obtains the results shown in the graph below.

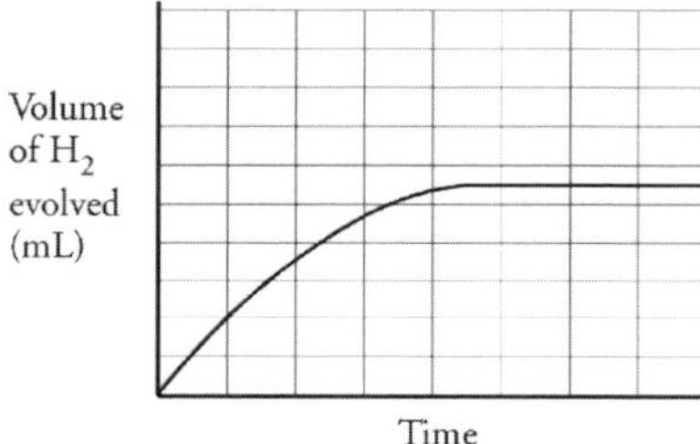

The student then repeats the experiment using the same amounts of zinc and hydrochloric acid but the temperature of the acid is 35°C. The results from the second experiment are plotted on the same axes as the first experiment. The most likely graph is

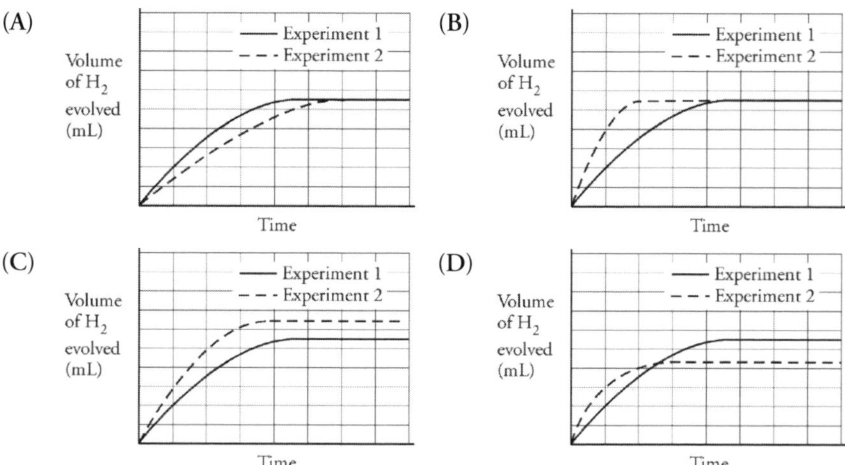

Item 53

When limestone, $CaCO_3$, reacts with hydrochloric acid, the reaction shown on the next page occurs:

$CaCO_3(s) + 2HCl(aq) \rightarrow CaCl_2(aq) + CO_2(g) + H_2O(l)$

Which of the following would **not** increase the rate of the reaction?

(A) Changing the temperature from 15°C to 25°C.
(B) Using finely powdered limestone.
(C) Increasing the volume of the container.
(D) Using 2.0 M acid instead of 1.0 M acid.

Question 54
Unless strict safety precautions are adhered to there is always a risk of an explosion at a flour mill, due to the presence of fine particles of flour. Which of the following statements is the best explanation for this?

(A) It is very easy to heat the fine particles of flour to their ignition temperature.
(B) The surface area of the flour particles is very large and thus combustion reactions are very rapid.
(C) The activation energy for the reaction of fine particles of flour is much lower than for larger particles.
(D) When flour is ground to fine particles the energy profile for the combustion reaction is changed.

Question 55
Acetone, CH_3COCH_3, and iodine, I_2, react according to the equation given below. A small amount of sulfuric acid is needed to catalyse the reaction.

$CH_3COCH_3(l) + I_2(aq) \rightarrow CH_3COCH_2I(aq) + HI(aq)$

A student determines which factors will change the rate of this reaction. Four experiments are carried out with different initial concentrations of acetone, iodine and sulfuric acid. The time taken to form a small amount of product is measured. This amount of product is the same for each experiment. The results are listed in the table below.

$[CH_3COCH_3]$	$[I_2]$	$[H^+]$	Time taken
0.100 M	0.100 M	0.010 mol L^{-1}	60 s
0.100 M	0.100 M	0.020 mol L^{-1}	30 s
0.200 M	0.100 M	0.010 mol L^{-1}	30 s
0.100 M	0.200 M	0.010 mol L^{-1}	60 s

The student deduces that the rate of the reaction

(A) depends only on the concentration of acetone.
(B) is not affected by the concentration of sulfuric acid.
(C) depends on the concentrations of acetone, iodine and acid.
(D) is only affected by the concentrations of acetone and acid.

Question 56
The gaseous reaction on the next page is an important step in the production of sulfuric acid. It is usually carried out at ~450°C in the presence of a solid vanadium(V) oxide catalyst.

$2SO_2(g) + O_2(g) \rightarrow 2SO_3(g)$

Which one of the following would **not** be expected to increase the rate of this reaction?

(A) Increasing the volume of the reaction vessel.
(B) Increasing the concentration of oxygen.
(C) Increasing the subdivision of the vanadium(V) oxide solid.
(D) Increasing the temperature to 550°C.

Question 57
An important reaction in the production of ammonia, NH_3, is given below.

$N_2(g) + 3H_2(g) \rightarrow 2NH_3(g); \quad \Delta H = -90 \text{ kJ mol}^{-1}$

If the reaction takes place in a sealed container, which of the following procedures would **not** cause the rate of the reaction to increase?

(A) Increasing the temperature.
(B) Adding an inert gas.
(C) Adding a suitable catalyst.
(D) Increasing the concentration of hydrogen.

Question 58
The energy profile for the reaction between SO_2 and O_2 to produce SO_3 is shown below: w, x, y and z are numerical values of the chemical energy.

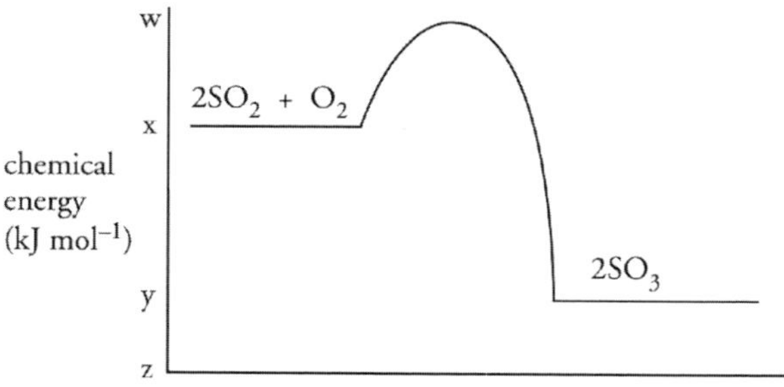

The activation energy of the left to right reaction would be calculated by

(A) w – x (B) w – y (C) w – z (D) x – y

Question 59
Students investigated the factors that changed the rate of reaction between dilute hydrochloric acid and a lump of magnesium. Which factor is **not** expected to increase the rate of this reaction?

(A) Using powdered magnesium.
(B) Using a more dilute solution of the acid.
(C) Heating the acid before it is added to the magnesium.
(D) Making sure the mixture is stirred constantly.

Question 60
Which one of the following energy profiles is most likely to be that of an explosive reaction?

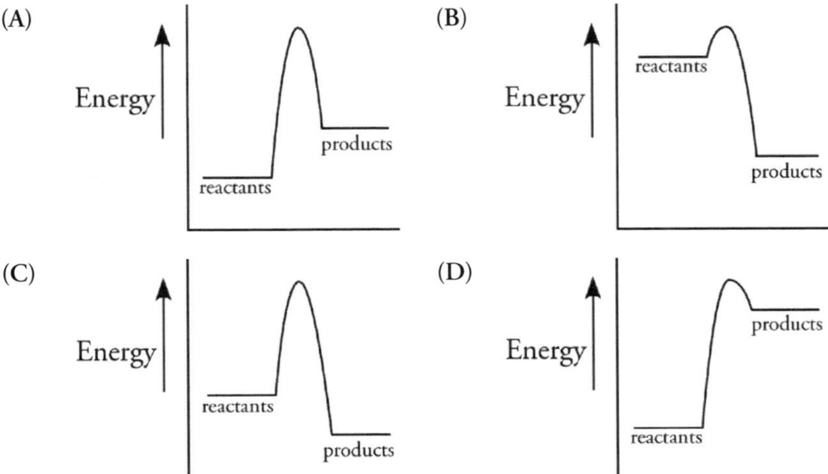

The following information refers to Questions 61 and 62.

The energy profile for a reaction is shown below.

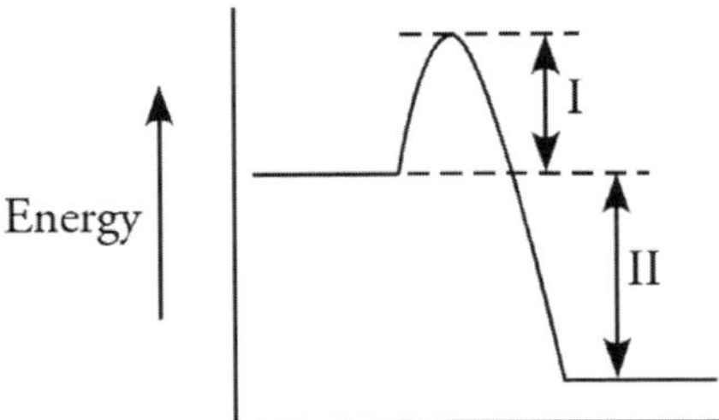

Question 61
ΔH for the reaction is indicated by the size of

(A) I (B) II (C) I + II (D) I – II

Question 62
If the reaction is carried out using a catalyst, this would

(A) decrease the size of both I and II.
(B) decrease the size of I but increase the size of II.
(C) increase the size of I.
(D) decrease the size of I.

Question 63
An important step in the production of sulfuric acid is the conversion of sulfur dioxide to sulfur trioxide. A temperature of ~450°C and a catalyst are used in this reaction.

$2SO_2(g) + O_2(g) \rightarrow 2SO_3(g)$

The purpose of the catalyst is to

(A) increase the number of collisions between SO_2 and O_2 molecules.
(B) increase the number of effective collisions between SO_2 and O_2 molecules.
(C) increase the amount of SO_3 produced.
(D) increase the activation energy of the reaction.

Extended Response Questions

(1) Chemical Reactions

Question 1
Write balanced formula equations for the following reactions.

(a) The reaction of phosphoric acid, H_3PO_4, with sodium hydroxide. (2 marks)
(b) The reaction of sodium with chlorine to form sodium chloride. (2 marks)
(c) The decomposition of mercury(II) oxide. (2 marks)
(d) The complete combustion of butane, C_4H_{10}, in air. (2 marks)
(e) The synthesis of ammonia, NH_3, from nitrogen and hydrogen. (2 marks)
(f) The reaction of aluminium oxide with sulfuric acid. (2 marks)
(g) The neutralisation of sulfuric acid with sodium hydrogen carbonate, $NaHCO_3$. (2 marks)

(Total = 14 marks)

Question 2
For each of the partial equations below: (i) state the most likely type of reaction and (ii) complete and balance the equation.

(a) $SO_2(g) + O_2(g) \rightarrow$ (2 marks)
(b) $Ba(OH)_2(aq) + HCl(aq) \rightarrow$ (2 marks)
(c) $Ba(NO_3)_2(aq) + Na_2SO_4(aq) \rightarrow$ (2 marks)
(d) $CaCO_3(s) + HCl(aq) \rightarrow$ (2 marks)
(e) $C_2H_6O(g) + O_2(g) \rightarrow$ (2 marks)
(f) $Au_2O_3 \rightarrow$ (2 marks)

(Total = 12 marks)

(2) Predicting Reactions of Metals

Question 3
A chemist places tin rods in each of four 0.2 M aqueous solutions. The solutes are respectively $AgNO_3$, $CuSO_4$, $FeSO_4$ and $ZnCl_2$. Describe what you would expect to happen in each of these experiments. Give reasons for your answers. Give equations for any reactions that occur. (Total = 4 marks)

Question 4

A student carries out four experiments with four different metals, I, II, III and IV. Pieces of the metals are heated strongly in air, added to cold water, added to dilute hydrochloric acid and added to a solution of silver nitrate. Some of the results obtained by the student are recorded in the table below.

	I	II	III	IV
Heat in air				Reacts
Cold H_2O	Reacts		Does not react	
HCl(aq)			Reacts	Does not react
Ag^+(aq)		Does not react		

(a) Use the results recorded in the table to deduce the activity series of these four metals. (3 marks)

(b) Give the name of a metal that could correspond to I, II, III and IV. (4 marks)
(Total = 7 marks)

Question 5

A student carries out experiments with four reductants, H_2, P, Q and R. Metal Q reacts with a solution of PSO_4 to produce metallic P. Gaseous hydrogen will reduce the cation R^{2+} and one other cation to their respective metals. RSO_4 solution will not react with metal P. Deduce the order of reactivity of the reductants (place the most reactive first).
Give reasons for your answer. (Total = 4 marks)

Question 6

A student performed the experiment shown in the diagram below as part of an investigation into the relative reactivity of metals. Initially the beaker contained 200.0 mL of 0.150 mol L^{-1} nickel chloride solution. After several hours the dark green colour of the solution had become lighter and a silvery grey deposit had formed on the piece of magnesium metal and on the bottom of the beaker. A small number of bubbles of gas also formed on the surface of the magnesium during this time.

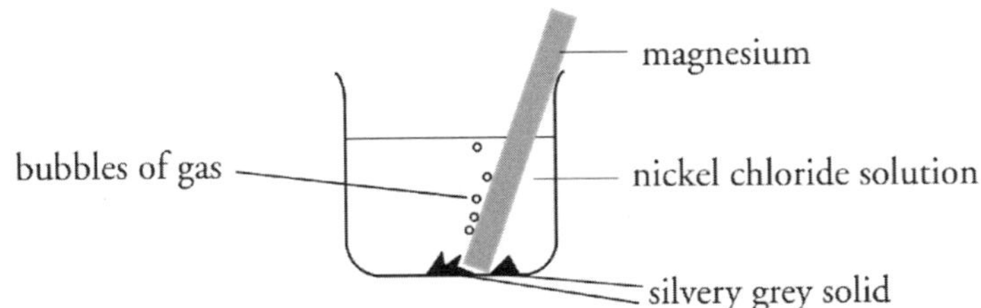

(a) Give an explanation for the changes observed by the student. (2 marks)

(b) Give a balanced oxidation–reduction equation for the production of the silvery grey solid. (1 mark)

(c) Identify the gas that is produced in this experiment and give a balanced equation for its formation. (2 marks)

The silvery grey solid was removed from the piece of magnesium and the beaker and was washed and dried. The mass of the solid was 0.880 g. The piece of magnesium was also washed and dried. The mass of magnesium had decreased by 0.401 g.

(d) Use the mass of silvery grey solid to calculate the expected loss in mass of the piece of magnesium. (2 marks)

(e) Explain why your answer to part (d) differs from 0.401 g. (1 mark)

(f) Assuming there has been no change in volume, calculate the concentration of the nickel chloride solution at the end of the experiment. (2 marks)

(Total = 10 marks)

Question 7

A chemist carried out reactions with three metals, X, Y and Z, and solutions of their nitrate salts. The observations below were made when clean metal surfaces were used.

I Metal Z dissolved in a 1 M YNO_3 solution, forming a deposit of metal Y.
II Metal X did not react with a 1 M $Z(NO_3)_3$ solution.
III Metal Y did not react with a 1 M $X(NO_3)_2$ solution.

(a) Use this information to place the three metals in order of increasing strength as reductants (put the least reactive first). Give reasons for your answer. (3 marks)

(b) The naturally occurring ores of these metals are XS, Y_2S and Z_2O_3. Which metal is likely to be the easiest to extract from its ore and which metal is likely to be the most difficult to extract? Give reasons for your answers. (2 marks)

(Total = 5 marks)

Question 8

6.537 g of solid zinc was added to 150 mL of 1.00 mol L^{-1} silver nitrate solution.

(a) Write a balanced equation for the reaction that occurs. (1 mark)
(b) For each of the species shown in the table below, calculate the number of moles present in the final mixture.

Chemical species	$Zn(s)$	$Zn^{2+}(aq)$	$Ag^{+}(aq)$	$Ag(s)$	$NO_3^{-}(aq)$
Amount, in moles, in final mixture					

(5 marks)

(Total = 6 marks)

Question 9

A student was given three metals and three electrolyte solutions and asked to measure the potential difference when the pairs of the metals and their electrolyte solutions were joined together. The student was given the metals copper, iron and silver; and the electrolyte solutions copper sulfate, iron(II) nitrate and silver nitrate.

(a) Which combination of the metals and electrolyte solutions are expected to give the largest potential difference? (1 mark)

(b) Using the metals and electrolyte solutions from part (a), sketch a diagram of a suitable experimental setup that the student could use. Label your diagram. (2 marks)

(c) Calculate the expected potential difference for the materials used in part (a). (1 mark)

(d) For the materials used in part (a), write the chemical equations for the reactions occurring at each of the metals and for the overall reaction. (2 marks)

(e) In experiments such as this one the theoretical potential difference often varies from the measured one. Suggest two steps the student should have taken to minimise this difference. (2 marks)

(Total = 8 marks)

Question 10

Metals in Group 1 have different physical and chemical properties from transition metals.

(a) Give an example of a physical property and an example of a chemical property that could be used to distinguish between a Group 1 metal and a transition metal. (2 marks)

(b) Choose a transition metal and give the formulae of two compounds, which demonstrate the variable oxidation states of this metal. (2 marks)

(Total = 4 marks)

Question 11

The position of the metal in the activity series is often correlated with other properties of the metal, such as atomic radius, ionisation energy and electronegativity.

(a) Why is the activity of metal expected to correlate with its atomic radius? (2 marks)

A shortened version of the activity series is given below along with the relevant atomic radius.

Metal activity series:	Zn >	Sn >	Pb >	Cu >	Ag >	Au
Atomic radius (pm)	133	151	175	128	144	144

(b) Using this data, comment on the correlation between the activity of a metal and its atomic radius. (2 marks)

(c) Give explanations for the expected correlation between the activity of a metal and (i) its ionisation energy and (ii) its electronegativity. (2 marks)

(Total = 6 marks)

Question 12

(a) The element tin is used to coat steel in 'tin' cans to prevent corrosion from occurring. The layer of tin is plated onto the steel can by electrolysis using a solution of tin(II) nitrate. This is called electroplating. The half-equation for the deposition of the tin is

$Sn^{2+}(aq) + ne^{-} \rightarrow Sn(s)$

(i) Justify whether the Sn^{2+} ion is being oxidised or reduced.
(ii) Justify whether the Sn^{2+} ion is the oxidant or the reductant.
(iii) How many electrons are required to plate each tin atom onto the can? (3 marks)

(b) Aluminium is obtained by the electrolysis of molten aluminium oxide dissolved in cryolite to lower the operating temperature. The simplified overall cell reaction is

$2Al_2O_3(cryolite) \rightarrow 4Al(l) + 3O_2(g)$

(i) Write the oxidation half-reaction and identify the species being oxidised.
(ii) Write the reduction half-reaction and identify the species being reduced.
(iii) How many electrons are transferred for every four atoms of aluminium produced?

(3 marks)
(Total = 6 marks)

Question 13

The EMFs and electrode polarities of two standard electrochemical cells are below. (Note that not all of these half-cells are listed in the electrochemical reactivity series provided in the data sheet.)

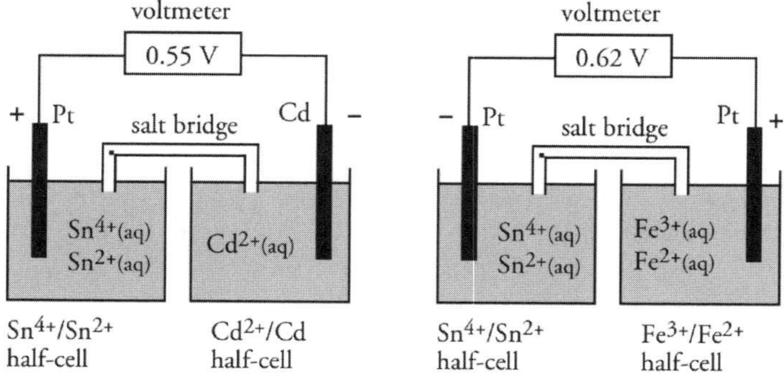

(a) From the information given above, deduce which species in the two cells is the strongest oxidising agent. Explain your reasoning. (2 marks)

(b) Give the equation for the reaction occurring at the anode in each cell. (2 marks)

(c) If a cell was constructed from the Fe^{3+}/Fe^{2+} and the Cd^{2+}/Cd half-cells, what would be the value for the EMF of the cell? (1 mark)

(Total = 5 marks)

Question 14

Explain the following:

(a) Iron objects in the desert or deep parts of the ocean do not rust. (2 marks)
(b) Although aluminium reacts with atmospheric oxygen it is used as a building material, e.g. in window frames. (2 marks)
(c) Sodium reacts rapidly with oxygen but is stored in oil rather than deoxygenated water. (2 marks)
(d) Gold does not react with water or atmospheric gases but is often alloyed with other metals before being used to make jewellery. (2 marks)

(Total = 8 marks)

Question 15

1.0 mol L^{-1} solutions of $AgNO_3$ and $NiCl_2$, pieces of Ag and Ni metal and a salt bridge can be used to produce a galvanic cell.

(a) Draw a simple arrangement showing how this could be done, and clearly label the positive and negative electrodes. (4 marks)

(b) Why is a salt bridge used in the galvanic cell? (1 mark)

(c) Give the formula of a compound that would be suitable to use in a salt bridge. (1 mark)

(d) Write the half-equations for the reactions occurring at each electrode and the overall cell reaction. (3 marks)

(Total = 9 marks)

Question 16

A cell is set up as shown in the diagram below.

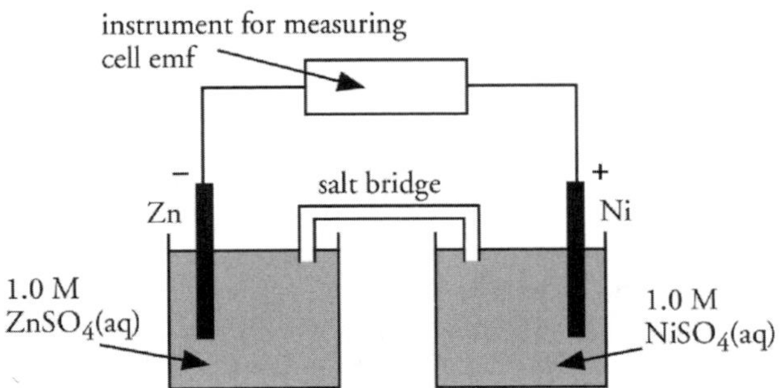

As current is drawn from this cell, describe

(a) what happens to the masses of the two electrodes. (2 marks)
(b) what happens to the concentrations of Zn^{2+}(aq) and of Ni^{2+}(aq). (2 marks)
(c) the purpose of the salt bridge. (2 marks)

(Total = 6 marks)

Question 17

Six experiments were carried out in which pairs of reagents were mixed. The pairs are indicated in the left-hand column of the table below. For those cases where the electrochemical series would predict that a reaction should occur, write a balanced chemical equation for the predicted reaction. Where you do not expect a reaction write 'no reaction'.

Reactants	Predicted reaction Yes/No	Equation
Fe^{2+}(aq)/Cl_2(g)		
$AgNO_3$(aq)/Sn(s)		
$SnCl_2$(aq)/Cu(s)		
Cd^{2+}(aq)/Ag(s)		
Ni^{2+}(aq)/Cd(s)		
Cl^-(aq)/I_2(aq)		

(Total = 9 marks)

Question 18

Consider the following electrochemical series.

$Cu^+(aq) + e^- \rightleftharpoons Cu(s) \qquad E° = 0.52$ V

$Cu^{2+}(aq) + e^- \rightleftharpoons Cu^+(aq) \qquad E° = 0.16$ V

Many solid compounds of copper(I) are known (such as solid copper(I) oxide, Cu_2O; solid copper(I) chloride, CuCl) and are quite stable. However, attempts to prepare solutions containing Cu^+(aq) are always unsuccessful. Use the information provided above to explain why solutions of Cu^+(aq) are unstable. (Total = 3 marks)

Question 19

The diagram below represents the cell constructed from cobalt, tin and solutions of their cations.

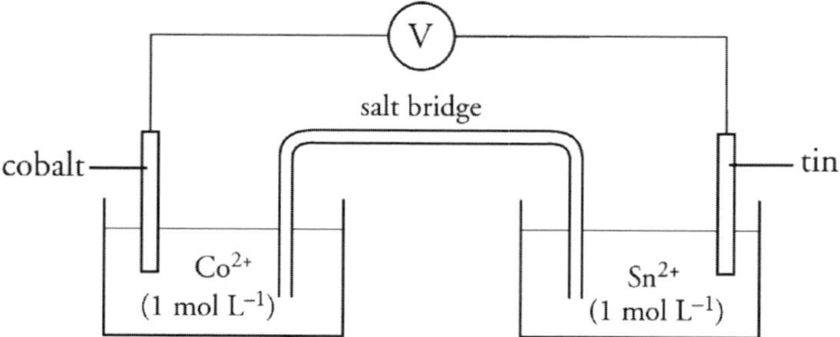

(a) Which material is the cathode in this cell? (1 mark)
(b) Write the overall equation for the redox reaction that occurs in this cell. (1 mark)
(c) Calculate the maximum potential (E°) that this cell could produce. (1 mark)
(d) In practice, the potential produced is often less than that predicted in part (c). Suggest a reason for this. (1 mark)

(Total = 4 marks)

Question 20

Some of the redox couples involving metals and their cations are shown in the table below along with their E° values.

Redox couple	**E° (V)**
Mn^{2+}/Mn	–1.03
Zn^{2+}/Zn	–0.76
Fe^{2+}/Fe	–0.44
Cd^{2+}/Cd	–0.40
Ni^{2+}/Ni	–0.23
Sn^{2+}/Sn	–0.14
Cu^{2+}/Cu	+0.34
Ag^{+}/Ag	+0.80
Au^{+}/Au	+1.68

Using only these redox couples predict, which combination of couples would give a cell voltage

(a) closest to 0.50 V
(b) closest to 1.00 V
(c) closest to 1.50 V
(d) closest to 2.00 V

(Total = 4 marks)

Question 21

The diagram on the next page shows a galvanic cell constructed from a Cu/Cu^{2+} half-cell and one containing metal Q and a solution of its nitrate salt.

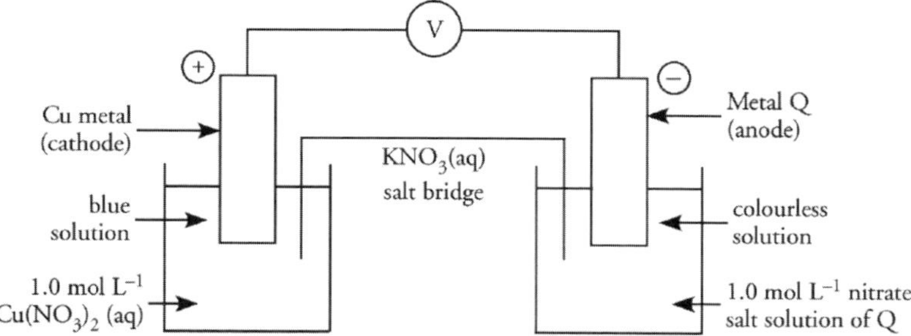

(a) Give an explanation for the change in colour expected in the copper half-cell. (2 marks)

(b) The theoretical potential difference expected for this cell is 1.52 V. Use the information in the data tables to deduce the identity of the metal Q. Give an explanation for your answer. (2 marks)

(Total = 4 marks)

(3) Rates of Reactions

Question 22

A student added 0.260 g of zinc to 100 mL of 1.00 mol L^{-1} hydrochloric acid in the equipment shown below. The temperature recorded was 20°C and the pressure was 101.3 kPa.

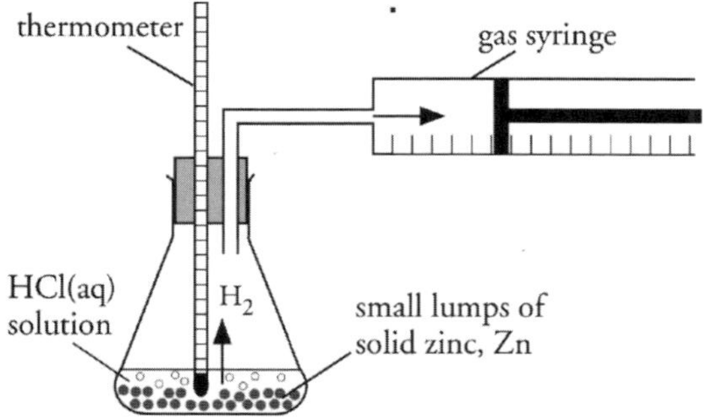

The student noted the volume of gas in the syringe at regular intervals and plotted the graph shown below.

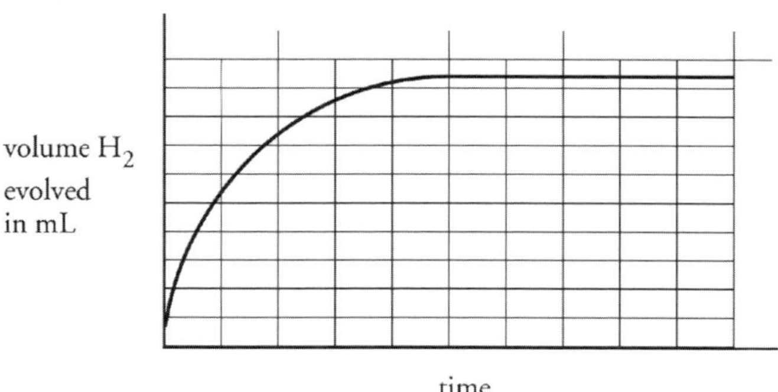

(a) Write an equation for the reaction between hydrochloric acid and zinc. (1 mark)

(b) Calculate the mass of hydrogen produced in the reaction. (2 marks)

(c) How did the rate of evolution of hydrogen change over the time taken for the reaction? (1 mark)

(d) Give an explanation for your answer to part (c). (2 marks)

(e) Propose two changes to the experiment that would increase the rate of evolution of hydrogen. (2 marks)

(f) In a second experiment, the student adds 0.260 g of zinc to 100 mL of 0.500 mol L^{-1} hydrochloric acid at a temperature of 20°C and again measures the volume of hydrogen evolved at regular intervals. On the diagram on the previous page sketch the line expected for this second experiment.
(1 mark)(Total = 9 marks)

Question 23

A student wishes to determine the rate of reaction between dilute hydrochloric acid and marble chips (calcium carbonate). He places 100 mL of 1.00 mol L^{-1} acid in an open flask and places the flask on a balance. He then adds 10.0 g of small lumps of calcium carbonate and records the mass every minute. His results are listed in the table below.

Time (min)	Mass of flask and contents (g)
0.0	225.67
1.00	225.13
2.00	224.69
3.00	224.30
4.00	223.99
5.00	223.75
6.00	223.59
7.00	223.52
8.00	223.49
9.00	223.49

(a) Write the equation for the reaction between calcium carbonate and hydrochloric acid. (1 mark)

(b) Calculate the amounts of each reactant placed in the flask. (2 marks)

(c) Which reactant is in excess? (1 mark)

(d) Why does the mass of the flask and contents decrease with time? (1 mark)

(e) Plot a graph of mass loss against time. (2 marks)

(f) Calculate the rate of reaction between
(i) 1 to 2 minutes and (ii) 5 to 6 minutes. (2 marks)

(g) How does the rate of reaction change over the course of the reaction? (1 mark)

(h) Give a reason for your answer to part (g). (1 mark)
(Total = 11 marks)

Question 24

The following reaction was originally part of the process for the production of sulfuric acid.

$SO_2(g) + NO_2(g) \rightarrow SO_3(g) + NO(g)$

The energy changes for this reaction are represented by the graph on the next page.

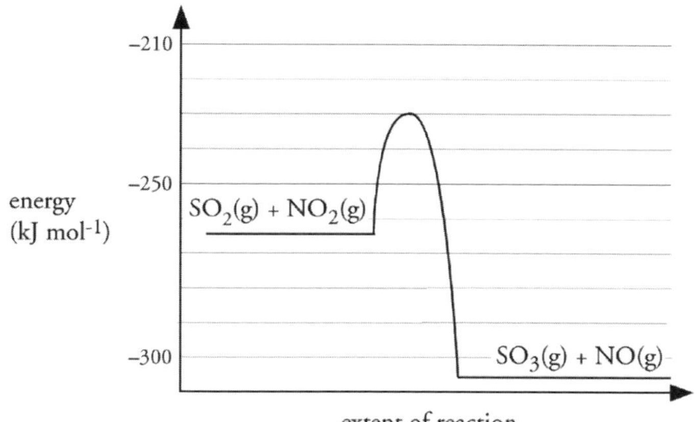

(a) From the graph, calculate the sign and magnitude of ΔH for the forward reaction (L → R). (2 marks)

(b) From the graph, calculate the activation energy for the reaction,

$SO_3(g) + NO(g) \rightarrow SO_2(g) + NO_2(g)$ (1 mark)

(c) The rate of this reaction increases with increasing temperature. Describe two reasons to explain this. (2 marks)

(d) If a suitable catalyst could be discovered for this process, how would the catalyst change

(i) the rate of reaction, (ii) the activation energy and
(iii) ΔH for the reaction?

In each case explain your answer.

(1 + 1 + 1 = 3 marks)
(Total = 8 marks)

Test: Reactive Chemistry

Multiple Choice Items

Question 1

The following sequence can be used to change sulfur into sulfuric acid.

$$\text{Rhombic sulfur} \xrightarrow[1]{\text{heat}} \text{Monoclinic sulfur} \xrightarrow[2]{\text{heat, oxygen}} SO_2 \xrightarrow[3]{\text{oxygen}} SO_3 \xrightarrow[4]{\text{water}} H_2SO_4$$

Rhombic and monoclinic are two allotropes of sulfur. The chemical changes in the above sequence are

(A) 1, 2, 3 and 4.
(B) 2, 3 and 4 only.
(C) 1 and 4 only.
(D) 2 and 3 only.

Question 2
A metal, Z, will react slowly with hot, dilute hydrochloric acid but does not react with boiling water. The metal is most likely to be

(A) copper (B) magnesium (C) silver (D) tin

Question 3
A metal undergoes a slow reaction with dilute hydrochloric acid. It does not react with cold water but will react with steam and undergoes rapid reaction with oxygen. The metal is most likely to be

(A) calcium (B) copper (C) silver (D) zinc

Question 4
From the information given in the data tables it would be expected that lead would be able to reduce

(A) all of Ag^+, Al^{3+}, Cu^{2+}, Fe^{2+}.
(B) Al^{3+} and Fe^{2+}.
(C) Ag^+ and Cu^{2+}.
(D) Cu^{2+} and Fe^{2+}.

Question 5
Metal M will displace copper from copper sulfate solution, silver from silver nitrate solution and tin a solution of tin(II) chloride. However metal M will not displace zinc fom zinc chloride solution. The most likely value for the E° of the M/M^{n+} half-cell is

(A) less than –0.76 V
(B) between –0.76 and –0.14 V
(C) between –0.14 and 0.34 V
(D) between 0.34 and –0.80 V

Question 6
The first ionisation energies of four metals, I, II, III and IV are given below.

Metal	I	II	III	IV
Ionisation energy (kJ mol^{-1})	509	744	596	556

The metal that would react most vigorously with water is expected to be

(A) I (B) II (C) III (D) IV

The information below refers to Question 7 and Question 8.

Magnesium reacts with bromine according to the following formula equation.

$Mg(s) + Br_2(g) \rightarrow MgBr_2(s)$

Question 7
The oxidation half-equation for this reaction is

(A) $Mg(s) \rightarrow Mg^{2+}(s) + 2e^-$
(B) $Br_2(g) + 2e^- \rightarrow 2Br^-(s)$
(C) $2Br^-(s) \rightarrow Br_2(g) + 2e^-$
(D) $Mg^{2+}(s) + 2e^- \rightarrow Mg(s)$

Question 8
The species that is reduced is

(A) Mg (B) Mg^{2+} (C) Br_2 (D) Br^-

Question 9
A student studied the rate of reaction between of calcium carbonate and an excess of hydrochloric acid. The volume of carbon dioxide evolved was measured at regular time intervals. The student carried out two experiments using different conditions. The graphs of his results are shown below.

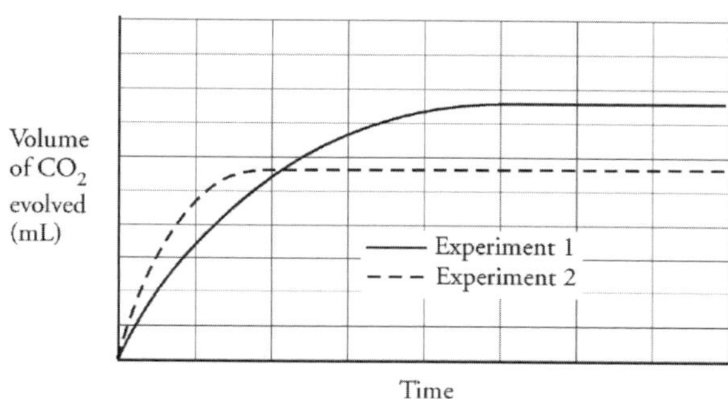

From the graphs it can be concluded that

(A) the quantities of reactants used were the same in both experiments and experiment 2 was conducted at a higher temperature.
(B) the quantities of reactants used were the same in both experiments and experiment 2 was conducted at a lower temperature.
(C) in experiment 2, less calcium carbonate was used and the experiment was conducted at a lower temperature.
(D) in experiment 2, less calcium carbonate was used but the concentration of the acid was higher.

Question 10
The rate of a chemical reaction will often change when factors, such as temperature, concentration of reactants, catalyst or surface area of a solid are changed. The three statements below are possible explanations for the change in rate.

I. The number of collisions between reacting particles has increased and hence the number of effective collisions has increased.
II. The proportion of effective collisions has increased.
III. The activation energy for the reaction has been reduced.

Which statements best explain the increase in the rate of reaction when the temperature is increased?

(A) I and II only (B) I, II and III
(C) II and III only (D) I and III only

Extended Response Questions

Question 1
Write balanced equations for the following reactions.

(a) Decomposition of solid ammonium nitrate into steam and nitrogen(I) oxide gas. (2 marks)

(b) Reaction of mercury with concentrated nitric acid to produce mercury(II) nitrate, water, and nitrogen(IV) oxide. (2 marks)

(c) Reaction of aqueous solutions of copper(II) sulfate and potassium iodide to form iodine, copper(I) iodide and potassium sulfate. (2 marks)

(Total = 6 marks)

Question 2
A partial activity series is given below.

Mn > Zn > Cd > Ni > Cu

The metals cadmium, copper, manganese, nickel and zinc were each added separately to 1.0 mol L^{-1} solutions of the nitrate salts of the same metals. Complete the table below to show whether or not a reaction was expected. Use "Y" if a reaction was expected and "N" if no reaction would occur. The boxes for Cu^{2+}/Zn and Cu/Zn^{2+} have been completed.

	$Cd^{2+}(aq)$	$Cu^{2+}(aq)$	$Mn^{2+}(aq)$	$Ni^{2+}(aq)$	$Zn^{2+}(aq)$
Cd(s)					
Cu(s)					N
Mn(s)					
Ni(s)					
Zn(s)		Y			

(4 marks)

Question 3
A galvanic cell was constructed from the Fe/Fe^{2+} and Ag/Ag^{+} redox couples as shown in the diagram below.

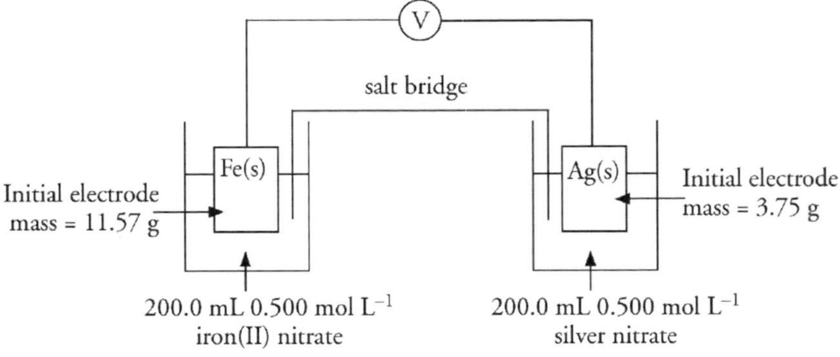

(a) Calculate the standard cell potential (E^{o}_{cell}) for this galvanic cell. (1 mark)

(b) Write the ionic equation for the overall cell reaction. (1 mark)

(c) When the cell had been operating for a period of time, the electrodes were removed, washed, dried and weighed. The mass of the silver electrode was 4.83 g.

(i) Calculate the final mass of the iron electrode. (3 marks)
(ii) Calculate the final concentration of the iron(II) nitrate solution, assuming there is no change in volume in the half-cells. (2 marks)
(Total = 7 marks)

Question 4
A home chemistry kit contains solutions of Sn^{2+}, Cu^{2+}, Fe^{3+}, a dilute acid and pieces of metallic copper, iron, lead and zinc.

(a) Describe an experiment in which Sn^{2+}(aq) would be oxidised to Sn^{4+}(aq). Give a balanced equation for the reaction. (2 marks)
(b) If a mixture of Cu^{2+}(aq) and Fe^{3+}(aq) was prepared, how could the Fe^{3+}(aq) be reduced without the Cu^{2+}(aq) reacting? Give a balanced equation for the reaction. (2 marks)
(c) Give a balanced equation for a reaction that could be used to prepare a sample of hydrogen gas. (1 mark)
(Total = 5 marks)

Question 5
Three electrochemical cells are set up as shown below. The cell voltage is shown on each voltmeter.

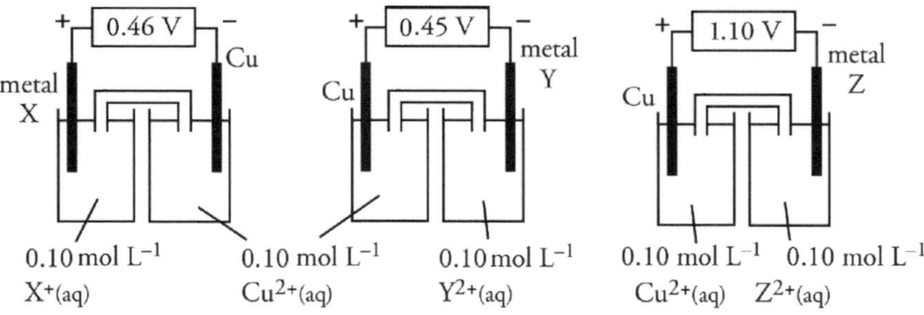

(a) From this information deduce the order of the four half-cells

Cu^{2+}/Cu X^+/X Y^{2+}/Y Z^{2+}/Z

in the electrochemical series. (List the one with the strongest reductant first.) (3 marks)
(b) If a cell was constructed from the Y^{2+}/Y and Z^{2+}/Z half-cells, deduce the polarity and the EMF of this cell. (2 marks)
(Total = 5 marks)

Question 6
Calculate the oxidation number of nitrogen in each of the following compounds.

(a) N_2H_4 (b) NH_2OH (c) HNO_2
(Total = 3 marks)

(Total = 40 marks)

Chapter 4

Drivers of Reactions

Multiple Choice Items

(1) Energy Changes in Chemical Reactions

Question 1
The following reaction is an important step in the industrial production of sulfuric acid.

$SO_2(g) + ½O_2(g) \rightarrow SO_3(g)$; $\Delta H = -99$ kJ mol^{-1}

For this reaction, which one of the following statements is correct?

(A) The enthalpy of the products is greater than that of the reactants and the reaction is exothermic.
(B) The enthalpy of the products is less than that of the reactants and the reaction is exothermic.
(C) The enthalpy of the products is greater than that of the reactants and the reaction is endothermic.
(D) The enthalpy of the products is less than that of the reactants and the reaction is endothermic.

Question 2
When potassium perchlorate, $KClO_4$, dissolves in water the temperature falls and the heat of solution is 41.4 kJ mol^{-1}. Which one of the following equations best represents this information?

(A) $KClO_4(s) \rightarrow K^+(aq) + ClO_4^-(aq)$; $\Delta H = +41.4$ kJ mol^{-1}
(B) $K^+(aq) + ClO_4^-(aq) \rightarrow KClO_4(s)$; $\Delta H = -41.4$ kJ mol^{-1}
(C) $KClO_4(s) \rightarrow K^+(aq) + ClO_4^-(aq)$; $\Delta H = -41.4$ kJ mol^{-1}
(D) $KClO_4(aq) \rightarrow K^+(aq) + ClO_4^-(aq)$; $\Delta H = +41.4$ kJ mol^{-1}

Question 3
When an endothermic reaction occurs

(A) the enthalpy of the products is less than that of the reactants.
(B) the surroundings gives energy to the reaction.
(C) the activation energy of the reaction is less than the enthalpy change for the reaction.
(D) the change in enthalpy is negative.

Question 4
One of the fuels often found in camping gas containers or portable lighters is butane, C_4H_{10}. The equation for the combustion of butane is

$2C_4H_{10}(g) + 13O_2(g) \rightarrow 8CO_2(g) + 10H_2O(g)$

This reaction is

(A) exothermic and the total chemical energy of the products is less than that of the reactants.
(B) endothermic and the total chemical energy of the products is less than that of the reactants.
(C) exothermic and the total chemical energy of the products is greater than that of the reactants.
(D) endothermic and the total chemical energy of the products is greater than that of the reactants.

Question 5
The equation that best represents the incomplete combustion of ethanol is

(A) $C_2H_5OH(l) + 3O_2(g) \rightarrow 2CO_2(g) + 3H_2O(g)$
(B) $C_2H_5OH(l) \rightarrow C_2H_4(g) + H_2O(g)$
(C) $C_2H_5OH(l) + 2O_2(g) \rightarrow CO_2(g) + C(s) + 3H_2O(g)$
(D) $2C_2H_5OH(l) + O_2(g) \rightarrow 2C_2H_4O(g) + 2H_2O(g)$

Question 6
For each mole of oxygen consumed, which one of the following fuels produces the largest amount of carbon dioxide?

(A) Methane, CH_4
(B) Ethyne, C_2H_2
(C) Ethene, C_2H_4
(D) Propane, C_3H_8

Question 7
The equations for four reactions are given below.

Reaction I: $KCl(g) \rightarrow K^+(g) + Cl^-(g)$
Reaction II: $C(s) + O_2(g) \rightarrow CO_2(g)$
Reaction III: $Na(g) \rightarrow Na^+(g) + e^-$
Reaction IV: $Cl_2(g) \rightarrow 2Cl(g)$

Which reaction is expected to have a heat of reaction of opposite sign from the other three?

(A) Reaction I
(B) Reaction II
(C) Reaction III
(D) Reaction IV

Question 8
Ammonium hydrogen carbonate, NH_4HCO_3, dissolves in water as follows:

$NH_4HCO_3(s) \rightarrow NH_4^+(aq) + HCO_3^-(aq)$

7.91 g of this salt is dissolved in 100 g of water in an insulated calorimeter. The temperature changes from 19.1°C to 12.9°C. The best estimate for the heat of reaction in kJ mol^{-1} is

(A) +0.259
(B) –2.59
(C) +25.9
(D) –25.9

Question 9
The molar heat of combustion of hexan-1-ol, $C_6H_{13}OH$, is 3984 kJ mol^{-1}. The alcohol is used to heat some water. 152 kJ of energy is transferred to the water with an efficiency of 45%. The mass of hexan-1-ol combusted to heat the water is closest to

(A) 0.57 g (B) 1.76 g (C) 3.90 g (D) 8.66 g

Question 10
Methanol, CH_3OH, was used as the fuel source for an experimental car. The car required ~2000 kJ of energy to travel every 1.00 km. The heat of combustion of methanol is 726 kJ mol^{-1} but only 30.0% of this energy was actually used to move the car. The maximum distance travelled by the car using 1.00 kg of methanol was approximately

(A) 2.75 km (B) 3.40 km (C) 11.3 km (D) 25.8 km

Question 11
When iron is heated in oxygen, iron(III) oxide, Fe_2O_3, is formed.

$$2Fe(s) + \frac{3}{2}O_2(g) \rightarrow Fe_2O_3(s);\ \Delta H = -825 \text{ kJ mol}^{-1}$$

The energy change when 1.00 mol of oxygen is formed in the decomposition of iron(III) oxide is

(A) 550 kJ released.
(B) 275 kJ released.
(C) 550 kJ absorbed.
(D) 275 kJ absorbed.

Question 12
When a hydrocarbon undergoes **complete** combustion in oxygen the products are

(A) carbon monoxide and water.
(B) carbon dioxide and water.
(C) carbon monoxide and hydrogen.
(D) carbon dioxide and hydrogen.

Question 13
Both ethanol, C_2H_5OH, and methanol, CH_3OH, have been suggested as alternative fuels for transport vehicles. The equations describing the complete combustion of ethanol and methanol are

$$C_2H_5OH(g) + 3O_2(g) \rightarrow 2CO_2(g) + 3H_2O(l)$$
$$2CH_3OH(g) + 3O_2(g) \rightarrow 2CO_2(g) + 4H_2O(l)$$

The heats of combustion of ethanol and methanol are 1368 kJ mol^{-1} and 726 kJ mol^{-1}. Separate experiments are conducted in which 1.0 mol of ethanol and 1.0 mol of methanol undergo complete combustion. In these experiments

(A) the combustion of methanol produces more carbon dioxide.
(B) more heat energy is released from the combustion of ethanol.
(C) less water is formed in the combustion of ethanol.
(D) the two experiments consume the same amount of oxygen.

Question 14

Methane, CH_4, ethane, C_2H_6, propane, C_3H_8, and butane, C_4H_{10}, have all been used as fuels. Their molar heats of combustion are given in the table below.

Fuel	Heat of combustion (kJ mol^{-1})
CH_4	890
C_2H_6	1560
C_3H_8	2220
C_4H_{10}	2877

When 1.00 g of each fuel is burnt, the fuel releasing the greatest amount of energy would be

(A) CH_4 (B) C_2H_6 (C) C_3H_8 (D) C_4H_{10}

Question 15

The energy profile for the combustion of methane is shown below.

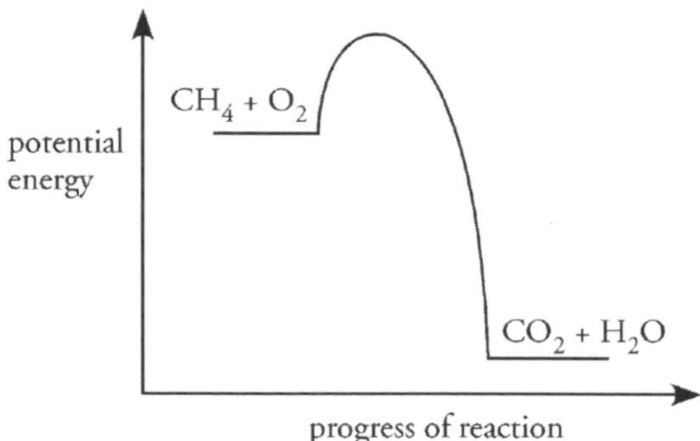

When 1 mol of methane reacts with excess oxygen, energy is

(A) absorbed from the surroundings and ΔH is positive.
(B) given to the surroundings and ΔH is positive.
(C) absorbed from the surroundings and ΔH is negative.
(D) given to the surroundings and ΔH is negative.

Question 16

The equation for the reaction of propane with oxygen is

$$C_3H_8(g) + 5O_2(g) \rightarrow 3CO_2(g) + 4H_2O(l); \Delta H = -2208 \text{ kJ mol}^{-1}$$

When 11 g of carbon dioxide is produced in this reaction, the energy change will be

(A) 552 kJ absorbed. (B) 552 kJ evolved.
(C) 184 kJ absorbed. (D) 184 kJ evolved.

Question 17

Many compounds can be used as fuels. The heat of combustion, in kJ g^{-1}, for four compounds are given in the table on the next page.

Fuel	Heat of combustion (kJ g^{-1})
Ethanol	29.7
Petrol (octane)	47.9
Butane	49.5
Propane	50.3

Identify the fuel whose heat of combustion is 2876 kJ mol^{-1}.

(A) Ethanol (B) Petrol (C) Butane (D) Propane

Question 18
The partial oxidation of methane is one step in the production of methanol.

$2CH_4(g) + O_2(g) \rightarrow 2CO(g) + 4H_2(g); \quad \Delta H = -74 \text{ kJ mol}^{-1}$

The activation energy for this reaction is 32 kJ mol^{-1}. The energy profile for this reaction is best represented by

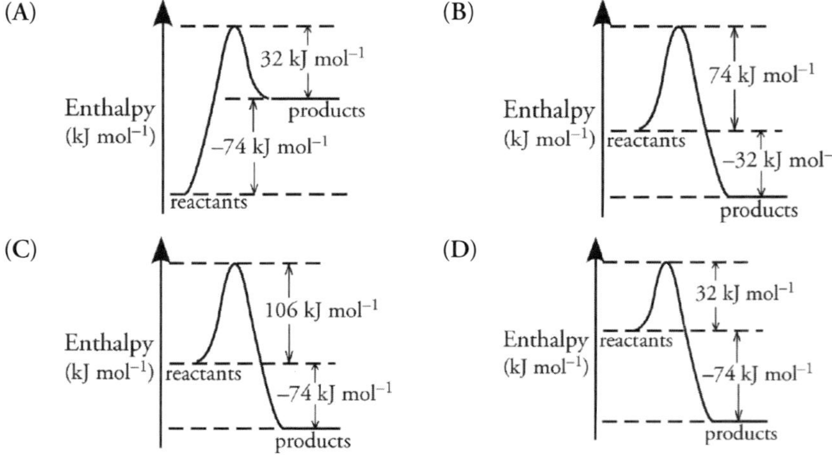

Question 19
To determine the heat of combustion of 1-butanol, a student used the apparatus shown below.

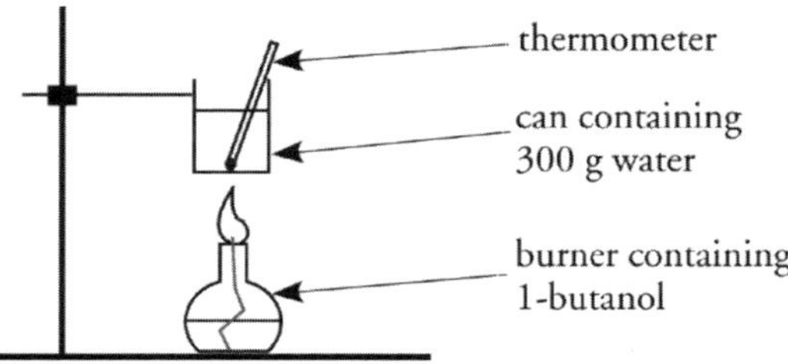

Some of the results obtained by the student are given below.

Mass of water heated = 300 g
Mass of 1-butanol burnt = 1.50 g
Initial temperature of water = 20.7°C

The student calculates that the molar heat of combustion of 1-butanol is 1530 kJ mol^{-1}. What was the final temperature of the water measured by the student?

(A) 24.7°C (B) 28.1°C (C) 37.2°C (D) 45.4°C

Question 20

Using a data table a student finds that the heat of combustion of 1-propanol is 2021 kJ mol^{-1}. What value would the student calculate for the heat of combustion of 1-propanol in kJ g^{-1}?

(A) 23.0 (B) 27.3 (C) 33.7 (D) 43.9

Question 21

To determine the heat of combustion of methanol a student used the apparatus shown below.

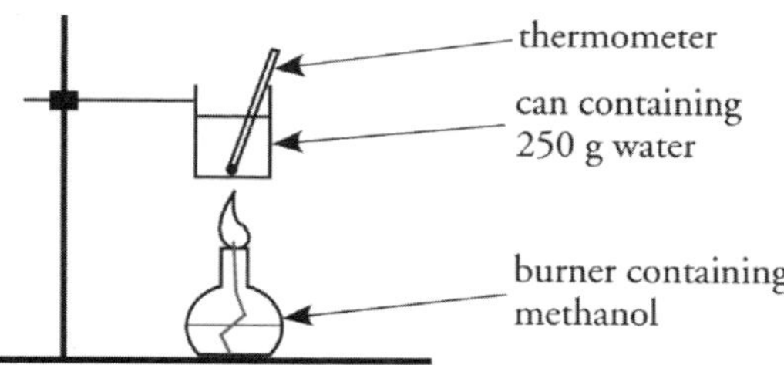

The following results were obtained.

Mass of burner at the start	125.58 g
Mass of burner at the end	124.38 g
Temperature of water at the start	20.6°C
Temperature of water at the end	36.6°C

From this data the student calculates the molar heat of combustion of methanol to be

(A) 446 kJ mol^{-1} (B) 535 kJ mol^{-1}
(C) 574 kJ mol^{-1} (D) 2140 kJ mol^{-1}

Question 22

When 3.27 g of zinc is added to 100 mL of 1.00 mol L^{-1} copper sulfate solution the following reaction occurs,

$$Zn(s) + CuSO_4(aq) \rightarrow ZnSO_4(aq) + Cu(s)$$

and the temperature of the solution rises by 24.0°C. If the specific heat of the solution is 4.20 J g^{-1} K^{-1} and its density is 1.0 g mL^{-1}, then ΔH for the reaction is

(A) +201 kJ mol^{-1}. (B) –201 kJ mol^{-1}.
(C) +101 kJ mol^{-1}. (D) –101 kJ mol^{-1}.

Question 23
The heat of solution of calcium bromide is given by the following equation,

$CaBr_2(s) \rightarrow Ca^{2+}(aq) + 2Br^-(aq)$; $\Delta H = -110$ kJ mol^{-1}

Crystals of calcium bromide form from a supersaturated solution of calcium bromide. The solution absorbs 5.5 kJ of energy. Which of following statements is correct?

(A) 10 g of crystals form and the temperature of the solution rises.
(B) 10 g of crystals form and the temperature of the solution falls.
(C) 20 g of crystals form and the temperature of the solution rises.
(D) 20 g of crystals form and the temperature of the solution falls.

Question 24
When barium hydroxide and ammonium cyanate are mixed, the following reaction occurs.

$Ba(OH)_2.8H_2O(s) + 2NH_4CNO(s) \longrightarrow Ba(CNO)_2(s) + 2NH_3(aq) + 10H_2O(l)$;
$\Delta H = +75$ kJ mol^{-1}

31.53 g of hydrated barium hydroxide (molar mass = 315.3 g mol^{-1}) is mixed with 6.0 g of ammonium cyanate (molar mass = 60 g mol^{-1}) in a calorimeter. The calorimeter constant is 150 J °C^{-1}. If the initial temperature is 20°C, the final temperature will be

(A) –30°C (B) –5°C (C) +45°C (D) +70°C

Question 25
One of the reactions involved in the production of methanol, CH_3OH, is

$CO_2(g) + 3H_2(g) \rightarrow CH_3OH(g) + H_2O(g)$; $\Delta H = -48$ kJ mol^{-1}

From this information it can be concluded that

(A) formation of 1 mol of water releases 24 kJ.
(B) when 3.0 g of hydrogen reacts 48 kJ of energy are released.
(C) reaction of 1 mol of carbon dioxide absorbs 48 kJ of energy.
(D) production of 2 mol of methanol would release 96 kJ of energy.

(2) Enthalpy and Hess's Law

Question 26
Methane reacts with oxygen according to the following equation

$CH_4(g) + 2O_2(g) \rightarrow CO_2(g) + 2H_2O(l)$; $\Delta_c H = -890$ kJ mol^{-1}

The energy change for this reaction is best described as

(A) exothermic, because the net strength of the bonds in the products is greater than the net strength of the bonds in the reactants.
(B) endothermic, because the net strength of the bonds in the products is greater than the net strength of the bonds in the reactants.
(C) exothermic, because the net strength of the bonds in the products is less than the net strength of the bonds in the reactants.

(D) endothermic, because the net strength of the bonds in the products is less than the net strength of the bonds in the reactants.

Question 27

The bond energy is the amount of energy required to break a bond. This is often given in kJ mol^{-1}. The bond energy for hydrogen is 436 kJ mol^{-1} and for oxygen is 498 kJ mol^{-1}. The molar heat of combustion of hydrogen is 241 kJ mol^{-1}. This information is summarised by the following equations:

$H_2(g) \rightarrow 2H(g)$; $\Delta H = +436$ kJ mol^{-1}
$O_2(g) \rightarrow 2O(g)$; $\Delta H = +498$ kJ mol^{-1}
$H_2(g) + \frac{1}{2}O_2(g) \rightarrow H_2O(l)$; $\Delta H = -241$ kJ mol^{-1}

The bond energy of the O–H bond is

(A) 222 kJ mol^{-1}
(B) 354 kJ mol^{-1}
(C) 463 kJ mol^{-1}
(D) 926 kJ mol^{-1}

Question 28

There are a number of oxides of nitrogen. The enthalpy changes for the formation of two of these oxides are given below.

$\frac{1}{2}N_2(g) + \frac{1}{2}O_2(g) \rightarrow NO(g)$; $\Delta H = +90$ kJ mol^{-1}
$\frac{1}{2}N_2(g) + O_2(g) \rightarrow NO_2(g)$; $\Delta H = +33$ kJ mol^{-1}

This information is also shown in the diagram below.

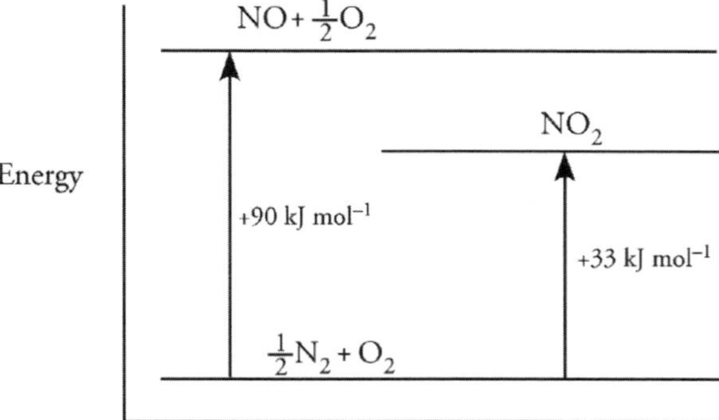

From this information the energy change, in kJ mol^{-1}, for the reaction

$2NO(g) + O_2(g) \rightarrow 2NO_2(g)$ will be

(A) –57
(B) +57
(C) –114
(D) +114

Question 29

The enthalpy changes for two reactions are given below.

Reaction I: $C(s) + 3H_2(g) \rightarrow C_2H_6(g)$; $\Delta H = -84$ kJ mol^{-1}
Reaction II: $C(s) + 2H_2(g) \rightarrow C_2H_4(g)$; $\Delta H = +52$ kJ mol^{-1}

From this information the enthalpy change, in kJ mol^{-1} for

Reaction III $C_2H_4(g) + H_2(g) \rightarrow C_2H_6(g)$ will be

(A) +137 (B) +32 (C) −32 (D) −137

Question 30

Three oxides of nitrogen are N_2O, N_2O_3 and N_2O_5. The energy changes when they form from nitrogen and oxygen are shown in the diagram below.

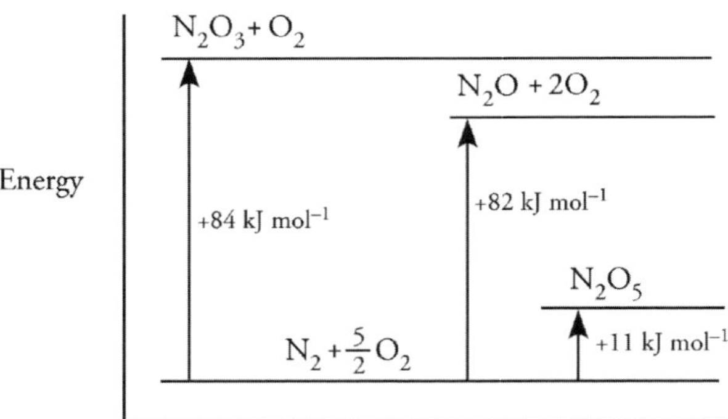

Which one of the following reactions will be exothermic?

(A) $N_2O(g) + O_2(g) \rightarrow N_2O_3(g)$
(B) $N_2O_5(g) \rightarrow N_2O(g) + 2O_2(g)$
(C) $N_2O_5(g) \rightarrow N_2O_3(g) + O_2(g)$
(D) $N_2O_3(g) + O_2(g) \rightarrow N_2O_5(g)$

Question 31

The energy diagram shown below contains the information from the following two combustion reactions.

$CH_4(g) + 2O_2(g) \rightarrow CO_2(g) + 2H_2O(l)$; $\Delta_c H = -890$ kJ mol^{-1} (1)
$CO(g) + ½O_2(g) \rightarrow CO_2(g)$; $\Delta_c H = -282$ kJ mol^{-1} (2)

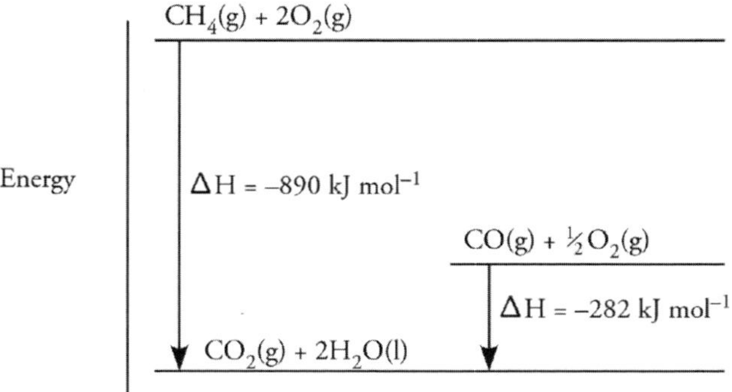

From the information above, ΔH for the reaction

$2CH_4(g) + 3O_2(g) \rightarrow 2CO(g) + 4H_2O(l)$ (3)

is most likely to be

(A) -608 kJ mol^{-1} (B) -1172 kJ mol^{-1}
(C) -1216 kJ mol^{-1} (D) -2344 kJ mol^{-1}

Question 32

The energies required to break the bonds in H_2, Br_2 and HBr are given in the equations below.

$H_2(g) \rightarrow 2H(g);$ $\Delta H = +436$ kJ mol^{-1}
$Br_2(g) \rightarrow 2Br(g);$ $\Delta H = +193$ kJ mol^{-1}
$HBr(g) \rightarrow H(g) + Br(g);$ $\Delta H = +366$ kJ mol^{-1}

From this information it is expected that the enthalpy change, in kJ mol^{-1}, for the reaction

$H_2(g) + Br_2(g) \rightarrow 2HBr(g)$ will be

(A) -263 (B) -103 (C) $+103$ (D) $+263$

Question 33

The following data may be used to calculate the energy change for the reaction and thus the strength of the H–S bond.

$H_2S(g) \rightarrow 2H(g) + S(g)$

$S(g) \rightarrow S(s);$ $\Delta H = -277$ kJ mol^{-1}
$H_2(g) \rightarrow 2H(g);$ $\Delta H = +436$ kJ mol^{-1}
$S(s) + H_2(g) \rightarrow H_2S(g);$ $\Delta H = -21$ kJ mol^{-1}

From this information the strength, in kJ mol^{-1}, of the H–S bond in H_2S is expected to be

(A) $+69$ (B) $+138$ (C) $+367$ (D) $+734$

(3) Entropy and Gibbs Free Energy

Question 34

For which one of the following changes will the entropy decrease?

(A) Ice changing into water.
(B) Ethanol mixing with water.
(C) Sodium chloride crystals forming from salt solution.
(D) Water being boiled.

Question 35

For which one of the following reactions will the entropy increase?

(A) $2C_2H_6(g) + 7O_2(g) \rightarrow 4CO_2(g) + 6H_2O(g)$
(B) $2C_2H_2(g) + 5O_2(g) \rightarrow 4CO_2(g) + 2H_2O(g)$
(C) $2SO_2(g) + O_2(g) \rightarrow 2SO_3(g)$
(D) $S(s) + 3F_2(g) \rightarrow SF_6(g)$

Question 36
Nitrogen(IV) oxide, NO_2, is readily converted into dinitrogen tetra-oxide, N_2O_4.

$2NO_2 \rightarrow N_2O_4$

If the entropy of NO_2 is 240 J mol^{-1} K^{-1} and that of N_2O_4 is 304 J mol^{-1} K^{-1}, then the entropy change, in J mol^{-1} K^{-1}, for the reaction is

(A) –64 (B) +64 (C) –176 (D) +176

Question 37
Which one of the following properties of a reaction is most likely to determine if the reaction will be spontaneous?

(A) The enthalpy of the reaction.
(B) The Gibbs free energy of the reaction.
(C) The activation energy of the reaction.
(D) The entropy of the reaction.

Question 38
An important step in the production of sulfuric acid is the conversion of sulfur dioxide into sulfur trioxide.

$2SO_2(g) + O_2(g) \rightarrow 2SO_3(g)$

If the entropies, in J mol^{-1} K^{-1}, of these substances are SO_2 = 248, O_2 = 205 and SO_3 = 257, then the entropy change, in J mol^{-1} K^{-1}, for the above reaction is

(A) –187 (B) –196 (C) +187 (D) +196

Question 39
When a solution of iodide ions is added to a solution containing ferric ions the following reaction occurs.

$2Fe^{3+}(aq) + 2I^{-}(aq) \rightarrow 2Fe^{2+}(aq) + I_2(aq)$

The entropies, in J mol^{-1} K^{-1}, of these substances are Fe^{3+}(aq) = –316, I^{-}(aq)= 106, Fe^{2+}(aq) = –138 and I_2(aq) = 137. The entropy change, in J mol^{-1} K^{-1}, for the above reaction is

(A) –431 (B) –281 (C) +209 (D) +281

The following information refers to questions 40 and 41.

The important step in the production of ammonia is the reaction

$N_2(g) + 3H_2(g) \rightarrow 2NH_3(g)$; $\Delta H = -92$ kJ mol^{-1}

At 25°C the entropy change for this reaction is –199 J mol^{-1} K^{-1}.

Question 40
At 25°C the Gibbs free energy change, in kJ mol^{-1}, for this reaction is

(A) –151 (B) –107 (C) –33 (D) +33

Question 41

At 25°C the reaction is too slow to be economical and the temperature is usually raised to ~450°C to increase the rate of reaction. Which one of the following statements is correct?

(A) Increasing the temperature causes ΔG to become more positive.
(B) Increasing the temperature causes ΔG to become more negative
(C) There is no change to ΔG when the temperature increases.
(D) The effect of the temperature increase on ΔG cannot be determined from the information given.

Extended Response Questions

(1) **Energy Changes in Chemical Reactions**

Question 1

The heats of combustion of three fuels are given in the table below.

Fuel	Molar Heat of Combustion (kJ mol^{-1})
methane, CH_4	890
propane, C_3H_8	2220
octane, C_8H_{18}	5470

The relevant equations for the complete combustion of each fuel are,

$CH_4(g) + 2O_2(g) \rightarrow CO_2(g) + 2H_2O(l)$
$C_3H_8(g) + 5O_2(g) \rightarrow 3CO_2(g) + 4H_2O(l)$
$C_8H_{18}(l) + 25/2O_2(g) \rightarrow 8CO_2(g) + 9H_2O(l)$

(a) For each fuel calculate the amount of energy released from the combustion of 1.00 kg of the fuel. (3 marks)

(b) Calculate the mass of carbon dioxide produced when each fuel produces 1000 kJ of energy. (3 marks)

(Total = 6 marks)

Question 2

When fuels are burnt in a limited supply of air incomplete combustion occurs. The products often contain carbon monoxide and carbon as well as carbon dioxide and water.

(a) Write the equation for the incomplete combustion of octane, C_8H_{18}, when ratio n(CO_2) : n(CO) : n(C) is 2 : 1 : 1. (3 marks)

The energy changes for two reactions when octane undergoes incomplete combustion are given in the following equations,

$C_8H_{18}(l) + 8\frac{1}{2}O_2(g) \rightarrow 8CO(g) + 9H_2O(l)$; $\Delta H = -3207$ kJ mol^{-1}
$C_8H_{18}(l) + 4\frac{1}{2}O_2(g) \rightarrow 8C(s) + 9H_2O(l)$; $\Delta H = -2323$ kJ mol^{-1}

(b) If the energy released when octane is completely burnt in air is 5470 kJ mol^{-1}, calculate the energy change for the reaction you have given in part (a). (3 marks)

(Total = 6 marks)

Question 3

The energy changes for three reactions are given below.

$C(s) + O_2(g) \rightarrow CO_2(g)$; $\Delta H = -394$ kJ mol^{-1}

$C(s) + \frac{1}{2}O_2(g) \rightarrow CO(g)$; $\Delta H = -111$ kJ mol^{-1}

$CO(g) + \frac{1}{2}O_2(g) \rightarrow CO_2(g)$; $\Delta H = -283$ kJ mol^{-1}

Construct a single energy profile diagram showing all three ΔH values (omit any activation energies). (Total = 3 marks)

Question 4

A student uses a simple calorimeter to determine the heat of solution of two solids, ammonium nitrate and potassium hydroxide. The calorimeter consists of a polystyrene cup, 100 mL of water, a stirrer and an accurate thermometer. His results are given in the table below.

	NH_4NO_3	KOH
Mass of solid (g)	4.192	3.496
Initial temperature (°C)	20.10	20.55
Final temperature (°C)	16.98	29.04

(a) For each solid calculate the heat of solution in kJ mol^{-1}. (4 marks)

(b) Propose one assumption made in this calculation. (1 mark)

(c) Identify one possible source of error in this experiment. (1 mark)

(d) For each reaction write a chemical equation that includes the heat of solution and identify whether these reactions are exothermic or endothermic. (4 marks)

(e) For each reaction draw an energy change diagram. Include reactants, products and the heat of solution. (2 marks)

(Total = 12 marks)

Question 5

The molar heat of combustion of liquid hexane, C_6H_{14}, is 4163 kJ mol^{-1}.

(a) Give balanced equation for the combustion of hexane. (2 marks)

(b) If the density of hexane is 0.660 g mL^{-1}, calculate the heat energy released when 1.00 L of liquid hexane, is completely burnt in air.

(3 marks)

(Total = 5 marks)

Question 6

The energy required by a typical Year 11 chemistry student is about 13 500 kJ per day. Glucose is oxidised in body cells according to the equation

$C_6H_{12}O_6(aq) + 6O_2(g) \rightarrow 6CO_2(g) + 6H_2O(l)$; $\Delta H = -2800$ kJ mol^{-1}

If all of the student's energy is derived from the oxidation of glucose, calculate the mass of glucose required each day.

(Total = 2 marks)

Question 7

Methane and methanol will both burn in air. The reactions are described by the equations

$CH_4(g) + 2O_2(g) \rightarrow CO_2(g) + 2H_2O(l);$ $\Delta H = -890 \text{ kJ mol}^{-1}$

$2CH_3OH(g) + 3O_2(g) \rightarrow 2CO_2(g) + 4H_2O(l);$ $\Delta H = -1452 \text{ kJ mol}^{-1}$

(a) If 2 mol of methane and 2 mol of methanol are completely burnt in separate experiments, which experiment will release the most energy? (1 mark)

(b) If each of the above reactions is used to produce 1000 kJ of energy, which one will release the most carbon dioxide? (2 marks)

(Total = 3 marks)

Question 8

The reaction between hydrogen and oxygen is described by the equation

$2H_2(g) + O_2(g) \rightarrow 2H_2O(g); \Delta H = -484 \text{ kJ mol}^{-1}$

(a) Draw an energy level diagram showing how the energy of the reactants is related to that of the products. Your diagram should also show ΔH and an activation energy. (3 marks)

(b) Describe how the strength of the bonds in the reactants is related to the strength of the bonds in the products. (1 mark)

(c) Would you expect the heat change for the reaction

$2H_2(g) + O_2(g) \rightarrow 2H_2O(l)$

to be greater than, less than or the same as the heat change in the first reaction? Explain your answer. (2 marks)

(Total = 6 marks)

Question 9

When 50.00 mL of 0.400 M HCl and 50.00 mL of 0.400 M NaOH, each at 21.00°C, were mixed in a polystyrene foam container, the temperature of the mixture reached 23.80°C.

(a) If 4.18 J of energy is required to raise the temperature of 1 mL of the solution by 1.00°C, then calculate the ΔH for the reaction

$H^+(aq) + OH^-(aq) \rightarrow H_2O(l)$ (4 marks)

(b) Why is polystyrene foam a good material to use in the container for this experiment? (1 mark)

(c) If the same container was used, what would be the temperature rise if 50.0 mL of 0.900 M HCl and 50.0 mL of 0.800 M NaOH were mixed? (2 marks)

In a second experiment 50.00 mL of 0.400 M HCl and 50.00 mL of 0.400 M ammonia, each at 20.00°C, were mixed in a polystyrene foam container. This time the final temperature was 22.48°C.

(d) Calculate a value for the heat of neutralisation of HCl and NH_3 in kJ mol^{-1}. (2 marks)

(e) If your answers to parts (a) and (d) are different, suggest a reason for this. (1 mark)

(Total = 10 marks)

Question 10

Natural gas consists largely of methane, CH_4, and is used as a source of energy in domestic gas supplies. In a laboratory using natural gas, a student uses a Bunsen burner to heat 300 mL of water. The temperature rises from 16.7°C to 49.6°C.

(a) Calculate the heat supplied to the water if the specific heat of water is 4.18 J $°C^{-1}$ g^{-1} and its density is 1.00 g mL^{-1}. (1 mark)

(b) If only 65% of the energy produced from the combustion of the gas is transmitted to the water, calculate the energy produced by the Bunsen burner. (1 mark)

(c) Write the equation for the combustion of methane. (1 mark)

(d) The student also measured the amount of gas used in the above experiment and found that 1.54 L at 115 kPa and 16.7°C were required. Calculate ΔH for the equation in part (c). (3 marks)

(Total = 6 marks)

Question 11

Decomposition of ethanal, CH_3CHO, occurs rapidly at 500°C, to give methane and carbon monoxide. The relevant equation is

$$CH_3CHO(g) \rightarrow CH_4(g) + CO(g); \ \Delta H = -20.0 \text{ kJ mol}^{-1}$$

(a) The activation energy for the reverse reaction is +210 kJ mol^{-1}. If the energy of ethanal is the zero of the energy, mark and label on the diagram below

(i) the energies of the reactants and products.
(ii) an uncatalysed reaction profile.
(iii) a possible catalysed reaction profile.

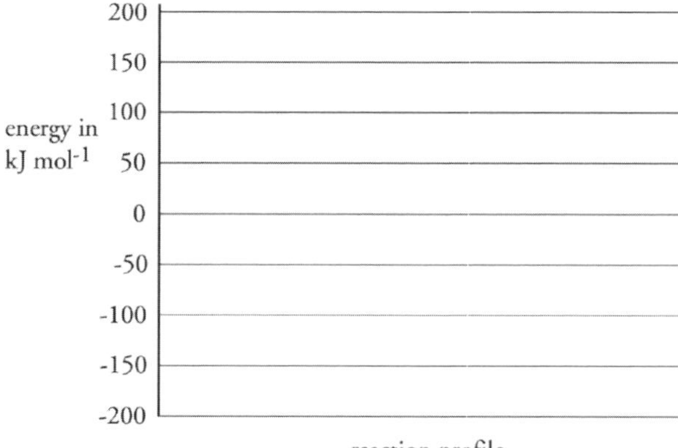

(4 marks)

(b) Calculate the mass of ethanal that reacts when 1000 kJ of energy are released. (2 marks)

(Total = 6 marks)

Question 12

A student is asked to determine the heat of combustion of methanol, CH_3OH, using the apparatus shown on the next page. 300 mL of water is placed in a metal can. The can is clamped above the flame from a spirit burner. The temperature of the water is measured before and after heating by the methanol burner. The burner is weighed before and after heating the water.

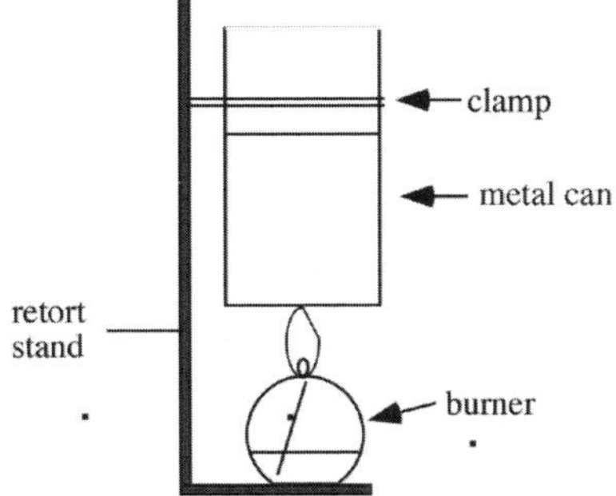

The student obtains the following results:

- mass of burner and methanol before combustion = 35.674 g
- mass of burner and methanol after combustion = 34.396 g
- temperature of water in can before heating = 16.3°C
- temperature of water in can after heating = 28.1°C

(a) Why was a metal can used rather than a glass container? (1 mark)

(b) How many mol of methanol were burnt? (2 marks)

(c) Calculate the heat given to the water in the can if the specific heat of water is 4.18 J $°C^{-1}$ g^{-1} and its density is 1.0 g mL^{-1}. (1 mark)

(d) From parts (b) and (c) calculate, in kJ mol^{-1}, the heat of combustion of methanol. (1 mark)

(e) The accepted value for the heat of combustion of methanol is 725 kJ mol^{-1}. Suggest two reasons why the value determined in part (d) is different from this value. (2 marks)

(Total = 7 marks)

Question 13

Dimethyl ether, CH_3OCH_3, is a gas at room temperature and has a boiling temperature of –25°C. It is increasingly being considered as an alternative to fossil fuels such as propane and diesel. Dimethyl ether readily undergoes complete combustion. Dimethyl ether can be synthesised from methanol by the following reaction

$$2CH_3OH(g) \rightarrow CH_3OCH_3(g) + H_2O(g); \qquad \Delta H = -24 \text{ kJ mol}^{-1}$$

The activation energy for this reaction is 23.4 kJ mol^{-1}.

(a) Draw an energy profile for this reaction. (3 marks)

(b) Give one advantage and one disadvantage for using dimethyl ether as a replacement for diesel. (2 marks)

(Total = 5 marks)

(2) Enthalpy and Hess's Law

Question 14

The bond strengths for a number of bonds are given in the table on the next page. In each case it is the energy required to break one mole of the bonds and to produce gaseous atoms.

Bond	Strength (kJ mol^{-1})	Bond	Strength (kJ mol^{-1})
C–H	414	O=O	498
C–C	346	C=O	804
H–O	463		

Use this information to calculate a value for the combustion of one mole of propane according to the equation below.

$C_3H_8(g) + 5O_2(g) \rightarrow 3CO_2(g) + 4H_2O(g)$ (Total = 4 marks)

Question 15
Copper forms two oxides, copper(I) oxide, Cu_2O and copper(II) oxide, CuO as shown in the equations below for Reactions I and II.

Reaction I: $2Cu(s) + \frac{1}{2}O_2(g) \rightarrow Cu_2O(s)$; $\Delta H = -169$ kJ mol^{-1}
Reaction II: $Cu(s) + \frac{1}{2}O_2(g) \rightarrow CuO(s)$; $\Delta H = -157$ kJ mol^{-1}

Use this information to calculate the enthalpy change in Reaction III.

Reaction III: $Cu_2O(s) \rightarrow Cu(s) + CuO(s)$ (Total = 2 marks)

Question 16
The enthalpy changes for a number of reactions are given below.

$C(s) + 2H_2(g) \rightarrow CH_4(g)$; $\Delta H = -74$ kJ mol^{-1}
$C(s) \rightarrow C(g)$; $\Delta H = +717$ kJ mol^{-1}
$\frac{1}{2}H_2(g) \rightarrow H(g)$; $\Delta H = +218$ kJ mol^{-1}
$CH_4(g) \rightarrow C(g) + 4H(g)$ $\Delta H = X$ kJ mol^{-1}

(a) From this information construct an energy level diagram that includes the four reactions. (2 marks)

(b) From your diagram determine a value for X. (1 mark)

(c) From your answer in part (b), calculate the average bond energy, in kJ mol^{-1}, for the C–H bond in methane, CH_4. (2 marks)
(Total = 5 marks)

Question 17
Use the information from the equations to answer the questions below.

$H_2(g) \rightarrow 2H(g)$; $\Delta H = +436$ kJ mol^{-1}
$O_2(g) \rightarrow 2O(g)$; $\Delta H = +498$ kJ mol^{-1}
$H_2O_2(l) \rightarrow H_2O_2(g)$ $\Delta H = +52$ kJ mol^{-1}
$H_2(g) + O_2(g) \rightarrow H_2O_2(l)$; $\Delta H = -188$ kJ mol^{-1}

(a) Calculate the enthalpy change, in kJ mol^{-1}, for the reaction

$H_2O_2(g) \rightarrow 2H(g) + 2O(g)$ (3 marks)

(b) If the strength of the O–H bond is 463 kJ mol^{-1}, calculate a value for the strength of the O–O bond in hydrogen peroxide. (2 marks)
(Total = 5 marks)

(3) Entropy and Gibbs Free Energy

Question 18

When lithium is added to a dilute acid the following reaction occurs.

$Li(s) + H^+(aq) \rightarrow Li^+(aq) + \frac{1}{2}H_2(g)$; $\Delta H = -278.3$ kJ mol^{-1}

(a) What is the expected sign for the entropy change for this reaction? Give a reason for your answer. (1 mark)

At 298 K the entropies, in J mol^{-1} K^{-1}, for the substances in the above equation are

$Li(s) = 28.0$; $H^+(aq) = 0$; $Li^+(aq) = 14.2$; $H_2(g) = 130.6$

(b) Calculate ΔS^o_{298} for the above reaction. (2 marks)

(c) Use the enthalpy value given above and your answer from part (b) to calculate the Gibbs free energy of the reaction at 298 K. (2 marks)

(d) Classify this reaction as spontaneous or non-spontaneous. Give a reason for your answer. (1 mark)

(Total = 6 marks)

Question 19

Heptane, C_7H_{16}, can be broken into smaller molecules by heating.

$C_7H_{16} \rightarrow CH_4(g) + 3C_2H_4(g)$; $\Delta H = +270$ kJ mol^{-1}

The entropies, in J mol^{-1} K^{-1}, of the three substances in this equation are

$C_7H_{16} = 428$; $CH_4 = 186$; $C_2H_4 = 220$

(a) Calculate ΔG for this reaction at 25°C. (3 marks)

(b) Calculate the temperature at which this reaction will become spontaneous. (2 marks)

(Total = 5 marks)

Question 20

The entropies, in J mol^{-1} K^{-1}, of a number of compounds are given in the table below.

Substance	Entropy	Substance	Entropy	Substance	Entropy
$CH_3OH(g)$	240	$C_2H_6(g)$	230	$H_2(g)$	131
$CH_4(g)$	186	$CO(g)$	198	$O_2(g)$	205
$C_2H_4(g)$	220	$CO_2(g)$	214	$H_2O(g)$	189

Use these values to calculate the entropy change for the reactions given below.

(a) $CO(g) + 2H_2(g) \rightarrow CH_3OH(g)$ (1 mark)

(b) $C_2H_4(g) + 3O_2(g) \rightarrow 2CO_2(g) + 2H_2O(g)$ (1 mark)

(c) $2CO(g) + O_2(g) \rightarrow 2CO_2(g)$ (1 mark)

(d) $C_2H_4(g) + H_2(g) \rightarrow C_2H_6(g)$ (1 mark)

(e) $2C_2H_6(g) + 7O_2(g) \rightarrow 4CO_2(g) + 6H_2O(g)$ (1 mark)

(f) $CH_4(g) + \frac{1}{2}O_2(g) \rightarrow CH_3OH(g)$ (1 mark)

(Total = 6 marks)

Question 21

At 25°C the entropies, in J mol^{-1} K^{-1}, of carbon dioxide, CO_2, magnesium oxide, MgO, and magnesium carbonate, $MgCO_3$ are 214, 27 and 66 respectively.

(a) Give an explanation for the variation in these values. (2 marks)

Magnesium carbonate can be decomposed to produce magnesium oxide and carbon dioxide.

$MgCO_3(s) \rightarrow MgO(s) + CO_2(g)$; $\Delta H = +100$ kJ mol^{-1}

(b) (i) Calculate the entropy change for this reaction. (1 mark)
(ii) Calculate ΔG for this reaction at 25°C. (1 mark)

(c) Is this reaction spontaneous or non-spontaneous at 25°C? (1 mark)

(d) (i) Calculate the temperature at which $\Delta G = 0$. (1 mark)
(ii) If magnesium carbonate is heated to this temperature, what changes are likely to occur? (1 mark)

(Total = 7 marks)

Question 22

The following information is available regarding the decomposition of hydrogen peroxide, H_2O_2.

$H_2O_2(aq) \rightarrow H_2O(l) + \frac{1}{2}O_2(g)$; $\Delta H = -95.0$ kJ mol^{-1}

	$H_2O_2(aq)$	$H_2O(l)$	$O_2(g)$
Entropy (J mol^{-1} K^{-1})	144	70	205

(a) Calculate the entropy change for the reaction given in the equation above. (2 marks)

(b) Use your answer from part (a) to calculate ΔG for the above reaction and show that this reaction is expeted to be spontaneous at 25°C. (2 marks)

(c) In contrast to the value of ΔG calculated in part (b), solutions of hydrogen peroxide are quite stable at 25°C. Suggest a reason for this lack of reactivity. (1 mark)

(Total = 5 marks)

Test: Drivers of Reactions

Multiple Choice Items

Question 1

Propane is often used as a fuel in portable barbecues. The equation for the reaction is

$C_3H_8(g) + 5O_2(g) \rightarrow 3CO_2(g) + 4H_2O(g)$

This reaction is

(A) exothermic and the total chemical energy of the products is less than that of the reactants.
(B) endothermic and the total chemical energy of the products is less than that of the reactants.
(C) exothermic and the total chemical energy of the products is greater than that of the reactants.
(D) endothermic and the total chemical energy of the products is greater than that of the reactants.

Question 2
If a catalyst is used in a chemical reaction, then the catalyst will change

(A) the enthalpy of the reaction.
(B) the Gibbs free energy of the reaction.
(C) the activation energy of the reaction.
(D) the entropy of the reaction.

Question 3
The energy required to break the bonds in H_2 and in Cl_2 is given below, along with the energy of reaction when H_2 reacts with Cl_2.

$H_2(g) \rightarrow 2H(g);$ $\Delta H = +436 \text{ kJ mol}^{-1}$
$Cl_2(g) \rightarrow 2Cl(g);$ $\Delta H = +242 \text{ kJ mol}^{-1}$
$H_2(g) + Cl_2(g) \rightarrow 2HCl(g);$ $\Delta H = -184 \text{ kJ mol}^{-1}$

From this information the energy required to break the H–Cl bond is

(A) 247 kJ mol^{-1}
(B) 431 kJ mol^{-1}
(C) 494 kJ mol^{-1}
(D) 862 kJ mol^{-1}

The following information refers to Questions 4 and 5.

Methane, CH_4, ethane, C_2H_6, ethyne, C_2H_2, and ethene, C_2H_4, could all be used as fuels. Their heats of combustion are given by the following equations.

$CH_4(g) + 2O_2(g) \rightarrow CO_2(g) + 2H_2O(l);$ $\Delta H = -890 \text{ kJ mol}^{-1}$
$C_2H_6(g) + 7/2O_2(g) \rightarrow 2CO_2(g) + 3H_2O(l);$ $\Delta H = -1560 \text{ kJ mol}^{-1}$
$C_2H_2(g) + 5/2O_2(g) \rightarrow 2CO_2\ g) + H_2O(l);$ $\Delta H = -1300 \text{ kJ mol}^{-1}$
$C_2H_4(g) + 3O_2(g) \rightarrow 2CO_2(g) + 2H_2O(l);$ $\Delta H = -1411 \text{ kJ mol}^{-1}$

Question 4
If 1.0 L of each fuel were burnt at 20°C and at 1 atmosphere pressure, the greatest amount of energy would be released by

(A) CH_4 (B) C_2H_6 (C) C_2H_2 (D) C_2H_4

Question 5
When 1.0 g of each fuel is burnt, the fuel releasing the least amount of energy would be

(A) CH_4 (B) C_2H_6 (C) C_2H_2 (D) C_2H_4

Question 6
The equation for the combustion of pentan-1-ol is

$$2C_5H_{11}OH(l) + 15O_2(g) \rightarrow 10CO_2(g) + 12H_2O(l)$$

and the molar heat of combustion for this alcohol is 3331 kJ mol^{-1}. The mass of water produced when 1500 kJ of energy is released is closest to

(A) 1.4 g (B) 15.4 g (C) 48.6 g (D) 97.3 g

Question 7
For butan-1-ol, C_4H_9OH, the molar heat of combustion is 2676 kJ mol^{-1}. If the combustion of this alcohol is used to heat water, the maximum mass of water that could be heated from 18.0°C to 38.0°C by 2.00 g of butan-1-ol is

(A) 0.059 kg (B) 0.45 kg (C) 0.86 kg (D) 0.96 kg

Question 8
A student determines a value for the heat of reaction when magnesium reacts with dilute hydrochloric acid.

$$Mg(s) + 2HCl(aq) \rightarrow MgCl_2(aq) + H_2(g)$$

0.243 g of magnesium is reacted with 100 mL of 1.00 mol L^{-1}. The temperature changes from 20.2°C to 31.1°C. The value of ΔH, in kJ mol^{-1}, for this reaction is

(A) +4.56 (B) –45.6 (C) +456 (D) –456

Question 9
The equation for the fermentation of glucose is

$$C_6H_{12}O_6(aq) \rightarrow 2C_2H_5OH(aq) + 2CO_2(g)$$

If the three substances involved in this reaction are arranged in decreasing order of their entropies, then the order would be

(A) $C_6H_{12}O_6(aq) > C_2H_5OH(aq) > CO_2(g)$
(B) $CO_2(g) > C_2H_5OH(aq) > C_6H_{12}O_6(aq)$
(C) $C_2H_5OH(aq) > CO_2(g) > C_6H_{12}O_6(aq)$
(D) $CO_2(g) > C_6H_{12}O_6(aq) > C_2H_5OH(aq)$

Question 10
The compound ammonium peroxydisulfate, $(NH_4)_2S_2O_8$ (M_r = 228.2), dissolves in water according to the following equation.

$$(NH_4)_2S_2O_8(s) \rightarrow 2NH_4^+(aq) + S_2O_8^{2-}(aq); \quad \Delta H = +37.0 \text{ kJ mol}^{-1}$$

In an experiment, 22.82 g of ammonium peroxydisulfate was dissolved in 100 g of water. If the initial temperature of the water was 19.5°C, then the final temperature was

(A) 8.9°C (B) 10.6°C (C) 18.6°C (D) 28.4°C

Question 11
The heat of combustion for three methyl esters is given in the table below.

Name	**Formula**	**$-\Delta H_c$ (kJ mol^{-1})**
Methyl pentanoate	$C_4H_9COOCH_3$	3558
Methyl hexanoate	$C_5H_{11}COOCH_3$	4211
Methyl heptanoate	$C_6H_{13}COOCH_3$	4863

One of the molecules found in biodiesel is methyl stearate, $C_{17}H_{35}COOCH_3$. The best estimate for the heat of combustion (in kJ mol^{-1}) of methyl stearate is

(A) –7178 (B) –12040 (C) –12632 (D) –13937

Question 12
The heats of solution of LiOH, NaOH, KOH and CsOH, along with their molar masses are given in the table below.

Compound	Molar mass (g mol^{-1})	Heat of solution (kJ mol^{-1})
LiOH	23.9	–23.6
NaOH	40.0	–44.5
KOH	56.1	–57.6
CsOH	149.9	–71.6

If 1.00 g of each of these compounds is dissolved separately in 100 mL of water, which one will produce the smallest temperature rise?

(A) LiOH (B) NaOH (C) KOH (D) CsOH

Extended Response Questions

Question 1
A student uses a calorimeter to determine the heat of reaction for the following processes.

Reaction I: $CuSO_4(s) + aq \rightarrow Cu^{2+}(aq) + SO_4^{2-}(aq)$
Reaction II: $CuSO_4.5H_2O(s) + aq \rightarrow Cu^{2+}(aq) + SO_4^{2-}(aq) + 5H_2O(l)$

For reaction I: 8.00 g of $CuSO_4$ was dissolved in 100 g of water at 18.6°C. The final temperature was 27.3°C.
For reaction II: 10.0 g of $CuSO_4.5H_2O$ was dissolved in 100 g of water at 18.6°C. The final temperature was 18.1°C.

(a) Use this information to calculate

(i) ΔH for reaction I. (3 marks)
(ii) ΔH for reaction II. (3 marks)

(b) Use Hess's Law to calculate a value of ΔH for the reaction

$CuSO_4(s) + 5H_2O(l) \rightarrow CuSO_4.5H_2O(s)$ (2 marks)

(Total = 8 marks)

Question 2

$C_{20}H_{42}$ is one of many compounds found in crude oil that is broken down to produce octane and ethene.

$C_{20}H_{42}(l) \rightarrow C_8H_{18}(g) + 6C_2H_4(g)$; $\Delta H = +660$ kJ mol^{-1}

(a) What is the expected sign for the entropy change for this reaction? Give two reasons for your answer. (2 marks)

The entropies, in J mol^{-1} K^{-1}, of the compounds in the above equation are

$C_{20}H_{42} = +752$ $C_8H_{18} = +467$ $C_2H_4 = +220$

(b) Calculate the entropy change for the reaction given above. (2 marks)

(c) Use your answer from part (b) and the information above to calculate the Gibbs free energy for this reaction at 25°C. (2 marks)

(d) Classify this reaction as spontaneous or non-spontaneous. Give a reason for your answer. (1 mark)

(e) Calculate the temperature at which ΔG will change sign. What is the significance of this temperature? (2 marks)

(Total = 9 marks)

Question 3

The heats of combustion for carbon, hydrogen and ethane are given in the equations for the three reactions below.

Reaction I $C(s) + O_2(g) \rightarrow CO_2(g)$; $\Delta H = -394$ kJ mol^{-1}

Reaction II $H_2(g) + \frac{1}{2}O_2(g) \rightarrow H_2O(l)$; $\Delta H = -286$ kJ mol^{-1}

Reaction III $C_2H_6(g) + 3\frac{1}{2}O_2(g) \rightarrow 2CO_2(g) + 3H_2O(l)$; $\Delta H = -1560$ kJ mol^{-1}

Use this information to calculate the enthalpy change for *Reaction IV:*

$2C(s) + 3H_2(g) \rightarrow C_2H_6(g)$ (Total = 3 marks)

Question 4

The bond dissociation energies for three bonds are given in the table below.

Bond	Energy (kJ mol^{-1})
Nitrogen to nitrogen in $N_2(g)$	+946
Oxygen to oxygen in $O_2(g)$	+498
Nitrogen to oxygen in $NO_2(g)$	+469

If the two nitrogen to oxygen bonds in NO_2 are the same, calculate the enthalpy change for the reaction

$\frac{1}{2}N_2(g) + O_2(g) \rightarrow NO_2(g)$ (Total = 3 marks)

Total = 35 marks

Answers: Properties and Structure of Matter

Multiple Choice Items

Question	Answer	Comments
1.	A.	Air, copper sulfate solution and iron chloride solution are mixtures.
2.	B.	Sugar is soluble in water and will recrystallise if the water is evaporated. Charcoal can be removed by filtration.
3.	C.	Filtration removes insoluble materials from solutions.
4.	C.	Homogeneous materials contain only one phase. Two liquids are present in "oil and water" and a liquid and a solid are present in "sand and water".
5.	A.	Filtration depends on the dissolving of one solid in a solvent whilst the other remains insoluble. The other methods depend on the different size and weight of particles.
6.	C.	Warming from –200°C means that –196°C would be the first boiling point reached. Nitrogen would boil first followed by argon and then oxygen.
7.	A.	Mass of water = 11.62 – 2.53 – 7.25 = 1.84 g % water present = (1.84 ÷ 11.62) × 100 = 15.83
8.	D.	In bromites the anion has the formula BrO_2^- and in bromates the formula is BrO_3^-.
9.	C.	Iron is a transition metal and can form Fe^{2+} or Fe^{3+} cations. Fe_2O_3 contains Fe^{3+} cations and this must be indicated in the name.
10.	D.	Na_2S is called sodium sulfide. In (B) and (C) the formulae are incorrect.
11.	D.	In this compound the cation is Cu^{2+}.
12.	C.	Any element will have a smaller mass than its compounds. Product 3 has the smallest mass and may be the pure element. Products 1, 2 and 4 and also substance A are more likely to be compounds.
13.	D.	Element 4 has the lowest values for thermal and electrical conductivity. Although element 2 is a liquid at room temperature it has a high density and good conducting values.
14.	A.	Compound Z is a gas at room temperature, while Y is a solid. The density of water at 25°C is approximately 1.0 g mL^{-1}. Compound X is denser than water. W is less dense than water.
15.	B.	In (A) lithium is a metal. In (C) all the elements are metals and in (D) iron is a metal. The elements in (B) are found in Groups 15, 16 and 17.

Question	Answer	Comments
16.	C.	The temperature range over which both VI and II are liquids includes room temperature.
17.	A.	Element II is a good conductor of heat and electricity and is also a liquid with a high density.
18.	A.	Element I is a solid at room temperature, is a good conductor of heat and electricity with a high density. It is most likely a metal and should have tensile strength.
19.	C.	Coloured compounds are most likely to be formed by transition metals. These metals usually have high densities and are very good conductors of heat and electricity.
20.	B.	The other answers all contain elements which are too chemically reactive to exist uncombined, e.g. in (A) the reactive elements are Al, Ca and Cl, in (C) all are reactive and in (D) F, Fe and K are reactive.
21.	C.	Most metals are malleable and ductile rather than brittle and many have high melting temperatures. The thermal and electrical conductivities of metals are generally higher than those of non-metals.
22.	B.	Elements in the same group of the table have similar chemical properties.
23.	A.	Since the elements have similar chemical properties they will be in the same group of the Periodic Table. For L, M and Q the melting temperatures increase with increasing relative atomic mass. Hence the properties of R will fit into this pattern.
24.	C.	Compounds of transition metals are most likely to be coloured.
25.	B.	Outside the central nucleus the electrons move in regions of space called orbitals. The electrons occupy very little of the available space. In chemical reactions atoms are not destroyed but are rearranged.
26.	D.	Protons and neutrons are much heavier than electrons but occupy a very small amount of space (the nucleus). The electrons move in a large volume outside of the nucleus.
27.	C.	40 is the mass number (protons + neutrons) and 20 is the atomic number (protons = no of electrons in a neutral atom).
28.	A.	The isotope of Sr has 38 protons and 52 neutrons, while the isotope of Zr has 40 protons and 50 neutrons.
29.	D.	Isotopes have the same atomic number but different mass numbers.
30.	B.	The number of neutrons is the difference between the mass number and the atomic number. Only in (B) is this difference constant.

Question	Answer	Comments
31.	D.	All the particles in (D) have more protons than electrons.
32.	A.	The mass number of this particle is 27+28 = 55 and its atomic number is 27. It has two more protons than electrons (27 to 25) and thus carries a charge of 2+.
33.	B.	Isotopes have the same atomic number but different mass numbers. I and II only differ in the number of electrons. IV is a different element to I, II and III.
34.	B.	Number of neutrons = mass number – atomic number
35.	D.	Atoms of the same element have the same number of protons, the same electron configurations and the same chemical properties.
36.	B.	The elements are in Groups 2, 3, 4 and 5 respectively. Elements in Group 3 have an outer shell configuration of s^2p^1.
37.	A.	Metals typically have 1, 2 or 3 outer shell electrons. (A) has 7 which places it on the right-hand side of the periodic table and thus a non-metal.
38.	C.	The third shell has enough space for 18 electrons.
39.	A.	This electron configuration has two completely filled shells. The element is not likely to react since there will be no tendency to gain or lose or share electrons (it is the configuration of the inert gas neon).
40.	C.	Their electron configurations are $1s^22s^22p^63s^23p^6$ (for P^{3-}) and $1s^22s^22p^6$ (for Mg^{2+}). These configurations are the same as those for the inert gases Ar and Ne.
41.	D.	All of these species have the electron configuration $1s^22s^22p^6$.
42.	C.	All d subshells contain 5 orbitals each of which can take 2 electrons.
43.	A.	Mg^{2+} has 10 electrons. The anion must also have 10 electrons and the element will have 8 protons.
44.	D.	The element Ti has two electrons in the 4s subshell and two electrons in the 3d. Three of these electrons are lost when Ti^{3+} is formed.
45.	B.	If the % of the lighter isotope is x, then the % of the heavier isotope is $100 - x$. $192.2 = \frac{191x + (100 - x)193}{100}$ $-80 = -2x$ and $x = 40$
46.	A.	If the % of the lighter isotope is x, then the % of the heavier isotope is 100 – x. $63.6 = \frac{63x + (100 - x)65}{100}$

Question	Answer	Comments
46(cont).	A.	$-140 = -2x$ and $x = 70$
47.	C.	(A) and (B) give relative atomic masses of 24.42 and 24.21, respectively. (D) gives a value that is too low (24.11).
48.	C.	The ground state electron configuration of calcium is $1s^2 2s^2 2p^6 3s^2 3p^6 4s^2$ since the 4s subshell is filled before the 3d subshell.
49.	B.	The colour seen in a flame test is caused by a species emitting energy. This happens when an electron in a higher energy level moves to a lower energy level. In (A) and (D) energy would be absorbed. In (C) the energy emitted would be greater than that emitted by (B).
50.	D.	In emission spectra the difference in energy between the two energy levels is emitted as light (electromagnetic radiation).
51.	B.	Bohr suggested that electrons in atoms could have only certain defined energies and occupy distinct orbits. For an electron to move from one orbit to another, energy had to be lost or gained.
52.	D.	Only Schrödinger proposed that within shells levels of similar energy exist, i.e. subshells.
53.	A.	Orbitals are part of Schrödinger's model (the quantum mechanical model) of the atom.
54.	B.	(A) is the ground state configuration of element 6. (C) is the configuration of an excited state of an anion, while (D) is the configuration of a cation.
55.	B.	Emission of a β–particle from an atom increases the atomic number by 1. This is expected when the n : p ratio is too high. Atoms can be radioactive without emitting a β–particle.
56.	B.	γ–rays are not deflected by an electric field but α– and β–particles are deflected.
57.	C.	In each reaction the atomic number increases by 1. To balance the equations x must have a nuclear charge of –1.
58.	C.	The two most important factors in determining the stability of an atom are its size and its n : p ratio. ^{238}U will be unstable since its atomic number is greater than 83. Both ^{3}H and ^{14}C have high n : p ratios and will emit a beta particle.
59.	D.	The sum of the mass numbers of Q and R is 235 + 1 – 3 = 233. The sum of the atomic numbers of Q and R = 92.
60.	B.	Thorium has an atomic number of 90. Atoms with an atomic number greater than 83 are unstable. These atoms are most likely to emit an alpha particle.

Question	Answer	Comments
61.	D.	1 hour corresponds to 3 half-lives for the ^{11}C isotope. After one half-life the amount decreases from 100% to 50%. During the second half-life the amount decreases from 50% to 25%. After 3 half-lives the amount of an isotope remaining will be 12.5%. Hence the initial amount of ^{11}C is $1.0 \times 10^{-4} \div 0.125$ g.
62.	A.	Atoms that have more protons than neutrons are most likely to be unstable.
63.	D.	All spontaneously decay and have an imbalance of protons and neutrons compared with stable isotopes. There are no stable isotopes of Tc. In the other alternatives the $^{14}_{7}N$, $^{40}_{20}Ca$, and $^{16}_{8}O$ isotopes are stable.
64.	D.	A nuclear reactor has a large number of neutrons needed for this transformation.
65.	B.	In (B) the mass numbers and positive charges balance. 27 + 1 = 24 + 4 and 13 + 0 = 11 + 2. This is not the case for the other options.
66.	B.	The electron configurations are 2.8.1 (for Na) and 2.8.8.1 (for K). The third shell for K is not full.
67.	C.	The third shell is full for both of these elements (2.8.18.2 for Zn and 2.8.18.8 for Kr). For all the other elements the third shell is only partly filled.
68.	C.	The reactivity decreases in going across a period, e.g. Na is more reactive than Mg which is more reactive than Al. The reactivity decreases going up a group, e.g. potassium is more reactive than sodium which is more reactive than lithium.
69.	D.	Early forms of the Periodic Table used atomic mass and chemical properties. Chemical properties are largely determined by the outer shell electron configuration.
70.	D.	In going down a group of elements in the Periodic Table, more electron shells are needed to accommodate the electrons. Only 2 shells are needed for the electrons of Be, Mg needs 3 shells, Ca 4 shells and Sr 5 shells. If more shells are used, then the atom increases in size.
71.	C.	All Group 1 elements form 1+ cations (since they have 1 electron in the outer shell) and there is no tendency to form 2+ cations. Going from Li to Cs, the outer shell electrons become further from the nucleus, have less attraction to the nucleus and hence are more easily removed.
72.	C.	In going down a group of elements in the Periodic Table, more electron shells are needed to accommodate the electrons. If more shells are used, then the atom increases in size. As the outer shell electrons get further from the nucleus they are easier

Question	Answer	Comments
72(cont).	C.	to remove and thus the first ionisation energy decreases.
73.	D.	Element number 16 is sulfur. Selenium is in the same group as sulfur.
74.	A.	Potassium is the most reactive metal of the four given and would be expected to have the smallest first ionisation energy, i.e. it loses its electrons most readily.
75.	C.	Element III has the smallest first ionisation energy and is expected to be the most reactive.
76.	C.	In going across the third period, the nuclear charge increases from 11+ to 18+ and all of the added electros go into the third shell. Thus the electrons are more strongly attracted to the nucleus by the increasing positive charge. This results in a decrease in the atomic radius. The increasing charge also means that more energy is needed to remove the outermost electron of the atom and thus the ionisation energy increases. The increasing nuclear charge also means that the atom can attract electrons more readily, i.e. the electronegativity increases.
77.	B.	These elements have *similar* chemical properties but not the same. The outer shell electron configuration is the same for each element (s^2p^5).
78.	B.	The size of the atoms increases going down Group 1, hence the atomic radius increases. When K is compared to Li the outer shell electron is further from the nucleus and less firmly held. Thus the ionisation energy decreases from Li to K.
79.	C.	In going across the Periodic Table, metallic character decreases (Na, Mg, Al are metals and P, S, Cl are non-metals) as does the atomic radius. The increasing nuclear charge means that more energy is needed to remove the outermost electron of the atom and thus the ionisation energy increases. Na reacts more vigorously with water than Mg and Al.
80.	D.	The element has 4 electrons in the outer shell, since four electrons are removed relatively easily (there is a sharp increase from 4 to 5). It cannot be carbon because carbon has only 6 electrons in total. This element has at least 8 electrons.
81.	A.	The size of an atom or ion will be determined by the nuclear charge and the number of electron shells. Na^+ and F^- have electrons in two shells, while Cl^- and K^+ use three shells. Na^+ has a nuclear charge of 11+ while the nuclear charge of F^- is 9+.
82.	C.	The nuclear charge of K is greater than that of Na. The K atom has electrons in 4 shells whereas Na has electrons in 3 shells. Thus K atoms will be larger than Na atoms. The ions, K^+ and Na^+ will be smaller than their respective atoms. Actual values are Na^+ 102 pm, Na 186 pm, K^+ 138 pm and K 227 pm.

Question	Answer	Comments
83.	B.	Going down a group the outer shell electrons get further away from the nucleus and thus easier to remove. The atomic radius increases but the electronegativity decreases. The number of outer shell electrons remains the same.
84.	A.	Two electrons are easily removed showing that the element has two electrons in the outer shell. (There is ~5 fold increase in the energy needed to remove the third electron. The ratio is much smaller for subsequent electrons, i.e. for the 3rd and 4th the ratio is ~1.4).
85.	D.	When Be and Li form cations the electron configuration will be the same as that of He. Ne is unreactive and has an atomic radius smaller than that of Mg.
86.	C.	Atomic radii decrease going across a group in the Periodic Table and electronegativities increase.
87.	B.	All the inert gases except helium have the outer shell configuration s^2p^6.
88.	C.	Transition metals are not highly reactive like Na and K. All the remaining properties are those of transition metals.
89.	C.	Main group metals are generally highly reactive, soft, have low ionisation energies and display one oxidation state. Transition metals are usually hard, form coloured compounds, have higher melting and boiling temperatures and have smaller atomic radii than main group metals.
90.	A.	When metals react they lose electrons. Going down Groups 1 and 2, the outermost (valence) electrons get further from the nucleus and are thus easier to remove. Hence the reactivity increases going down the group.
91.	A.	Metals with low reactivity are easiest to obtain from their ores or to be found uncombined.
92.	C.	Covalent bonds are formed between atoms of non-metals. Non-metals generally have high electronegativities.
93.	B.	The polarity of a covalent bond depends upon the difference in electronegativity of the two elements. For these bonds the electronegativity differences are Q–R = 0.38, Q–X = 1.40, Q–Z = 0.86, R–X = 1.78, R–Z = 1.24 and X–Z = 0.54. For the bonds X–X and Z–Z the differences are 0.
94.	B.	Ions are formed by the transfer of outer shell electrons from metal to non-metal atoms. Both atoms gain full outer shells and a positive or negative charge. There is electrostatic attraction between the positive and negative ions in the crystal.
95.	D.	An element with six outer shell electrons will gain two electrons and become an anion with the stability of a full 3p subshell and the electron configuration of argon.

Question	Answer	Comments
96.	D.	The elements carbon, nitrogen and chlorine are non-metals and these elements form covalent oxides. Manganese, which is a transition metal, forms both Mn^{2+} and Mn^{4+} ions so can have ionic oxides with the formulae MnO and MnO_2.
97.	B.	Non-metals achieve the stability of a full outer shell by sharing electrons between two atoms. A covalent bond consists of a shared pair of electrons, one originally from each atom.
98.	A.	In (A) the C atom forms three C–H bonds and one C–P bond, while the P atom forms two more bonds to H. (B) is CH_3CN which has a triple bond, (C) has a C to O double bond. In (D) each N forms one single bond to O and one double bond to O.
99.	B.	Two aluminium atoms each donate three outer shell electrons, two to each of three oxygen atoms so that all ions formed have the stability of full outer shells. Both aluminium and oxide ions then have the same electron configuration which is that of neon.
100.	B.	Calcium atoms have two outer shell electrons and fluorine atoms have seven. A calcium atom will therefore donate two electrons, one to each of two fluorine atoms so that all atoms have the stability of full outer shells. Thus the formula is CaF_2.
101.	C.	The number of bonding pairs plus the number of non-bonding pairs of electrons determine the shape of the molecule. The electron pairs repel each other and get as far apart as possible.
102.	B.	Ammonia is a triangular pyramid. Nitrogen atoms form three covalent bonds to three hydrogen atoms and there is also a non-bonding electron pair on the nitrogen atom.
103.	C.	C_2H_2, HCl and N_2 are all linear molecules. PCl_3 has a triangular pyramid shape.
104.	D.	Fluorine is the most electronegative element so the difference in electronegativity between F and H is greater than that between C, N and O and hydrogen.
105.	D.	PH_3 is an unsymmetrical triangular pyramid and the molecule is polar with a permanent dipole. CO_2, CH_4, and CF_4 are all symmetrical and non-polar as they have no permanent dipole.
106.	C.	M atoms have 2 outer shell electrons and X atoms have 7 outer shell electrons. When ionic bonds form, M atoms donate 2 electrons, one to each of 2 X atoms, so that all three atoms have the stability of full outer electron shells. Thus the formula is MX_2.
107.	C.	J atoms have 3 outer shell electrons, oxygen atoms have 6 outer shell electrons, chlorine atoms have 7 outer shell electrons. *Oxide:* two J atoms donate 3 electrons per atom, two to each of 3 oxygen atoms, so that all atoms have the stability of full outer

Question	Answer	Comments
107 (cont).	C.	electron shells. Thus the formula is J_2O_3. *Chloride:* an J atom donates 3 electrons per atom, one to each of 3 chlorine atoms, so that all atoms have the stability of full outer electron shells. Thus the formula is JCl_3.
108.	A.	PF_3 is a covalent molecule formed when a P atom shares three of its five outer shell electrons, one with each of three F atoms. The molecule has three covalent bonds and one non-bonding electron pair, i.e. eight outer shell electrons.
109.	D.	CH_4O will have only single bonds between its atoms. C forms *3* C–H bonds and *1* C–O bond. O also forms *1* O–H bond.
110.	D.	F atoms have seven outer shell electrons so only share one electron to gain a full outer electron shell. C, N and O atoms all share more than one electron to gain full outer shells.
111.	A.	Definition.
112.	C.	All three forms conduct electricity. In carbon nanotubes the layers are similar to the layers in graphite and graphene but rolled into tubes. In each form, electrons are delocalised throughout the layers.
113.	B.	In diamond each carbon is covalently bonded to 4 other carbon atoms. In graphite and buckyballs each carbon is covalently bonded to 3 other carbon atoms. In each of these forms the carbon atoms are in rings and the fourth electron from each carbon is delocalised around the ring or throughout the layer.
114.	C.	Three electrons from each carbon atom form covalent bonds with three other carbon atoms in the same layer. The remaining electron from each carbon atom is delocalised through the layer.
115.	A.	In B and C some of the carbon atoms have only three bonds. In D the atoms have six bonds.
116.	D.	When metals are bent or stretched the inter particle bonds must be overcome and then reform in the new position. Statements I, II and III are true but not relevant to the properties of malleability and ductility.
117.	C.	Delocalised outer shell electrons in metals are able to move through the metal under the influence of an applied potential difference. This makes the metal an electrical conductor.
118.	A.	The attractive forces between particles must be overcome for the metal to melt or boil. The stronger the forces of attraction the higher the melting or boiling points.
119.	B.	Density is defined as mass per unit volume. The greater the number of particles, and therefore mass, in a given volume of metal, the greater its density.

Question	Answer	Comments
120.	A.	Na_2CO_3 as it is an ionic compound and forms an ionic lattice in which each ion is surrounded by ions of opposite charge.
121.	A.	All four molecules are quite polar and their dipoles (in debye) decrease in the order $CH_3F \cong CH_3Cl > CH_3Br > CH_3I$ (6.2, 6.2, 6.0 and 5.4). However there are also dispersion forces that will contribute to the intermolecular attractions. These are dependent on the number of electrons present (18e, 26e, 44e and 62e). Thus there is a larger change in dispersion forces. The boiling points (in °C) are $CH_3F = -78 < CH_3Cl = -24 < CH_3Br = 3.6 < CH_3I = 42$
122.	B.	Molecular substances often (but not always) have low boiling temperatures. Some elements (e.g. O_2, N_2, F_2 etc.) are composed of molecules. Many molecular substances are liquids (H_2O, Br_2) or solids (I_2) at room temperature. They generally do not conduct electricity.
123.	B.	HF is very soluble in water because it forms hydrogen bonds with water molecules. Butan-1-ol is slightly soluble in water. The –OH group forms hydrogen bonds with water molecules but the $CH_3CH_2CH_2CH_2–$ part of the molecule does not. Both O_2 and propane are only slightly soluble in water since they are either non-polar or only slightly polar molecules and do not readily form bond to water molecules.
124.	A.	Both methanol and ethanol exhibit hydrogen bonding and have one –OH group per molecule. The magnitude of the dispersion forces will be higher in ethanol as it is a larger molecule.
125.	C.	All the molecules have intermolecular dispersion forces but aminomethane contains a –N–H bond, and is the only molecule that also exhibits hydrogen bonding. Its boiling point is expected to be (and is) higher than that of the other alternatives.
126.	A.	If a substance is hard and brittle and has high melting and boiling temperatures, it indicates that the attractive forces between particles are strong. Much energy is needed to overcome them.
127.	D.	The strength of ionic bonds is such that temperatures higher than room temperature are needed to overcome them and cause melting. The arrangement is alternate positive and negative ions as each ion is surrounded in the lattice by and attracted to, oppositely charged ions.
128.	C.	Molecular substances have weak intermolecular bonding, but covalent network and layer lattices have strong covalent bonding throughout. Thus molecular substances have much lower melting and boiling points than covalent lattices.

Question	Answer	Comments
129	D.	This requires the breaking of strong covalent bonds between hydrogen and oxygen in the water molecule. The other alternatives require weak intermolecular bonding to be overcome.

Extended Response Questions

Question 1

The properties of the ionic compound, zinc iodide, are different from those of the metal, zinc and the non-metal, iodine. A mixture of zinc and iodine would show some of the properties of the individual materials. For example, in the mixture some of it would melt at 114°C and the rest would melt at 420°C. The densities of the mixture would be part way between 4.9 and 7.14 g mL^{-1}. (Total = 3 marks)

Question 2

(a) In fractional distillation the substances are separated according to their boiling temperatures. The mixture of liquids is heated until it boils. Substances are collected according to their boiling temperatures. The liquid with the lowest boiling temperature boils first and is thus collected first. The least volatile compound will have the highest boiling temperature and will be collected last. (2 marks)

(b) Pentanol will remain in the flask. It has a higher boiling temperature than butanol (boiling temperature 117.7°C), which is the second fraction. (2 marks)

(c) The first fraction is either methanol, ethanol or propanol. These all have a boiling temperature less than 117.7°C. Since the boiling temperature of the first fraction is not given, no decision can be made about which one of these it is. (1 mark)

(Total = 5 marks)

Question 3

(a) At 80°C, 362 g of sugar will dissolve in 100 g of water.
50 g of sugar will dissolve in (100 ÷ 362) × 50.0 = 13.8 g of water. (1 mark)

(b) 100 g of water will dissolve 38.1 g of salt at 80°C.
13.8 g of water will dissolve (38.1 ÷ 100) × 13.8 = 5.26 g of salt. (1 mark)

(c) Mass of salt not dissolved = 50.0 –5.3 = 44.7 g (1 mark)

(d) At 0°C mass of sugar that dissolves in 13.8 g of water = (179 ÷ 100) × 13.8
= 24.7 g
Mass of sugar that crystallises from solution at 0°C = 50.0 – 24.7
= 25.3 g (1 mark)

(e) Mass of salt that dissolves in 13.8 g of water at 0°C = (35.7 ÷ 100) × 13.8
= 4.93 g (1 mark)

(Total = 5 marks)

Question 4

(a) To ensure that all of the water had been removed from the crucible. (1 mark)

(b) Mass of water = 65.00 – 59.57 = 5.43 g
Mass of hydrated sodium carbonate = 65.00 – 56.38 = 8.62 g
% water = (5.43 ÷ 8.62) × 100 = 63.0%
(3 marks)

(c) Safety procedures include
- wearing safety spectacles
- wearing laboratory coat
- not touching hot equipment (allow crucible to cool) (2 marks)

(Total = 6 marks)

Question 5

Mass of water removed = 6.04 – 4.77 = 1.27 g
Mass of hydrated copper sulfate = (1.27 ÷ 36.1) × 100 = 3.52 g
Mass of NaCl 6.04 – 3.52 = 2.52 g
(Total = 3 marks)

Question 6

(i) An element is a pure substance consisting of atoms which all have the same number of protons. Atoms of an element cannot be broken down into simpler substances by chemical means.

(ii) Compounds are formed from atoms of more than one element joined by chemical bonds. The chemical bonds form from the outer shell electrons of the atom. Compounds consist of molecules or ions.

(iii) Mixtures do not have a fixed composition. They can be physically separated into, and have the properties of, the components from which they are made.
(Total = 1 + 1 + 1 = 3 marks)

Question 7

Mixture	Separation Method
Liquid air	Fractional distillation
Coffee grounds in water	Filtration
Blood cells in plasma	Centrifuging
Gold particles in crushed rock	Sedimentation
Lumps in flour	Sieving
Useful metal ores from worthless rock	Froth flotation
Dissolved salts from water	Crystallisation
Liquids with different boiling points	Distillation
Vegetable oil and water	Separating funnel
Magnetic and non-magnetic substances	Magnetism

(Total = 5 marks)

Question 8

1. Place the mixture on a large sheet of paper with a strong magnet underneath the paper. Draw the iron filings to one side of the paper using the magnet. Iron filings are the only magnetic substance present.

2. Add sufficient water to the remaining mixture of substances to dissolve the salt. Filter, heat the salt solution to evaporate the water. Gold and naphthalene will form a residue in the filter paper.
   The ionic compound salt is water soluble. Metallic gold and covalent naphthalene are not.
3. Add water to the mixture of gold and naphthalene in a large bowl.
   Gold is heavy and will sink to the bottom.
4. Naphthalene is less dense and can be washed out of the bowl into another container. Most of the water can be poured off and the remaining substances left to dry.

(Total = 8 marks)

Question 9

(a) Cr_2O_3 (b) KNO_3 (c) $MgCO_3$ (d) $HgCl_2$
(e) $Al(OH)_3$ (f) Li_3PO_4 (g) $NaHCO_3$ (h) CaF_2
(i) Ba_3N_2 (j) $FeSO_4$

(Total = 10 × ½ = 5 marks)

Question 10

(a) lithium bromide (b) aluminium sulfate
(c) lead(II) sulfide (d) chromium(III) bromide
(e) zinc nitrate (f) potassium oxide
(g) nickel(II) hydroxide (h) copper(II) phosphate
(i) iron(III) chloride (j) silver iodide

(Total = 10 × ½ = 5 marks)

Question 11

Element X is a non-metal. The electrical conductivity of this element is very small.
Element Z is a transition metal. Z has a higher density than element Y and also has higher melting and boiling temperatures. This is typical of transition metals.
Element Y is a main group metal. Y is a good conductor of heat and electricity but the density, melting and boiling temperatures are all lower thanthose of Z.

(Total = 5 marks)

Question 12

(a) Any three of:

Non Metals	Metals
Brittle	Malleable and ductile
Poor thermal and electrical conductors	Good thermal and electrical conductors
May be solids, liquids or gases	Most are solids
Reflective surfaces if crystalline	Lustrous

(3 marks)

(b) (i) nitrogen, oxygen, fluorine, chlorine, or any of the inert gases
(ii) bromine
(iii) boron, carbon, silicon, phosphorus, sulfur, selenium, tellurium

(1 + 1 + 1 = 3 marks)
(Total = 6 marks)

Question 13
Metals are better conductors of heat and electricity than non-metals or semi-metals. However a range of values exist.

Element	Thermal conductivity ($J\ s^{-1}\ m^{-1}\ K^{-1}$)	Electrical conductivity ($MS\ m^{-1}$)	Metal, semi-metal, non-metal
bromine	0.12	10^{-16}	non-metal
chromium	94	7.9	metal
germanium	60	10^{-4}	semi-metal
iodine	0.45	10^{-13}	non-metal
indium	82	12	metal
nickel	91	14	metal
osmium	88	11	metal
phosphorus	0.24	10^{-15}	non-metal
tellurium	3	10^{-4}	semi-metal
titanium	22	2.3	metal

(Total = 5 marks)

Question 14
(a) Lithium, Li, beryllium, Be and carbon in the form of graphite are all solids at room temperature that conduct heat and electricity. (3 marks)

(b) (i) Phosphorus, P, and sulfur, S, are solid non-metals.
(ii) Chlorine, Cl, and argon, Ar, are gaseous non-metals. (2 marks)

(c) Caesium, Cs, is the most reactive 'alkali' metal and lithium, Li, is the least reactive. (2 marks)
(Total = 7 marks)

Question 15
(a) The atomic number is an integer and is the number of protons in the nucleus of an atom. It is given the symbol Z. All atoms of the same element have the same atomic number; e.g. all atoms of oxygen have an atomic number of 8. (2 marks)

(b) The mass number is an integer and is the sum of the number of protons and the number of neutrons. It is given the symbol A. Many atoms of oxygen have a mass number of 16. This means that these atoms have 8 protons and 8 neutrons in the nucleus. (2 marks)

(c) Atoms which have the same atomic number but different mass numbers are called isotopes. Isotopes have the same number of protons but different numbers of neutrons, e.g. ${}^{16}_{8}O$ and ${}^{17}_{8}O$ are isotopes of oxygen. Both have 8 protons. The first has 8 neutrons but the second atom has 9 neutrons. (2 marks)
(Total = 6 marks)

Question 16

(a)

Species	Protons	Neutrons	Electrons	Neutral atom, cation, anion
I	12	12	12	neutral atom
II	10	12	10	neutral atom
III	9	10	10	anion
IV	12	14	10	cation
V	14	14	14	neutral atom
VI	13	14	10	cation

(3 marks)

(b) I and IV are isotopes since they have the same number of protons but different numbers of neutrons. (1 mark)

(c) ${}^{27}_{13}Al^{3+}$ (1 mark)

(Total = 5 marks)

Question 17

		Electron configuration	Number of neutrons	
(a)	${}^{21}_{10}Ne$	$1s^22s^22p^6$	21 – 10 = 11	(1 mark)
(b)	${}^{17}_{8}O$	$1s^22s^22p^4$	17 – 8 = 9	(1 mark)
(c)	${}^{27}_{12}Mg$	$1s^22s^22p^63s^2$	27 – 12 = 15	(1 mark)
(d)	${}^{30}_{14}Si$	$1s^22s^22p^63s^23p^2$	30 – 14 = 16	(1 mark)
(e)	${}^{40}_{19}K$	$1s^22s^22p^63s^23p^64s^1$	40 – 19 = 21	(1 mark)

(Total = 5 marks)

Question 18

	Number of protons	Number of neutrons	Electron configuration
${}^{7}_{4}Be$	4	7 – 4 = 3	$1s^22s^2$
${}^{14}_{7}N$	7	14 – 7 = 7	$1s^22s^22p^3$
${}^{37}_{17}Cl$	17	37 – 17 = 20	$1s^22s^22p^63s^23p^5$
${}^{33}_{15}P$	15	33 – 15 = 18	$1s^22s^22p^63s^23p^3$

(8 marks)

Question 19

(a) This is an emission spectrum (the hydrogen has given out light). (1 mark)

(b) The electron occupies the n = 1 level when the atom is in its ground state, i.e. the level with lowest energy. (1 mark)

(c) Hydrogen atoms gain energy from the electrical discharge. Electrons are moved from the n = 1 levels to higher levels. The electrons then return to a level of lower energy. The difference in energy between the two levels (the excess energy) is emitted as light. (2 marks)

(d) The energy of each line is the difference in energy between two levels.
Energy of line = Energy of higher level – Energy of lower level
The values are shown in the table below.

Line(Energy kJ mol^{-1})	Energy of higher level (kJ mol^{-1})	Energy of lower energy (kJ mol^{-1})	Difference in Energy (kJ mol^{-1})
W (182.4)	–145.7 (n = 3)	–328.1 (n = 2)	–145.7 – (–328.1) = 182.4
X (246.1)	–82.0 (n = 4)	–328.1 (n = 2)	–82.0 – (–328.1) = 246.1
Y (276.0)	–52.1 (n = 5)	–328.1 (n = 2)	–52.1 – (–328.1) = 276.0
Z (291.4)	–36.7 (n = 6)	–328.1 (n = 2)	–36.7 – (–328.1) = 291.4

(3 marks)

(e) An electron jump from n = 6 to n = 1 will produce the line of highest energy (energy = –36.7 – (–1313.2) = 1276.5 kJ mol^{-1}) (1 mark)

(Total = 8 marks)

Question 20

(a) The outer shell electron configurations are Li $2s^1$, Na $3s^1$ and K $4s^1$. (3 marks)

(b) Flame tests are examples of emission spectra. These spectra are produced when an electron moves from an energy level of high energy to one of lower energy. The difference in energy between the two levels is given out as light of a particular colour ($\Delta E = hf$). In the three elements the electron levels will have different numerical values. Hence when the electron movements occur, different amounts of energy (and thus different colours) will be released for the three elements, i.e. ΔE for Li is different from ΔE for Na, which is different from that for K. (3 marks)

(Total = 6 marks)

Question 21

(a) RAM(Pb) = (203.973 × 0.014) + (205.975 × 0.283) + (206.976 × 0.263) + (207.977 × 0.440) = 207.09 (2 marks)

(b) The RAM of this sample of lead is lower than that from other sources. This sample may have derived from a source that was richer in ^{238}U or ^{235}U or had less ^{232}Th. (2 marks)

(Total = 4 marks)

Question 22

Rutherford: Suggested that atoms consisted of a very small positively charged **nucleus** surrounded by the electrons. He did not make significant contributions to the areas of electron shells, subshells and orbitals. (2 marks)

Bohr: Suggested that electrons are arranged in shells around the nucleus. He did not make significant contributions to the areas of the nucleus, subshells and orbitals. (2 marks)

Schrödinger: Suggested that electrons occupied regions of space around the nucleus called orbitals. Orbitals with the same energy are grouped together in subshells. His theory suggested that there are major electron energy levels within an atom called shells. He did not make significant contributions to the understanding of the nucleus. (2 marks)

Chadwick: Showed that as well as heavy positively charged particles (protons) the nuclei of atoms also contained heavy neutral particles (neutrons).

He did not make significant contributions to the areas of electron shells, subshells and orbitals. (2 marks)

(Total = 8 marks)

Question 23

(a) In an atom or ion when all of the electrons are in their lowest possible energy states, the atom or ion is said to be in its ground state. If any of the electrons are not in the lowest possible energy level, then the atom or ion is in an excited state. (1 mark)

(b) One or more of the electrons has been moved to a higher energy level from where it is usually found. (1 mark)

(c) When an electron in an excited state moves to a state of lower energy the difference in energy (ΔE) is emitted as light. This amount of energy will have a specific frequency, f, as $\Delta E = hf$. (Frequency is inversely proportional to wavelength.) (2 marks)

(d) 6 lines could be produced if just the first 4 shells were used. The electron movements that would give emission lines are (the ground state = 1):
$4 \rightarrow 3$; $4 \rightarrow 2$; $4 \rightarrow 1$; $3 \rightarrow 2$; $3 \rightarrow 1$; $2 \rightarrow 1$; (2 marks)

(e) If the excited states increase in energy 2 to 3 to 4, then the $4 \rightarrow 1$ transition would have the highest energy. (1 mark)

(Total = 7 marks)

Question 24

(a) oxygen, O (the atom has 8 electrons) (1 mark)

(b) The process would release energy, since the electron has moved from a subshell of high energy to one of lower energy (4s to 3s). (2 marks)

(c) $1s^2 2s^2 2p^4$ (1 mark)

(Total = 4 marks)

Question 25

(a) X and Y are neutrons ($^{1}_{0}n$) since in each case the mass number increases by one unit but the atomic number remains constant. Z is a β–particle ($^{0}_{-1}e$) since the mass number is constant and the atomic number increases by one unit. (3 marks)

(b) $^{241}_{95}Am \rightarrow ^{237}_{93}Np + ^{4}_{2}He$ (2 marks)

(Total = 5 marks)

Question 26

(a) There are no stable nuclei with an atomic number greater than 83. The atomic number of astatine is 85 thus ^{219}At is expected to be unstable. (1 mark)

(b) Loss of an alpha particle decreases the atomic number by 2 and the mass number by 4 units. When a beta particle is lost from an atom the atomic number increases by 1 but there is no change in the mass number. For an atom of $^{235}_{92}U$ to change into an atom of $^{227}_{89}Ac$, two alpha particles and one beta particle must be lost. Loss of two more alpha particles will convert $^{227}_{89}Ac$ into $^{219}_{85}At$. One possible pathway is shown on the next page.

$$^{235}_{92}U \xrightarrow{\alpha} {}^{231}_{90}Th \xrightarrow{\alpha} {}^{227}_{88}Ra \xrightarrow{\beta} {}^{227}_{89}Ac \xrightarrow{\alpha} {}^{223}_{87}Fr \xrightarrow{\alpha} {}^{219}_{85}At$$

(3 marks)
(Total = 4 marks)

Question 27

(a) A nucleus will be unstable if its atomic number is greater than 83. Smaller nuclei will be unstable if their neutron to proton ratio is too high or too low. (2 marks)

(b) $^{232}_{90}Th \rightarrow {}^{228}_{88}Ra + {}^{4}_{2}He$ (1 mark)

(c) These two isotopes differ by 4 mass units. To change one to the other one, one alpha particle and two beta particles must be lost. There are three ways this might happen.

$$^{228}_{88}Ra \xrightarrow{\alpha} {}^{224}_{86}Rn \xrightarrow{\beta} {}^{224}_{87}Fr \xrightarrow{\beta} {}^{224}_{88}Ra$$

$$^{228}_{88}Ra \xrightarrow{\beta} {}^{228}_{89}Ac \xrightarrow{\beta} {}^{228}_{90}Th \xrightarrow{\alpha} {}^{224}_{88}Ra$$

$$^{228}_{88}Ra \xrightarrow{\beta} {}^{228}_{89}Ac \xrightarrow{\alpha} {}^{224}_{87}Fr \xrightarrow{\beta} {}^{224}_{88}Ra$$

(2 marks)

(d) The conversion of $^{214}_{82}Pb$ into $^{214}_{83}Bi$ is an example of beta emission. In this process a neutron is converted into a proton and an electron is emitted.

$^{214}_{82}Pb \rightarrow {}^{214}_{83}Bi + {}^{0}_{-1}e$ (1 mark)

(Total = 6 marks)

Question 28

(a) In ^{15}O the ratio of neutrons to protons is less than 1.0 (7÷8), hence this isotope is likely to decay by either electron capture or positron emission. In ^{19}O the neutron to proton ratio is greater than 1.0 (11÷8) and this isotope is likely to decay by emitting a beta particle. (2 marks)

(b) $^{15}_{8}O + {}^{0}_{-1}e \rightarrow {}^{15}_{7}N$ or $^{15}_{8}O \rightarrow {}^{15}_{7}N + {}^{0}_{1}e$

$^{19}_{8}O \rightarrow {}^{19}_{9}F + {}^{0}_{-1}e$ (2 marks)

(Total = 4 marks)

Question 29

(a) $^{24}_{11}Na \rightarrow {}^{24}_{12}Mg + {}^{0}_{-1}e$ (1 mark)

(b) $^{39}_{20}Ca \rightarrow {}^{39}_{19}K + {}^{0}_{1}e$ (1 mark)

(c) $^{103}_{46}Pd + {}^{0}_{-1}e \rightarrow {}^{103}_{45}Rh$ (1 mark)

(d) $^{131}_{53}I \rightarrow {}^{131}_{52}Te + {}^{0}_{-1}e$ (1 mark)

(Total = 4 marks)

Question 30

The nuclear equations for the two processes are given below.

Method 1 $^{241}_{95}Am + {}^{1}_{0}n \rightarrow {}^{242}_{95}Am \rightarrow {}^{242}_{96}Cm + {}^{0}_{-1}e$ (2 marks)

Method 2 $^{239}_{94}Pu + {}^{4}_{2}He \rightarrow {}^{242}_{96}Cm + {}^{1}_{0}n$ (2 marks)

(Total = 4 marks)

Question 31

(a) Increases

F has electrons in 2 shells, Cl uses 3 shells, Br uses 4 shells and I uses 5 shells. Going from one period to the next adds on an extra shell of electrons and increases the volume and radius of the atom. (2 marks)

(b) Decreases

These elements will react by gaining an electron or by sharing an electron. To gain an electron a substance must be able to remove an electron from another material. The strength with which an atom can attract electrons will determine how reactive it is. F attracts extra electrons more strongly than Cl. The extra electron goes into the second shell on F but into the third shell on Cl and so is more strongly held on F. (2 marks)

(c) Decreases

All these elements have a core charge of +7. However electrons attracted by F atoms will be attracted to the second shell, but for iodine any electrons will be attracted to the fifth shell, which is further from the nucleus. The attraction for iodine will be weaker than that for fluorine. (2 marks)

(Total = 6 marks)

Question 32

(a) Magnesium, calcium and barium have similar chemical properties (1 mark)

(b) Barium atoms are larger than magnesium atoms and thus the outer shell electrons are less strongly held than the outer shell electrons in Mg atoms. (2 marks)

(c) $1s^22s^22p^63s^23p^64s^2$ (1 mark)

(d) The electron configuration of a calcium ion, Ca^{2+}, is $1s^22s^22p^63s^23p^6$, i.e. the Ca atom has lost the two outer shell electrons (4s electrons). (1 mark)

(e) A magnesium atom has the electron configuration $1s^22s^22p^63s^2$ and has electrons in 3 shells. The electron configuration of a Mg^{2+} ion is $1s^22s^22p^6$ and only 2 shells are used. The outermost electrons of a Mg atom are thus further from the nucleus and the atom is larger than the cation. (1 mark)

(Total = 6 marks)

Question 33

(a) (i) F (ii) Ne (iii) F (iv) Co (v) S (5 marks)

(b) The core charge increases from Na to Cl (+1 to +7). Hence the ability of an atom to attract another electron increases in the same order. (2 marks)

(Total = 7 marks)

Question 34

(a) Atomic radius: This decreases in going from Li to F. The core charge increases from Li to F resulting in an increased attraction for the outer shell electrons. These are pulled closer to the nucleus. (2 marks)

Electronegativity: This increases from Li to F. The increasing core charge attracts the outer shell electrons more strongly. Hence F atoms will have greater electron attracting power than atoms of Li. (2 marks)

(b) (i) The energy required to remove an electron completely from an atom. (1 mark)

(ii) In sodium the outermost electron is further from the nucleus than it is in lithium. Hence the atomic radius of sodium is greater than that of lithium. There is a weaker attraction for the outermost electron in sodium than for the electron in lithium, hence the ionisation energy is smaller.

(2 marks)
(Total = 7 marks)

Question 35

(i) J and Q. The electronegativities are low and similar. (2 marks)
(ii) J and L or J and M or Q and L or Q and M. There is a large difference in electronegativity. (2 marks)
(iii) L and M. Both electronegativities are high and the difference between them is > 0.4 units. (2 marks)
(iv) Pure covalent bonding results when the electronegativity difference is < 0.4 units. There is no combination of these four elements that gives such a difference. (2 marks)

(Total = 8 marks)

Question 36

(a)

Element	Na	Mg	Al	Si	P	S	Cl
oxide	*Na_2O*	*MgO*	*Al_2O_3*	*SiO_2*	P_2O_5	*SO_3*	Cl_2O_7
fluoride	NaF	*MgF_2*	*AlF_3*	SiF_4	*PF_5*	SF_6	ClF_5

(4 marks)

(b)

Element	Na	Mg	Al	Si	P	S	Cl
oxide	Na_2O	MgO	Al_2O_3	SiO_2	P_2O_5	SO_3	Cl_2O_7
fluoride	NaF	MgF_2	AlF_3	SiF_4	PF_5	SF_6	ClF_5
bonding	*ionic*	*ionic*	*ionic*	*covalent*	*covalent*	*covalent*	*covalent*

(2 marks)

(c) The electron configurations of the atoms increases from 2.8.1 (for Na) to 2.8.7 (for Cl). In the oxides the number oxygen atoms that combine with 2 atoms of each element increases steadily from 1 (for Na) to 7 (for Cl), i.e. as the number of outer shell electrons increases so does the number of O atoms. The trend is similar in the fluorides. The formulae of the fluorides, from Na to S is MF_n, where n increases from 1 to 6, again in line with the change in electron configuration (Cl does not complete the sequence). (2 marks)

(Total = 8 marks)

Question 37

	Elements	Formula	Electron Configurations
(a)	lithium and phosphorus	Li_3P	$1s^2$ and $1s^22s^22p^63s^23p^6$
(b)	sodium and sulfur	Na_2S	$1s^22s^22p^6$ and $1s^22s^22p^63s^23p^6$
(c)	potassium and oxygen	K_2O	$1s^22s^22p^63s^23p^6$ and $1s^22s^22p^6$
(d)	calcium and fluorine	CaF_2	$1s^22s^22p^63s^23p^6$ and $1s^22s^22p^6$
(e)	aluminium and chlorine	$AlCl_3$	$1s^22s^22p^6$ and $1s^22s^22p^63s^23p^6$
(f)	magnesium and nitrogen	Mg_3N_2	$1s^22s^22p^6$ and $1s^22s^22p^6$

(Total = 12 marks)

Question 38

(a) +4 (b) +2 (c) +1 (d) +3
(e) +3 (f) +2 (g) +3 (h) +2 (Total = 8 marks)

Question 39

(a) S = 4 and F = 1 (1 mark)
(b) N = 3 and H = 1 (1 mark)
(c) P = 5 and Cl = 1 (1 mark)
(d) H = 1, O = 2 and S = 6 (1 mark)

(Total = 4 marks)

Question 40

(a) (i) aluminium $1s^2 2s^2 2p^6 3s^2 3p^1$
(ii) calcium $1s^2 2s^2 2p^6 3s^2 3p^6 4s^2$
(iii) fluorine $1s^2 2s^2 2p^5$
(iv) sulfur $1s^2 2s^2 2p^6 3s^2 3p^4$

(1 + 1 + 1 + 1 = 4 marks)

(b)

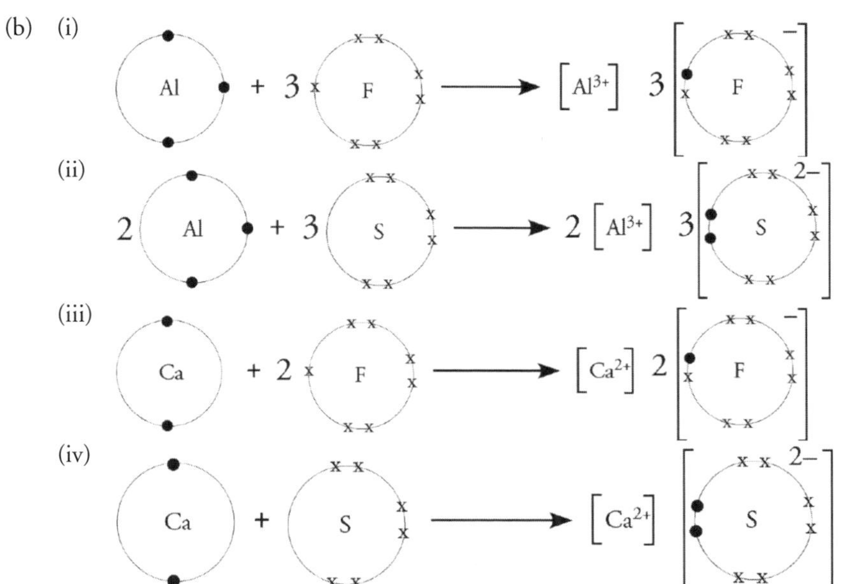

(Only outer shell electrons are shown) (4 marks)

(Total = 8 marks)

Question 41

(a) H—C≡N—

(b) H—S—H

(c) H—O—N=O

(d) $H_2C=O$

(e) SiF_4 (Si bonded to four F)

(f) H—O—C(H)=O

(Total = 6 marks)

Question 42

	Molecule	Shape	Polar/non-polar
(a)	F_2	linear	non polar
(b)	CH_2O	triangular planar	polar
(c)	CCl_4	tetrahedral	non polar
(d)	HCN	linear	polar
(e)	BF_3	triangular planar	non polar

(Total = 10 marks)

Question 43

(a) H—C≡C—H

or

N≡C—C≡N

(b) 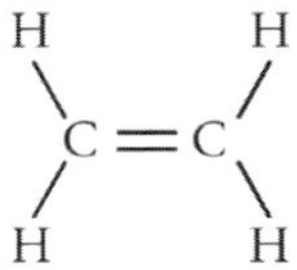 H₂C=CH₂ structure (H, H / C=C / H, H) or C_2F_4

(c) 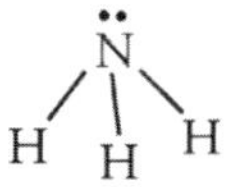 NH_3 structure (N with lone pair bonded to H, H, H) or NF_3

(d) 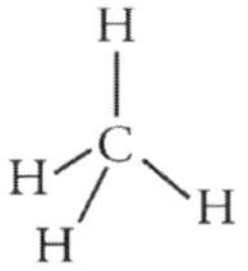 CH_4 structure (C bonded to H, H, H, H) or CF_4

(Total = 4 marks)

Question 44

(a) 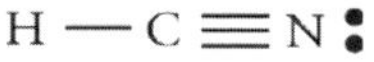 H—C≡N:

(b) H—S—H with two lone pairs on S

(c) O=N—O—H with lone pairs on N and O atoms

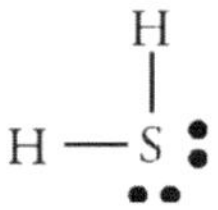

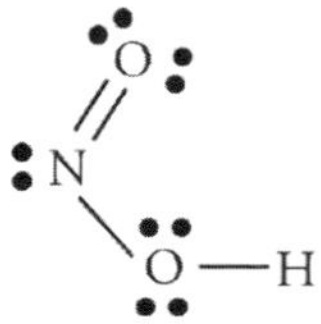

(d) 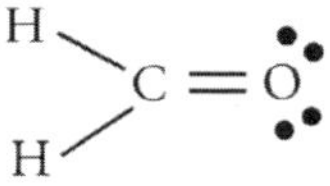 $H_2C=O$ with two lone pairs on O

(e) 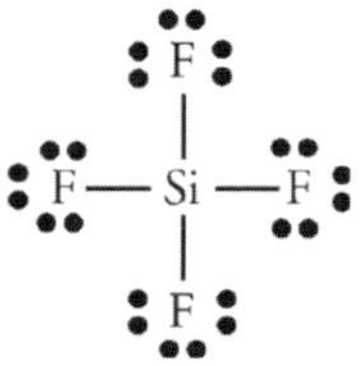 SiF_4: F—Si—F with F above and below, each F with three lone pairs

(f) H—C(=O)—O—H with two lone pairs on each O

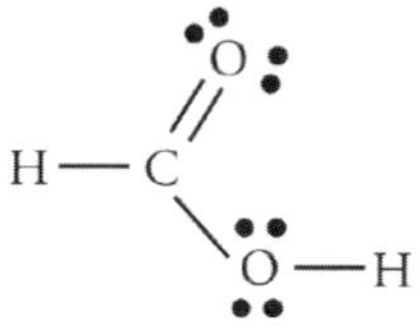

(Total = 1 + 1 + 1 + 1 + 1 + 1 = 6 marks)

Question 45

(a)	Nitrogen covalency	Formula of oxide
	1	N_2O
	2	NO
	3	N_2O_3
	4	NO_2
	5	N_2O_5

(5 marks)

(b) NO and NO_2. Nitrogen atoms have an odd number of electrons and oxygen atoms have an even number. Those molecules from above that have a single N atom will have an unpaired electron. (2 marks)

(Total = 7 marks)

Question 46

(a) Allotropes are different physical forms of the same chemical element. Their chemical bonding may differ in strength, nature and direction. (1 mark)

(b) In diamond each carbon atom is covalently bonded to four other carbon atoms. There is covalent bonding between the atoms throughout the lattice. In graphite each carbon atom is covalently bonded to three other carbon atoms. The carbon atoms are arranged in layers. There are dispersion forces between the layers. (2 marks)

(c) (i) Diamond has strong bonding throughout its structure. Graphite has weak bonding between the layers. (1 mark)

(ii) In graphite one electron from each carbon atom is delocalised throughout the layer. This allows conduction of electricity. Diamond has no delocalised electrons. (1 mark)

(iii) The distance between the layers of atoms in graphite is greater than the length of the covalent bonds in diamond. Hence the atoms in diamond are closer together and the density is greater. (1 mark)

(d) (i) The strong bonding between carbon atoms in diamond make it harder than the rock etc. that it cuts. (1 mark)

(ii) Diamond transmits and reflects light. It also produces a white light spectrum, making it attractive as jewellery. (1 mark)

(iii) The weak bonding between the layers of carbon atoms in graphite is overcome when a pencil is moved across paper leaving a trail of carbon on the paper. (1 mark)

(iv) The very high melting point of graphite makes it a suitable container for other high melting point substances. (1 mark)

(v) Graphite is an electrical conductor but also is relatively inert chemically. It can be shaped so is suitable as an electrode. (1 mark)

(Total = 11 marks)

Question 47

The bonding in carbon nanotubes is similar to the bonding in graphite. The atoms are arranged in layers with each carbon atom covalently bonded to three other carbon atoms to form six membered rings. One electron per carbon atom is delocalised throughout the layer. In carbon nanotubes the layers are rolled into a tube. Along the direction of the tube the bonding is very strong making the material stiff. The delocalised electrons mean that the material is a good conductor of heat and electricity. (3 marks)

Question 48

(a) 60 ^{12}C atoms will have a relative moleular mass of $60 \times 12 = 720$. Hence the largest peak in the spectrum is due to $^{12}C_{60}^{+}$ ions. The peak with a mass to charge ratio of 721 is caused by a positive ion in which one ^{12}C atom has been replaced by a ^{13}C atom, i.e. ($59 \times {}^{12}C + 1 \times {}^{13}C$). Similarly the peak at 722 is caused by a positive ion containing 58 ^{12}C atoms and two ^{13}C atoms. (3 marks)

(b) The area of each peak is proportional to the number of molecules producing that peak. Hence in the sample of C_{60} there are 18 molecules containing only ^{12}C atoms, 12 molecules containing 59 ^{12}C plus 1 ^{13}C and 4 molecules with 58 ^{12}C and 2 ^{13}C.

The total number of carbon atoms = $(18 + 12 + 4) \times 60 = 34 \times 60 = 2040$.

The number of ^{13}C atoms = $12 + 8 = 20$

% ^{13}C atoms = $(20 \div 2040) \times 100 = 0.9804$; i.e. 0.98% (3 marks)

(c) The C_{60} fullerene will contain small numbers of molecules containing 3 or 4 or 5 atoms of ^{13}C. These would increase the percentage of ^{13}C calculated using the method outlined on the previous page. (2 marks)

(Total = 8 marks)

Question 49

A. This is an ionic material. In the solid state the ions are not free to move around and the material is a non-conductor of electricity. In solution or when molten the ions are free to move and thus conducts.

B. This is a covalent molecular material. The intermolecular forces of attraction are broken at a moderate temperature and it is a non-conductor.

C. This is a covalent network material. It is a non-conductor and the attractive forces between the particles are hard to overcome.

D. This material is a metal. It is malleable, conducts and has a high melting temperature.

(Total = 4 marks)

Question 50

(a) *Sodium:* metallic bonding, attraction between positive ions in 'sea' of delocalised outer shell electrons.

Chlorine: non-polar covalent molecules with intermolecular dispersion forces bonding. Each Cl atoms shares one electron to form a Cl_2 molecule.

Sodium chloride: ionic bonding, attraction between oppositely charged ions in a fixed continuous array.

(2 marks)

(b) The intermolecular bonds in chlorine are weak dispersion forces between molecules but in sodium chloride the bonds between ions are strong ionic bonds. When melting occurs the inter-particle bonds are overcome and the solid structure breaks down. More energy is required to overcome strong bonds than weak bonds and the melting point of sodium chloride is much higher than that of chlorine. (2 marks)

(Total = 4 marks)

Question 51

(a) (i) Na^+ and F^- (ii) Mg^{2+} and O^{2-} (2 marks)

(b) All of the ions, Na^+, F^-, Mg^{2+} and O^{2-}, have the same electron configuration, $1s^2 2s^2 2p^6$. (1 mark)

(c) Although all four ions have the same electron configuration, the attractive force between magnesium and oxide ions is higher that between sodium and fluoride ions (approximately four times). The charge on the ions results from the transfer of two electrons in magnesium oxide rather than one in the case of sodium fluoride. (2 marks)

(Total = 5 marks)

Question 52

(a) Potassium $1s^2 2s^2 2p^6 3s^2 3p^6 4s^1$

Chromium $1s^2 2s^2 2p^6 3s^2 3p^6 3d^4 4s^2$ (2 marks)

(b) Both potassium and chromium have metallic bonding. The positive nuclear charge of chromium is greater than that of potassium, therefore electrons are more strongly attracted to the nucleus and the chromium atom has a smaller radius than the potassium atom. Potassium only has one electron in the fourth shell that is delocalised but chromium has both electrons in the third and fourth shells that are delocalised. This means that the metallic bonding in chromium is stronger than that in potassium as positive metal ions and delocalised electrons are closer and the number of delocalised electrons is higher. (2 marks)

(c) Potassium and chromium:
-are both reductants and react chemically by forming positive ions
-both have a metallic lustre (potassium rapidly oxidises in air). (2 marks)

(d) Any two of:

Potassium	*Chromium*
Single valency	Several valencies
Compounds white	Compounds coloured
Soft, low melting point	Hard, high melting point
Very reactive metal	Lower reactivity

(2 marks)
(Total = 8 marks)

Question 53

(a)

	CH_3Cl	CH_3Br	CH_3I
Number of electrons	26	44	62

(3 marks)

(b) The attractive forces due to dipole-dipole bonding should be approximately the same for each compound since the dipoles are approximately the same. However the dispersion forces will increase from CH_3Cl to CH_3Br to CH_3I since the number of electrons is increasing in this order. (2 marks)
(Total = 5 marks)

Question 54

(a)

propane dimethyl ether ethanol

(3 marks)

(b) Dimethyl ether and ethanol are isomers. They both have the molecular formula, C_2H_6O. (1 mark)

(c) Propane has $(3 \times 6) + 8 = 26$ electrons
Dimethyl ether has $(2 \times 6) + 6 + 8 = 26$ electrons
Ethanol has $(2 \times 6) + 6 + 8 = 26$ electrons (1 mark)

(d) The size of the dispersion forces between molecules depends on the number of electrons in the molecule and the shape of the molecule. These three molecules have the same number of electrons and very similar molecular shapes. The size of the dispersion forces should be approximately the same for the three molecules. (2 marks)

(e) The only attractive force between propane molecules will be dispersion forces. Dimethyl ether will have similar dispersion forces acting between its molecules. Dimethyl ether molecules also have a small molecular dipole. Oxygen has a higher electronegativity than carbon. The C–O bonds are polar with the oxygen atom being slightly negative and the carbon atom slightly positive. The small molecular dipole in dimethyl ether means that the intermolecular forces are slightly larger in dimethyl ether than they are in propane. Thus there is a small increase in boiling temperature. Ethanol contains an O–H bond. Hydrogen bonding occurs between ethanol molecules so the intermolecular forces are larger in ethanol than dimethyl ether. Hence the boiling temperature of ethanol is higher than that of dimethyl ether. (3 marks)

(Total = 10 marks)

Question 55

Solid magnesium chloride exists as a crystalline ionic lattice in which each ion is surrounded by ions of opposite charge. The ionic bonds between ions are fixed in length, strength and direction. There are no delocalised electrons.

For an electric current to flow, a substance must contain charged particles that are free to move. When magnesium chloride melts or dissolves in water, the crystal structure breaks down and the ions are able to move and carry an electric current.

(Total = 3 marks)

Question 56

When water is converted into steam, heat energy overcomes the **intermolecular** hydrogen bonds and dispersion forces and the liquid becomes a gas. The water molecules become independent of each other but no chemical reaction occurs and the molecules are unchanged. This is a physical change.

When an electric current is passed through water, electrical energy overcomes the **intramolecular** covalent bonds between hydrogen and oxygen, the water molecules decompose and new substances (hydrogen and oxygen) are formed. This is a chemical change. (Total = 4 marks)

Test: Properties of Matter and Atomic Structure

Multiple Choice Items

Question	Answer	Comments
1.	B.	A mixture of petrol and water would form two layers.
2.	C.	Element Q has high electrical and thermal conductivity, and high density compared with the other alternatives.
3.	B.	Mass of water removed = (5.34 – 3.14) g = 2.20 g. % water = (2.20 ÷ 5.34) × 100 = 41.2%
4.	C.	In A, $Li(NO_3)_2$ should be $LiNO_3$; in B, AgO should be Ag_2O; in D, $CuBr_3$ should be CuBr or $CuBr_2$ and $NaCO_3$ should be Na_2CO_3.
5.	A.	(B) is the definition of atomic number, (C) is a mass and (D) is the difference between mass number and atomic number.
6.	B.	The mass number is placed at the top left of the element symbol and the atomic number at the bottom left.
7.	A.	${}_{12}Mg^{2+}$ has 10 electrons (electron configuration of neon). The other alternatives have 18 electrons (the electron configuration

Question	Answer	Comments
7(cont).	A.	of argon).
8.	B.	The atomic number is subtracted from the mass number.
9.	D.	The calcium ion has 2 less electrons than the neutral atom, which has 20 electrons.
10.	D.	C–12, O–16, Zn–65 and Mg–24 are all stable nuclei. All the nuclei in D are unstable.
11.	C.	Iso-electronic species have the same electron configuration. Potassium has the electron configuration $1s^22s^22p^63s^23p^64s^1$. The other species have the configuration $1s^22s^22p^63s^23p^6$.
12.	B.	Lines in an *emission* spectrum, are caused by electrons moving from a *higher* energy shell to a *lower* energy shell.

Extended Response Answers

Question 1

(a) $1s^22s^22p^63s^23p^63d^64s^2$ (1 mark)

(b) Iron is classified as a transition metal because it has a partially filled "-d-" subshell. (1 mark)

(c) The electron configuration of Fe^{3+} is $1s^22s^22p^63s^23p^63d^5$. (1 mark)

(Total = 3 marks)

Question 2

(a) Line **d** is at the lowest wavelength and thus has the highest energy. (1 mark)

(b) Since this is an emission spectrum, the lines are caused by electrons moving from a high energy level to one of lower energy. The energies of the four lines increase a < b < c < d.
a: the electron moves from n = 2 to n = 1
b: the electron moves from n = 3 to n = 1
c: the electron moves from n = 4 to n = 1
d: the electron moves from n = 5 to n = 1 (4 marks)

(c) The line of highest energy is that of lowest wavelength. Energy emitted is equal to the energy difference between energy levels, therefore the highest energy line corresponds to the greatest difference in energy levels. (3 marks)

(Total = 8 marks)

Question 3

If the percentage of $^{203}Tl = x$ then the percentage of $^{205}Tl = 100 - x$.

Hence $[202.97x + 204.97(100 - x)]/100 = 204.38$

$202.97x + 20497 - 204.97x = 20438$

$-2.00x = -59$ and $x = 29.5\%$

Hence $\%\ ^{203}Tl = 29.5$ and $\%\ ^{205}Tl = 70.5$ (4 marks)

Question 4

(a) chromium(III) oxide

(b) potassium sulfate

(c) copper(I) chloride

(d) barium carbonate

(Total = 4 marks)

Question 5

(a) $^{18}_{9}F + ^{0}_{-1}e \rightarrow ^{18}_{8}O$ (1 mark)

(b) $^{31}_{14}Si \rightarrow ^{31}_{15}P + ^{0}_{-1}e$ (1 mark)

(c) $^{26}_{13}Al \rightarrow ^{26}_{12}Mg + ^{0}_{1}e$ (1 mark)

(d) $^{213}_{83}Bi \rightarrow ^{209}_{81}Tl + ^{4}_{2}He$ (1 mark)

(Total = 4 marks)

(Total = 35 marks)

Test: Periodicity and Bonding

Multiple Choice Items

Question	Answer	Comments
1.	B.	Due to the increasing positive charge on the nucleus, from left to right across the periodic table, the atomic radius decreases and the electronegativity increases.
2.	A.	Metal atoms lose their outer shell electrons to gain the extra stability of full shells, but gain a positive charge as the number of protons in the atom exceeds the number of electrons. Positively charged ions are called cations.
3.	D.	The ionisation energies of electrons in the same shell increase as more electrons are removed, but there is a much larger difference in ionisation energy between that of the last electron in a shell and the first electron to be removed from the next inner shell. D has 3 outer shell electrons with similar energies and a large jump to the ionisation energy of the fourth electron.
4.	A.	The graphs show 2 electrons of similar ionisation energy for elements I and II, then a larger energy difference to the ionisation energy of the third electron.
5.	C.	All ions have the same number of electrons (18) but the S^{2-} has the smallest nuclear charge.
6.	D.	Element IV has two outer shell electrons and will transfer one to each of two chlorine atoms to produce a chloride with the formula MCl_2.
7.	B.	Nitrogen atoms have five outer shell electrons, so share three electrons with other atoms to gain the stability of a full outer shell. Thus they form three covalent bonds.
8.	B.	H_2O and H_2S are both V-shaped molecules. CO_2 is linear, NH_3 is triangular pyramidal, BF_3 is triangular planar and CH_4 is tetrahedral.

Question	Answer	Comments
9.	D.	The metal structure model considers the outer shell electrons of metal atoms to be delocalised. Thus positive metal ions exist in a regular array with bands ('a sea') of delocalised electrons between them. Forces of attraction exist between the positive metal ions and the delocalised electrons.
10.	C.	Diamond exists as a covalent network lattice in which each carbon atom forms four strong covalent bonds to four other carbon atoms. Methane is a molecular substance whose molecules have strong covalent bonds within the molecule but weak dispersion forces between them. The bonds, which must be overcome when a change of state occurs, are covalent bonds in diamond but dispersion forces in methane, thus methane has a much lower melting and boiling point.
11.	D.	C and O have different electronegativities and the C=O bonds are polar covalent bonds. However since CO_2 is a linear molecule the bond polarities cancel out and the molecule is non-polar.
12.	B.	Electrical conductors must contain either electrons or ions that are able to move. Solid ionic compounds are crystalline with ions in fixed positions, and no delocalised electrons. When the ionic compound melts, the ionic bonds are overcome and the ions are able to move. Thus the molten salt is a conductor.
13.	B.	The four molecules have the same number of electrons and similar molar masses. Hence the dispersion forces between the molecules in these substances will be similar. $C_3H_7NH_2$ and $C_2H_5NHCH_3$ will also have hydrogen bonding between their molecules. This will be greater for $C_3H_7NH_2$. The boiling temperatures (in °C) are C4H10 = –0.5; $C_3H_7NH_2$ = 48.5; $C_2H_5NHCH_3$ = 36.5 and $(CH_3)_3N$ = 2.9.
14.	A.	Both electronegativities are greater than 2.0 and there is a large difference between the two values (1.11 units).
15.	D.	The electronegativity of the halogens decreases in the order F>Cl>Br>I. The smallest electronegativity difference will be between C and I. This will give the smallest molecular dipole.

Extended Response Answers

Question 1

(a) Electronegativity is the ability of an atom to attract electrons. Metals have low electronegativities (~0.7 to ~1.9 and non-metals have higher values, typically ~2.0 to 4.0. (2 marks)

(b) Core charge is the effective nuclear charge felt by the outer shell electrons. It is the difference between the nuclear charge (atomic number) and the number of inner shell electrons. It is also equal to the number of electrons in the outer shell. For sulfur (Z = 16), the core charge is +6 (16 – 10). (2 marks)

(c) The first ionisation energy is the amount of energy needed to remove one electron from an atom in the gaseous phase. Ionisation energy usually has units of kJ mol^{-1}. Normally one of the outer shell electrons would be removed first.

(2 marks)

(Total = 6 marks)

Question 2

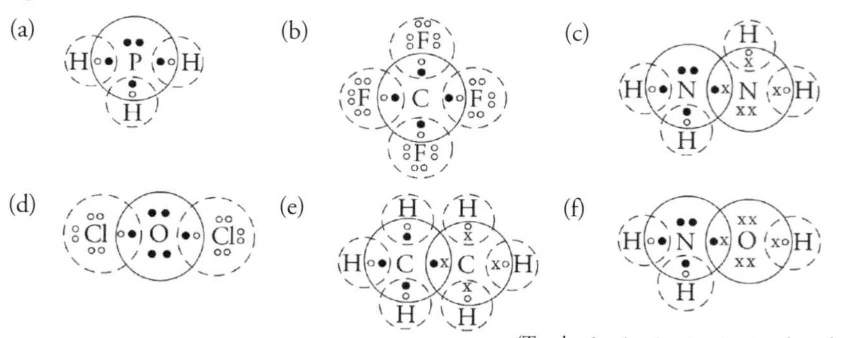

(Total = 1 + 1 + 1 + 1 + 1 + 1 = 6 marks)

Question 3

Carbon dioxide is a molecular substance. Each molecule consists of a C atom bonded to two O atoms by carbon oxygen double covalent bonds. Only weak dispersion forces are possible between the molecules and the substance is a gas at room temperature. Silicon dioxide is a network lattice. In this structure each Si atom forms single covalent bonds to four O atoms. Each O atom is covalently bonded to two Si atoms. The lattice extends in three dimensions and the substance is a solid at room temperature.

(Total = 4 marks)

Question 4

CF_4 is a symmetrical molecule. Although each C–F bond is polar because of the molecular symmetry, the bond polarities cancel each other out. (2 marks)

Question 5

(a) Methane, CH_4, is a non-polar molecule. The only forces of attraction between the molecules are dispersion forces. These are very weak and hence methane is a gas at room temperature. Water is a polar molecule. As well as dispersion forces there are hydrogen bonds between the molecules. Hence the intermolecular attractions are much greater in water and it is a liquid. (2 marks)

(b) Ammonia is a polar molecule. The polar N–H bonds can form hydrogen bonding with water molecules. Hence ammonia is soluble in water. (1 mark)

(c) Iodine is a non-polar molecule. It does not form hydrogen bonds to water molecules and thus has low solubility in water. The dispersion forces between the iodine molecules are comparable to the dispersion forces between the hexane molecules. Hence iodine is soluble in hexane. (1 mark)

(Total = 4 marks)

(Total = 37 marks)

Answers: Introduction to Quantitative Chemistry

Multiple Choice Items

Question	Answer	Comments
1.	C.	Answer (A) does not allow for the mass of hydrogen used in the reaction, i.e. $m(Cu_2O) + m(H_2) = m(Cu) + m(H_2O)$
2.	B.	$m(O_2) = m(CO_2) + m(H_2O) - m(CH_4) = 4.4 + 3.6 - 1.6$
3.	B.	$4Fe(s) + 3O_2(g) \rightarrow 2Fe_2O_3(s)$
4.	D.	(B) can be eliminated since z must be ½ w. Also to balance N atoms w = 2x + y which eliminates (A) and (C).
5.	A.	Stoichiometry is the quantitative relationship between the reactants and the products in a chemical reaction. It can refer to masses, ratios or numbers of atoms or molecules.
6.	C.	$\% \text{ mass loss} = \frac{(20.79 - 18.71) \times 100}{(20.79 - 15.16)} = 36.9\%$
7.	D.	Relative mass of $NaHCO_3 = 23 + 1 + 12 + 48 = 84$ For equation (A) $\% \text{ mass loss} = \frac{44 \times 100}{84} = 52.4\%$ For equation (B) $\% \text{ mass loss} = \frac{106 \times 100}{168} = 63.1\%$ For equation (C) $\% \text{ mass loss} = \frac{34 \times 100}{168} = 20.2\%$ For equation (D) $\% \text{ mass loss} = \frac{62 \times 100}{168} = 36.9\%$
8.	D.	This is the definition of the unit.
9.	B.	This is the definition of relative atomic mass. RAM's have no units. The answers (A), (C) and (D) all have the units of mass.
10.	A.	Definition.
11.	C.	(C) is the definition of molar mass and has units of g mol^{-1}. (A) and (D) are the relative formula mass of the substance.
12.	B.	Definition of Avogadro's number
13.	D.	2 mol of KI are required to produce 1 mol of K_2SO_4.
14.	B.	$M_r(Ca(OH)_2) = 40.08 + (2 \times 16) + (2 \times 1.01) = 74.1$ or 74 to 2 significant figures.
15.	A.	$n(KCl) = n(K) = 0.25$ mol mass K $= 0.25 \times 39.1 = 9.78$ g
16.	B.	mass H in compound = n(H) in compound × 1.00 For A mass H = $(20 \div 16) \times 4 = 5$ g For B mass H = $(36 \div 18) \times 2 = 4$ g

Question	Answer	Comments
16(cont).	B.	For C mass H = $(10 \div 2) \times 2 = 10$ g For D mass H = $(40 \div 58) \times 10 = 6.9$ g
17.	B.	$n(Na_3PO_4) = 16.4 \div 164 = 0.10$ mol; $n(Na) = 3 \times 0.10 = 0.30$
18.	C.	$n(Fe_2(SO_4)_3) = 40.0 \div 400 = 0.1$ mol. Each mole of iron sulfate contains 12 mole of O atoms. n(O atoms) = $0.1 \times 12 = 1.2$ mol
19.	C.	n(N atoms) = $0.15 \times 3 = 0.45$ mol mass of N = $0.45 \times 14 = 6.3$ g
20.	C.	Formula mass = (RAM X × 2) + (16 × 5) = 182 (RAM X × 2) = 182 – 80 = 102 RAM X = 102 ÷ 2 = 51
21.	D.	Formula mass $Cr_2O_3 = (52 \times 2) + (16 \times 3) = 152$ g mol^{-1}
22.	D.	Formula mass $Li_2SO_4 = (6.9 \times 2) + 32.1 + (16 \times 4) = 109.9$ $n(Li_2SO_4) = 2.20 \div 109.9 = 0.020$
23.	C.	$n(UF_6) = \frac{5.84}{352}$; $n(F) = \frac{6 \times 5.84}{352} = 0.0995$
24.	B.	Formula mass $Mn_2O_3 = (54.9 \times 2) + (16 \times 3) = 157.8$ $n(Mn_2O_3) = 5.00 \div 157.8 = 0.0317$ mol $n(O) = 3 \times 0.0317 = 0.0951$; mass oxygen = 0.0951×16
25.	C.	$n(O_2) = 3 \times n(SO_2) \div 2 = (3 \times 9.6) \div (64 \times 2) = 0.225$ mol Mass $O_2 = 0.225 \times 32 = 7.2$ g
26.	D.	Since X is in excess the reaction will stop when all of Y has been consumed. Y is the limiting reactant.
27.	A.	36 mol of NH_3 will react with 27 mol of O_2 (alternatively 30 mol of O_2 would react with 40 mol of NH_3). Since the ratio of NH_3 to N_2 is 2 : 1 then 18 mol of N_2 will be produced.
28.	D.	Molar ratio $n(S) : n(O_2)$ is 1 : 1. $n(O_2)$ is 64/32 = 2.0. Hence mass S reacting = $2.0 \times 32 = 64$ g. Mass S remaining = 160 – 64 = 96 g.
29.	A.	$n(CH_4) = 3.2/16 = 0.20$ mol; $n(O_2) = 3.2/32 = 0.10$ mol. Since molar ratio is 1:2 then 0.10 mol of O_2 reacts with 0.050 mol of CH_4, i.e.CH_4 is in excess. $n(CH_4) = n(CO_2)$. Mass $CO_2 = 0.050 \times 44 = 2.2$ g
30.	B.	$n(Cl^-) = n(AgCl) = \frac{0.177}{143.32} = 1.235 \times 10^{-3}$ mol Mass Cl $= 1.235 \times 10^{-3} \times 35.45 = 0.04378$ g $\% Cl = \frac{0.04378 \times 100}{1.75} = 2.50$
31.	B.	$\% O = \frac{4 \times 16 \times 100}{(2 \times 39.10) + 32.06 + 64} = 36.73$

Question	Answer	Comments
32.	A.	In this compound 126.9 g of iodine combines with 5 × 19 g of fluorine. Formula mass of compound = 126.9 + 95 = 221.9 % F = (95 ÷ 221.9) × 100 = 42.81
33.	A.	% C = (mass C ÷ molar mass compound) × 100. For the four compounds the values are A = 40.0%; B = 38.71%; C = 39.1%; D = 37.5%
34.	D.	% O = 100 – 18.78 – 28.98 = 52.24% Mass O = (6.4 × 52.24) ÷ 100 = 3.34 g
35.	C.	% Cl = 100 – 45.53 = 54.47% Mass Cl = (6.25 × 54.47) ÷ 100 = 3.40 g
36.	B.	Mass sulfur = 5.65 – 1.72 – 1.64 = 2.29 g % sulfur = (2.29 ÷ 5.65) × 100 = 40.53
37.	A.	Molar mass of propanoic acid = 36 + 6 + 32 = 74 g mol^{-1}. Mass of 1.5 mole = 74 × 1.5 = 111 g.
38.	D.	Each molecule of ethane contains 8 atoms. Thus 0.1 mole contains 0.1 × 6 × 10^{23} × 8 atoms. 1 mole of ethane weighs 24 + 6 = 30 g. Thus 1.0 g is (1 ÷ 30) mol and contains (2 ÷ 30) mole of C. 1 molecule of ethane would weigh 30 ÷ (6 × 10^{23}) g, that is 5 × 10^{-23} g.
39.	B.	Molar mass of methane = 12 + 4 = 16 g mol^{-1}. n(H) = (4 × 4) ÷ 16 = 1.0 mol number of H atoms = 1.0 × 6.0 × 10^{23}
40.	C.	For each of the answers the number of atoms present is A = 0.10 × 2 × 6 × 10^{23} = 1.2 × 10^{23} B = 4 × 6 × 10^{22} = 2.4 × 10^{23} C = (1.0 ÷18) × 3 × 6 × 10^{23} = 1 × 10^{23} D = 0.05 × 14 × 6 × 10^{23} = 4.2 × 10^{23}
41.	C.	% H = 100 – 80 = 20 n(H) 20 ÷ 1 = 20; n(C) = 80 ÷ 12 = 6.67 ratio n(H):n(C) = 20:6.67 = 3:1
42.	D.	% O = 100 – 38.8 = 61.2 n(Cl) = 38.8 ÷ 35.5 = 1.093; n(O) = 61.2 ÷ 16 = 3.825 ratio n(Cl):n(O) = 1.093:3.825 = 1:3.5 or 2:7
43.	B.	Formula mass of CH_2O = 12 + 2 + 16 = 30 Molecular formula is 90 ÷ 30 = 3 times empirical formula
44.	C.	Molar mass of compound = 176 ÷ 2 = 88 g mol^{-1} Molar mass of empirical formula = 24 + 4 + 16 = 44 Molecular formula is 88 ÷ 44 = 2 times empirical formula
45.	C.	Mass Sn reacted = 3.561 – 2.374 = 1.187 g n(Sn) = 1.187 ÷ 118.7 = 0.0100 mol

Question	Answer	Comments
45(cont).	C.	n(I) = 5.076 ÷ 126.9 = 0.0400 mol Simplest ratio n(I) : n(Sn) is 0.0400 : 0.0100, i.e. 4 : 1
46.	C.	The general equation for complete combustion of a hydrocarbon is C_xH_y + oxygen → xCO_2 + $y/2H_2O$ Since equal numbers of moles of CO_2 and H_2O are formed: x = y/2 and y = 2x, i.e. n(H) = 2n(C) If n(C) = 5 mol, then n(H) = 10 mol and formula is C_5H_{10}.
47.	D.	Molar mass of $C_3H_6O_3$ = 36 + 6 + 48 = 90 %C = (36 ÷ 90) × 100 = 40%
48.	B.	% C in each compound *A* = 50%; *B* = 63.2%; *C* = 60%; *D* = 51.8%.
49.	B.	n(KI) = 1.50 × 0.2 mol = 0.3 mol, $n(Pb(NO_3)_2)$ = 0.5 × 0.15 mol = 0.075 mol $2KI + Pb(NO_3)_2 \rightarrow 2KNO_3 + PbI_2$ mol ratio KI : $Pb(NO_3)_2$ = 2:1 0.3 mol KI requires 0.15 mol $Pb(NO_3)_2$; $Pb(NO_3)_2$ is in excess mol ratio $Pb(NO_3)_2$: PbI_2 = 1 : 1, $n(PbI_2)$ = 0.075 mol $m(PbI_2)$ = 0.075 × (207.2 + (2 × 126.9)) = 34.6 g
50.	B.	m(Cu) = 6.0 × 63.54 = 381.2 g. $n(O_2) = (4.0 \times 10^{22}) \div (6 \times 10^{23})$; $m(O_2)$ = 0.067 × 32 = 2.13 g $m(Hg) = (2.4 \times 10^{23}) \times 200.6 \div (6 \times 10^{23})$ = 80 g
51.	D.	Mass of In reacting = 2.298 – 1.532 = 0.766 g n(In) = 0.766 ÷ 114.8 = 0.006672 mol Mass of I reacting = 2.54 g n(I) = 2.54 ÷ 126.9 = 0.0200 mol Ratio I:In = 0.0200: 0.006672 = 3:1
52.	C.	The concentrations of the four solutions, in mg mL^{-1}, are test tube 1 = 50.0; test tube 2 = 20.0; test tube 3 = 5.0 and test tube 4 = 10.0. Hence test tube 3 will be the palest pink.
53.	A.	Mass of $KMnO_4$ = 100/1000 = 0.10 g Volume of solution = 5.0/1000 = 0.0050 L Concentration in g L^{-1} = 0.10 ÷ 0.0050 = 20
54.	B.	Mass $CaBr_2$ = 0.30 × 200 = 60 g Volume = 150 ÷1000 = 0.15 L Concentration = 60 ÷ 0.15 = 400 g L^{-1}
55.	A.	The amounts of each compound, in mol, are (A) = 20.0/74.6 = 0.268; (B) = 30.0/101.1 = 0.297; (C) = 40.0/102.9 = 0.388; (D)= 20.0/58.4 = 0.342. The corresponding concentrations, in mol L^{-1}, are 2.68, 2.97, 3.88 and 3.42.
56.	C.	The concentration is 0.75 mole in 1.0 L of *solution*. 0.75 mol of $CaBr_2$ is 0.75 × 200 = 150 g/L or 0.15 g/mL.

Question	Answer	Comments
57.	C.	Dilution only involves adding water, the number of moles of solute is unchanged.
58.	D.	Mass of KBr = 39.1 + 79.9 = 119 g. Volume of water required is (119 × 100) ÷ 60 = 198 mL
59.	B.	$n = cv$, n(KNO_3) = 2.2 × 0.75 = 1.65 mol. Mass (KNO_3) = n × M_r = 1.65 × 101.1 = 166.8 g.
60.	A.	Mass of bleach = 35.0 × 0.200 = 7.0 g Volume of solution needed = mass ÷ new concentration = 7.0 ÷ (5.0 ÷ 1000) = 1400 mL Volume water needed = 1400 – 200 mL = 1200 mL (1.2 L)
61.	A.	M_r(NaClO) = 74.44 In 1.00 L m(NaClO) = (0.711 × 74.44) = 52.92g Mass NaClO in 100 g of solution = (52.92/1000) × 100 = 5.30% m/m
62.	C.	$n = cv$, n($Pb(NO_3)_2$) = 0.5 × 0.5 mol, = 0.25 mol
63.	B.	Mass of NH_3 = 6.3 mg = 6.3/1000 g = 0.0063 g This mass is in 100 mL. Mass in 1 L is 0.063 g.
64.	C.	n($AgNO_3$) = 2.00/169.9 = 0.0118 mol c($AgNO_3$) = 0118/0.300 = 0.0392 mol L^{-1}
65.	B.	n($CuCl_2$) = 5.70/134.44 mol = 0.0423 mol. c($CuCl_2$) = 0.0423/0.75 = 0.0565 mol L^{-1}
66.	B.	molar ratio $AlCl_3$: Cl^- = 1 : 3, c(Cl^-) = 3 × 1.2 = 3.6 mol L^{-1}
67.	C.	n(Cl^-) = 3 × (c × v) = 3 × (0.5 × 0.5) = 0.75 mol
68.	B.	n($Fe(NO_3)_2$ = c × v = 2.50 × 0.200 = 0.500 mol. M_r($Fe(NO_3)_2$ = 55.85 + 28.02 + 96 = 179.87 Mass ($Fe(NO_3)_2$) = 179.87 × 0.5 = 89.94 = 89.9 g (3 sig fig)
69.	B.	The amount of NO_3^- in each solution is (A) = 0.4 × 0.45 = 0.18 mol; (B) = 2 × 0.5 × 0.3 = 0.30 mol; (C) = 3 × 0.25 × 0.3 = 0.225 mol; (D) = 4 × 0.3 × 0.2 = 0.24 mol
70.	B.	$c_1v_1 = c_2v_2$; 2.0 × 0.200 = 0.500 × c_2; c_2 = 0.80 mol L^{-1}
71.	C.	1.5 × 0.3 = 0.5 × v_2, hence v_2 = 0.90 L or 900 mL, volume of water added = 900 – 300 = 600 mL
72.	D.	1 ppm = 1 g solute in 10^6 g solution or 10^6 mL 1 ppm is also 1 mg in 10^3 mL or 1 L For each example the concentrations are (A) = (5.0 × 1000)/5.0 = 1000 ppm (B) = (0.5 × 1000 × 1000)/500 = 1000 ppm (C) = 0.1 × 1000 = 100 ppm (D) = (50 × 1000)/100 = 500 ppm

Question	Answer	Comments
73.	D.	210 ppm is 210 mg in 1.0 L (1000 mL). Mass SO_2 added = 0.75 × 210 = 157.5 mg i.e. 158 mg (3 sig fig)
74.	C.	The volume of alcohol in each example is (A) = (5.3 × 350)/100 = 18.6 mL; (B) = (12.5 × 150)/100 = 18.8 mL; (C) = (12.0 × 200)/100 = 24.0 mL (D) = (40.0 × 50)/100 = 20.0 mL
75.	A.	$n(K_2SO_4)$ = c × v = (0.5 × 0.26) = 0.13 mol. = $n(SO_4^{2-})$ $n(Al_2(SO_4)_3$ = (1.7 × 0.43) = 0.731 mol $n(SO_4^{2-})$ = 3 × 0.731 = 2.193 mol total $n(SO_4^{2-})$ = 0.13 + 2.193 mol = 2.323 mol. total volume = 430 + 260 mL = 690 mL $c(SO_4^{2-})$ = 2.323/0.69 = 3.37 mol L^{-1}
76.	D.	$2KI + Pb(NO_3)_2 \rightarrow 2KNO_3 + PbI_2$ mol ratio KI : $Pb(NO_3)_2$ = 2 : 1 n(KI) = m/M_r = 7.70/166 = 0.0464 mol Hence $n(Pb(NO_3)_2)$ = 0.0464/2 mol = 0.0232 mol $vol(Pb(NO_3)_2)$ = n/c = 0.0232/2.0 L = 0.0116 L = 11.6 mL
77.	A.	0.045 mol L^{-1} $AlCl_3$ contains 3 × 0.45 mol = 0.135 mol Cl^- ions in 1.0 L. 1 mol Cl^- ions is contained in 1.0/0.135 = 7.41 L.
78.	D.	$c(PbCl_2)$ = (1.08/278.1) ÷ 0.1 = 0.0388 mol L^{-1}. $c(PbCl_2)$ = 1.08/0.1 = 10.8 g L^{-1}or 10800 mg L^{-1} (≡ ppm).
79.	D.	n(NaCl) = (0.25 × 1000 ÷ 58.45) × 0.4 = 1.7 mol. Other answers are (A) = 1.2 mol, (B) = 0.205 mol, (C) = 0.12 mol.
80.	B.	$n(Na_2CO_3)$ = 0.15 × 0.020 = 0.0030 mol $n(AgNO_3)$ = 0.25 × 0.030 = 0.0075 mol Since the molar ratio is 1 : 2 0.0030 mol of Na_2CO_3 reacts with 0.0060 mol of $AgNO_3$, i.e. $AgNO_3$ is in excess. $n(Ag_2CO_3)$ = $n(Na_2CO_3)$ = 0.0030 mol mass (Ag_2CO_3) = 0.0030 × 275.8 = 0.827 g
81.	B.	Gay-Lussac stated in his Law of Combining Gas Volumes that in a gaseous chemical reaction, at constant temperature, the ratios of reacting gas volumes are small whole numbers. John Dalton proposed an Atomic Theory, Robert Boyle demonstrated the relationship between gas pressure and gas volume and Avogadro suggested that at the same *T* and *P* equal volumes of gases contained the same number of molecules.
82.	C.	Boyle's law states that for a given mass of gas at a fixed temperature the volume varies inversely with the pressure, i.e. as the pressure increases the volume decreases. Hence as *p* increases 1/*p* decreases and *V* decreases.

Question	Answer	Comments
83.	A.	(B) is a statement of Boyle's law. (C) is true but not Charles' law. (D) is incorrect.
84.	D.	Charles demonstrated the relationship between gas volume and absolute temperature. For Boyle, Gay-Lussac and Avogadro, see answer to question 81.
85.	C.	In any gas at any temperature there will be a range of kinetic energies. Thus not all neon atoms in the sample will have the same kinetic energy at a certain temperature but their average kinetic energy is proportional to the temperature.
86.	A.	Increasing the volume decreases the number of particles per unit area and therefore decreases the rate of collision of particles with the container walls.
87.	D.	As the volume occupied by the gas particles is negligible compared with the total volume of the gas, each gas behaves as though it were the only gas in the container.
88.	C.	$P_1V_1 = P_2V_2$, $V_2 = 101.3 \times 1.5/ 95.3 = 1.59$ L
89.	A.	$P_1V_1 = P_2V_2$, $P_2 = 99.5 \times 0.5/0.125 = 398$ kPa
90.	B.	0°C ≡ 273 K, therefore to convert °C to K, 273 is added. $(-139 + 273) = 134$ K
91.	C.	Since P and T are the same for all gases then V/n = constant. The syringes contain equal masses hence $V \times M_r$ = constant. The gas with the largest molar mass will occupy the smallest volume. $M_r(SO_3)/M_r(CH_4) = 80 \div 16 = 5$
92.	C.	New volume of weather balloon = $500 \times 240/298$ L = 402 L.
93.	D.	Volume of fluorine = $5.9 \times 2.3/0.35$ L = 39 L.
94.	B.	The volume of a gas at fixed temperature and pressure conditions depends on the number of particles, and whether the gas behaves as an ideal gas with no attractive forces between particles. Thus (B) which compares the volumes of one mole of each of two monatomic inert gases is the only correct answer.
95.	D.	The lower the pressure of a gas the greater the interparticle distance and the less likelihood of interparticle attractions.
96.	A.	Molar volume of gas = $nRT/P = (1 \times 8.31 \times 233)/75$ L. = 25.8 L.
97.	B.	New volume of air bubble = $2 \times 1.5 \times 10^{-3} \times 273/255$ mL = 3.2 mL. Increase in volume = 3.2 – 1.5 = 1.7 mL.
98.	A.	All four gases might have some interparticle dispersion forces attraction, but there is also the possibility of hydrogen bonding between ammonia molecules.

Question	Answer	Comments
99.	B.	n(gas) = PV/RT = (156 × 5.00)/(8.31 × 308) mol = 0.305 mol. 0.305 – 0.083 = 0.222 mol.
100.	D.	New $P(N_2)$ = (101.3 × 75 × 298)/(293 × 57.3) kPa = 135 kPa.
101.	A.	Since the amount of hydrogen does not change $n(H_2)$ is constant and PV/RT = constant. Then P × 146/T = 2P × V/2T, therefore V = 146 mL
102.	D.	If the gas samples are at the same temperature their average kinetic energy will be the same. Since P, T and V are the same for both gases then $n(SO_2)$ = $n(O_2)$ hence (A) and (C) are incorrect.
103.	D.	The formula of the compound is N_xO_y and the equation for decomposition is $2N_xO_y \rightarrow xN_2 + yO_2$. Under these conditions equal volumes contain equal moles hence x = 2 and y = 5.
104.	D.	Since *n* and *P* are constant then *T*/*V* = constant. Then T = (291 × 475)/450 = 307.2 K or 34°C.
105.	C.	If product volume is 60 mL and the ratio $CO_2 : SO_2$ is 1 : 2, $V(CO_2)$ = 20 mL and $V(SO_2)$ = 40 mL Thus $V(CS_2)$ = 20 mL and $V(O_2)$ = 3 × 20 = 60 mL
106.	A.	Volume ratio O_2 : HCl = 1 : 4, Thus 50 mL of oxygen reacts with 4 × 50 = 200 mL of HCl Volume of water is negligible at room temperature. So product volume = 2 × $v(O_2)$= 100mL
107.	A.	100 mL of CH_4 reacts with 200 mL of O_2 producing 100 mL of CO_2 and 200 mL of steam. Total reactant gas volume = total product gas volume and there is no overall volume change.
108.	B.	In the first container, n(air) = (2 × 3)/RT. For the second container n(air) = (3 × 2)/RT. Hence total n(air) = 12/RT. When the containers are connected V(total) = 5.0 L and P(final) = [(12/RT) RT]5.0 = 2.4 atm.
109.	C	n(gas) = PV/RT = 100 × 7.82/8.31 × 300 = 0.3137 mol. M (gas) = m/n = 11.94/0.3137 = 38.06 g mol^{-1}. $M(F_2)$= 38 g mol^{-1}.
110.	B.	Since V and T are the same then P is proportional to n. The relative mass of Q is greater than that of J and thus n(Q) will be less than n(J).

Extended Response Questions

Question 1

(a) $Mg(s) + 2H_2O(g) \rightarrow Mg(OH)_2(s) + H_2(g)$ (2 marks)

(b) $Ca(s) + 2HCl(aq) \rightarrow CaCl_2(aq) + H_2(g)$ (2 marks)

(c) $4Na(s) + O_2(g) \rightarrow 2Na_2O(s)$ (2 marks)

(Total = 6 marks)

Question 2

(a) $2Cr(s) + 3O_2(g) \rightarrow 2Cr_2O_3(s)$ (2 marks)

(b) $Pb(s) + 2Cl_2(g) \rightarrow PbCl_4(s)$ (2 marks)

(c) $2K(s) + 2H_2O(l) \rightarrow 2KOH(aq) + 2H_2(g)$ (2 marks)

(d) $2Al(s) + 6H_2O(g) \rightarrow 2Al(OH)_3(s) + 3H_2(g)$ (2 marks)

(e) $2Fe(s) + 6HCl(aq) \rightarrow 2FeCl_3(aq) + 3H_2(g)$ (2 marks)

(f) $2Al(s) + 3H_2SO_4(aq) \rightarrow Al_2(SO_4)_3(aq) + 3H_2(g)$ (2 marks)

(Total = 12 marks)

Question 3

(a) $2NaHCO_3(s) \rightarrow Na_2CO_3(s) + CO_2(g) + H_2O(g)$ (2 marks)

(b) mass lost = 5.163 – 3.258 = 1.905 g
% mass loss = (1.905 ÷ 5.163) × 100 = 36.90% (2 marks)

(c) mass lost = 4.687 – 3.207 = 1.480 g
This mass is 36.90% of the mass of $NaHCO_3$.
Hence (1.480 ÷ mass $NaHCO_3$) × 100 = 36.90
mass $NaHCO_3$ = (1.480 ÷ 36.90) × 100 = 4.01 g
% purity $NaHCO_3$ = (mass $NaHCO_3$ ÷ mass of sample) × 100
% purity $NaHCO_3$ = (4.01 ÷ 4.687) × 100 = 85.6% (2 marks)

(Total = 6 marks)

Question 4

No. of atoms of He produced in 10 days = $6.2 \times 10^{10} \times 60 \times 60 \times 24 \times 10$
$= 5.357 \times 10^{16}$

n(He) produced in 10 days = $3.68 \times 10^{-7} \div 4.0 = 9.2 \times 10^{-8}$ mol

No. of atoms of He in 1.0 mol = $5.357 \times 10^{16} \div 9.2 \times 10^{-8} = 5.82 \times 10^{23}$

(Total = 4 marks)

Question 5

(a) $Cu(s) + 4HNO_3(aq) \rightarrow Cu(NO_3)_2(aq) + 2H_2O(l) + 2NO_2(g)$ (2 marks)

(b) $2C_2H_6(g) + 7O_2(g) \rightarrow 4CO_2(g) + 6H_2O(l)$ (2 marks)

(c) $P_4(s) + 10F_2(g) \rightarrow 4PF_5(g)$ (2 marks)

(d) $Al_2(SO_4)_3(aq) + 3BaCl_2(aq) \rightarrow 2AlCl_3(aq) + 3BaSO_4(s)$ (3 marks)

(e) $2Pb(NO_3)_2(s) \rightarrow 2PbO(s) + O_2(g) + 4NO_2(g)$ (3 marks)

(Total = 12 marks)

Question 6

(a) [(14.01 + 2.02) × 2] + 12.01 + 16.00 = 60.07 g mol^{-1} (1 mark)

(b) $(22.99 \times 2) + 32.06 + (16.00 \times 4) + 10 \times (2.02 + 16.00) = 322.24\ g\ mol^{-1}$ (1 mark)

(c) $(39.10 \times 3) + 55.85 + 6 \times (12.01 + 14.01) = 329.27\ g\ mol^{-1}$ (1 mark)

(Total = 3 marks)

Question 7

(a) Molar mass of $CH_3COOH = 60.06\ g\ mol^{-1}$
$n(CH_3COOH) = 3.60 \div 60.06 = 0.0599$ mol (1 mark)

(b) No. of molecules $= 0.0599 \times 6.022 \times 10^{23} = 3.61 \times 10^{22}$ (1 mark)

(c) $n(O) = 2 \times 0.0599 = 0.1198$ mol (1 mark)

(d) Each molecule contains 8 atoms.
Total no. of atoms $= 8 \times 3.61 \times 10^{22} = 2.888 \times 10^{23}$ (1 mark)

(Total = 4 marks)

Question 8

(a) mass of oxygen in the indium oxide = 6.06 – 5.00 = 1.06 g
$n(In) = 5.0 \div 75 = 0.0667$; $n(O) = 1.06 \div 16 = 0.0663$
ratio $n(In) : n(O) = 0.0667 : 0.0663 = 1 : 1$
The scientists had assumed that the formula of indium oxide was InO. (3 marks)

(b) From the revised formula, $\frac{n(In)}{n(O)} = \frac{2}{3}$ and $n(O) = 0.0663$ mol, hence
$n(In) = (0.0663 \times 2) \div 3 = 0.0442$ mol

$RAM(In) = \frac{5.0}{0.0442} = 113$ (modern value = 114.8) (3 marks)

(Total = 6 marks)

Question 9

(a) Relative formula mass of bornite = 5(63.55) + 55.85 + 4(32.1) = 502.0 (1 mark)

(b) $\% Cu = \frac{5 \times 63.55 \times 100}{502.0} = 63.30\%$; $\% Fe = \frac{55.85 \times 100}{502.0} = 11.13\%$

$\% S = \frac{4 \times 32.1 \times 100}{502.0} = 25.57\%$ (3 marks)

(c) Mass of copper $= \frac{1000 \times 63.30}{100} = 633.0$ g (2 marks)

(Total = 6 marks)

Question 10

(a) $\%N\ (urea) = \frac{2 \times 14 \times 100}{12 + 16 + 2(14 + 2)} = 46.67\%$;

$\%N\ ((NH_4)_2SO_4) = \frac{2 \times 14 \times 100}{2(14 + 4) + 32.1 + 4(16)} = 21.20\%$

$\%N\ (NH_4NO_3) = \frac{2 \times 14 \times 100}{14 + 4 + 14 + 3(16)} = 35.0\%$ (3 marks)

(b) $n(N) = \frac{2 \times 100}{80} = 2.5$ mol (2 marks)

(c) $n(N) = \frac{2 \times 500}{132} = 7.58$ mol; mass (N) = 7.58 × 14 = 106 g (2 marks)
(or (21.20 × 500) ÷ 100)

(Total = 7 marks)

Question 11

(a) The relative molecular mass is the mass of 1 molecule of a substance compared to the mass of 1 atom of ^{12}C taken as 12 exactly. (2 marks)

(b) The molar mass is the mass, in grams, of 1 mole of a substance. (2 marks)
(Total = 4 marks)

Question 12

(a) Molar mass of propane = 36 + 8 = 44 g mol^{-1} (1 mark)

(b) $n(C_3H_8) = 11 \div 44 = 0.25$ mol (1 mark)

(c) Number of molecules = $0.25 \times 6 \times 10^{23} = 1.5 \times 10^{23}$ (1 mark)

(d) $n(H) = n(C_3H_8) \times 8 = 0.25 \times 8 = 2.0$ mol (1 mark)

(e) Number of atoms in each molecule = 3 + 8 = 11
Total number of atoms = $11 \times 1.5 \times 10^{23} = 1.65 \times 10^{24}$ (1 mark)
(Total = 5 marks)

Question 13

(a) $n(C) = (1.20 \times 10^{23}) \div (6.02 \times 10^{23}) = 0.199$ mol (1 mark)

(b) Mass C = 0.199 × 12.01 = 2.39 g (1 mark)

(c) Each molecule of ethane contains 2 atoms of carbon, thus the number of molecules will be half the number of atoms of carbon.

Number of molecules = $(1.20 \times 10^{23}) \div 2 = 6.0 \times 10^{22}$ (1 mark)

(d) Every 2 atoms of carbon are combined with 6 atoms of hydrogen.
Number of hydrogen atoms = $3 \times (1.20 \times 10^{23}) = 3.60 \times 10^{23}$ (1 mark)

(e) $n(C_2H_6) = n(C) \div 2 = 0.0997$ mol
Mass $(C_2H_6) = 0.0997 \times 30.08 = 3.00$ g (2 marks)
(Total = 6 marks)

Question 14

(a) Relative formula mass of Na_2CO_3 = 2(22.99) + 12.01 + 3(16.0) = 106.0
(1 mark)

(b) Mass Na_2CO_3 = 0.250 × 106.0 = 26.5 g (1 mark)

(c) n(Na) = 2 × 0.250 = 0.500 mol (1 mark)

(d) n(O) = 3 × 0.250 = 0.750 mol; mass oxygen = 0.75 × 16 = 12.0 g (2 marks)
(Total = 5 marks)

Question 15

(a) Mass oxygen = 15.00 – 3.89 = 11.11 g (1 mark)

(b) n(N) = 3.89 ÷ 14 = 0.278 mol; n(O) = 11.11 ÷ 16 = 0.694 mol (2 marks)

(c) Ratio n(O) : n(N) = 0.694 ÷ 0.278 = 2.5 : 1; simplest ratio is 5 : 2
Hence empirical formula is N_2O_5. (2 marks)
(Total = 5 marks)

Question 16

(a) $n(H) = 0.12 \div 1.0 = 0.12$ mol; $n(C) = 0.48 \div 12 = 0.04$ mol (2 marks)

(b) ratio $n(H) : n(C) = 0.12 : 0.04 = 3 : 1$; hence empirical formula is CH_3. (2 marks)

(c) The formula CH_3 has a molar mass of $12 + 3 = 15$ g mol^{-1}. Since the actual molar mass is 30.0 g mol^{-1} then the molecular formula must be 2 × the empirical formula. Molecular formula is C_2H_6.
(Alternatively let molecular formula = $(CH_3)_x = C_xH_{3x}$. then $30.0 = 12x + 3x$ and $x = 2$) (2 marks)

(Total = 6 marks)

Question 17

(a) $n(CO_2) = 3.14 \div 44 = 0.0714$ mol (1 mark)

(b) 1 mole of CO_2 contains 1 mole of C; hence $n(C) = 0.0714$ mol (1 mark)

(c) Mass of C = $0.0714 \times 12 = 0.856$ g (1 mark)

(d) Mass of H = $1.00 - 0.856 = 0.144$ g (1 mark)

(e) $n(H) = 0.144 \div 1.0 = 0.144$ mol; $n(C) = 0.0714$ mol
Ratio $n(H):n(C) = 0.144:0.0714 = 2.02:1$; or 2:1
Empirical formula is CH_2. (2 marks)

(f) Molar mass of compound = $14.0 \div 0.25 = 56.0$ g mol^{-1}.
Molecular formula is $(CH_2)_x$.
Hence $56.0 = 12x + 2x$ and $x = 4$
Molecular formula is $(CH_2)_4$ or C_4H_8. (2 marks)

(Total = 8 marks)

Question 18

$n(O) = (9.0 \times 10^{22}) \div (6 \times 10^{23}) = 0.15$ mol; $n(H) = 0.40 \div 1.0 = 0.40$ mol. Ratio $n(C) : n(H) : n(O) = 0.15 : 0.40 : 0.15 = 1 : 2.67 : 1$. Simplest whole number ratio is 3 : 8 : 3 and the empirical formula is $C_3H_8O_3$.

(Total = 3 marks)

Question 19

(a) % oxygen = 100 – 50.0 – 8.33 – 19.44 = 22.23% (1 mark)

(b)

	carbon	hydrogen	nitrogen	oxygen
%	50.0	8.33	19.44	22.23
no mole	50.0 ÷ 12 = 4.17	8.33 ÷ 1.0 = 8.33	19.44 ÷ 14 = 1.39	22.23 ÷ 16 = 1.39
÷ smallest	4.17 ÷ 1.39 = 3.0	8.33 ÷ 1.39 = 5.99 = 6.0	1.0	1.0

Hence empirical formula is C_3H_6NO (3 marks)

(c) Molar mass of compound = $21.6 \div 0.15 = 144$ g mol^{-1}. (1 mark)

(d) Molecular formula is $(C_3H_6NO)_x$
Hence $36x + 6x + 14x + 16x = 144$ i.e. $72x = 144$ and $x = 2$
Molecular formula is $C_6H_{12}N_2O_2$. (2 marks)

(Total = 7 marks)

Question 20

(a)

	Carbon	Hydrogen	Oxygen
%	38.71	9.68	100 – 38.71 – 9.68 = 51.61
no mole	38.71 ÷ 12 = 3.226	9.68 ÷ 1.0 = 9.68	51.61 ÷ 16 = 3.226
÷ smallest	3.226 ÷ 3.226 = 1.00	9.68 ÷3.226 = 3.00	3.226 ÷ 3.226 = 1.00

Hence empirical formula is CH_3O (3 marks)

(b) Molar mass of CH_3O = 31 g mol^{-1}. Since the molar mass of the compound is 62 g mol^{-1} the molecular formula must be 62/31 = 2 times the empirical formula, i.e. $C_2H_6O_2$. (2 marks)

(Total = 5 marks)

Question 21

(a) Mass of oxygen produced = 5.21 – (3.51 + 1.45) g = 0.25 g oxygen (1 mark)

(b) (i) $n(PbNO_3)_2)$ = 5.21/ (207.2 + 28.02 + 96) = 0.0157 mol

(ii) n(PbO) = 3.51/ (207.2 + 16) = 0.0157 mol

(iii) $n(NO_2)$ = 1.45/(14.01 + 32) = 0.0315 mol

(iv) $n(O_2)$ = 0.25/32 = 0.00781 mol

(1 + 1 + 1 + 1 = 4 marks)

(c) Molar ratio $(PbNO_3)_2$:PbO : (NO_2) : O_2 = 0.0157 : 0.0157 : 0.0315 : 0.00781

i.e. 2 : 2 : 4 : 1

Equation is $2Pb(NO_3)_2(s) \rightarrow 2PbO(s) + 4NO_2(g) + O_2(g)$ (2 marks)

(Total = 7 marks)

Question 22

(a) Molar ratio Na_2CO_3 : $AgNO_3$ = 1 :2

$n(AgNO_3)$ = 1.62/(107.87 + 14.01 + 48) mol = 9.536 x 10^{-3} mol

$n(Na_2CO_3)$ = 9.536 x 10^{-3}/2 = 4.768 × 10^{-3} mol

$m(Na_2CO_3)$ = 4.768 x 10^{-3} x (22.99 x 2 + 12.01 + 48) = 0.505 g (3 marks)

(b) $n(Ag_2CO_3)$ = $n(Na_2CO_3)$ = 4.768 × 10^{-3} mol

$m(Ag_2CO_3)$ = 4.768 × 10^{-3} × (215.74 + 12.01 + 48) = 1.32 g (2 marks)

(Total = 5 marks)

Question 23

(a) Molar ratio $CrCl_3$: NaOH = 1 : 3

$n(CrCl_3)$ = 2.35 × 10^3/(52.00 + 106.35) = 14.84 mol

n(NaOH) = 3 × 14.84 = 44.52 mol

m(NaOH) = 44.52 × 40.00 = 1781 g or 1.78 kg (2 marks)

(b) $n(Cr(OH)_3)$ = $n(CrCl_3)$ = 14.84 mol

$m(Cr(OH)_3)$ = 14.84 × (52 + 48 + 3.03) = 1529 g or 1.53 kg

n(NaCl) = n(NaOH) = 44.52 mol

m(NaCl) = 44.52 × (22.99 + 35.45) = 2602 g or 2.60 kg (4 marks)

(Total = 6 marks)

Question 24

(a) Molar ratio SO_2 : O_2 = 2 : 1

$n(SO_2)$ = 100/(32.06 + 32) = 1.56 mol

$n(O_2)$ required = 1.56/2 = 0.781 mol
$n(O_2)$ supplied = 100/32 = 3.13 mol
O_2 is in excess by 3.13 – 0.781 = 2.34 mol
Mass O_2 remaining = (2.34 × 32) = 75.0 g (3 marks)

(b) $n(SO_3)$ = $n(SO_2)$ = 1.56 mol
$m(SO_3)$ = 1.56 × 80.06 g = 125 g
Or: mass SO_3 formed = mass of SO_2 + mass of O_2 reacting
= 100 + 25 = 125 g

(2 marks)
(Total = 5 marks)

Question 25

(a) To allow more air into the crucible to react with the magnesium. (1 mark)

(b) Mass of Mg = 15.86 – 15.67 = 0.19 g; n(Mg) = 0.19 ÷ 24.3 = 0.007819 mol
Mass of O = 15.96 – 15.86 = 0.10 g; n(O) = 0.10 ÷ 16 = 0.00625 mol
Ratio n(Mg) : n(O) = 0.007819/0.00625 : 1.0 = 1.25 : 1 or 5 : 4
Empirical formula of magnesium oxide is Mg_5O_4. (3 marks)

(c) The mass of oxygen is too low for the mass of Mg. Either some of the magnesium remained unreacted or some magnesium oxide escaped from the crucible during the heating process. (2 marks)
(Total = 6 marks)

Question 26

(a) To remove any remaining zinc iodide. (1 mark)

(b) Mass of zinc reacting = 26.58 – 26.04 = 0.54 g;
n(Zn) = 0.54 ÷ 65.4 = 0.008257 mol
Mass of iodine = 28.66 – 26.58 = 2.08 g
n(I) = 2.08 ÷ 126.9 = 0.01639 mol
Ratio n(Zn) : n(I) = 0.008257 : 0.01639 = 1.0 : 1.99, i.e. 1 : 2
Empirical formula zinc iodide = ZnI_2. (3 marks)
(Total = 4 marks)

Question 27

(a) RFM (malachite) = (63.54 × 2) + 12.01 + (16 × 5) + (1.01 × 2) = **221.1**
(1 mark)

(b) $\frac{127.08}{221.1} \times 100\%$ = **57.5%** (2 marks)

(c) $\frac{57.5}{100} \times 500$ kg = **287 kg** (3 sig fig) (3 marks)

(Total = 6 marks)

Question 28

n(Cu) = 0.203 ÷ 63.55 = 0.003194 mol
Mass O = 0.256 – 0.203 = 0.053 g
n(O) = 0.053 ÷ 16.0 = 0.003313
Ratio n(O) : n(Cu) = 0.003313 : 0.003194 = 1.04 : 1.0; i.e. 1 : 1
Empirical formula of copper oxide is CuO
(Total = 3 marks)

Question 29

The molecular formula is $C_5H_{10}O_2$ and the molar mass is 102.1 g mol^{-1}.

Mass of C in 1.0 mole = 5 × 12.01 = 60.05 g
% C = (60.05 × 100) ÷ 102.1 = 58.81%
Mass of H in 1.0 mole = 10.08 g
%H = (10.08 × 100) ÷ 102.1 = 9.87%
Mass of O in 1.0 mole = 32.0 g
% O = (32.0 × 100) ÷ 102.1 = 31.34%

(Total = 3 marks)

Question 30

(a) Mass C = (4.761 ÷ 44.01) × 12.01 = 1.299 g
% C = (1.299 ÷ 2.167) × 100 = 59.96%
Mass H = (2.605 ÷ 18) × 2 = 0.289 g
% H = (0.289 ÷ 2.167) 100 = 13.36%
% O = 100 – 59.96 – 13.36 = 26.68% (3 marks)

(b)

	C	H	O
n	= 59.96 ÷ 12.01 = 4.992	= 13.36 ÷ 1.008 = 13.25	26.68 ÷ 16 1.668
÷ smallest	4.992 ÷ 1.668 = 2.992	13.25 ÷ 1.668 = 7.944	1.668 ÷ 1.668 = 1.0
whole number ratio	3	8	1

Empirical formula = C_3H_8O (2 marks)

(c) The molecular formula of a compound is either the same as its empirical formula or a simple multiple of this formula. If C_3H_8O is doubled the formula becomes $C_6H_{16}O_2$. Now there are too many hydrogen atoms to bond to the carbon atoms. The maximum number of hydrogen atoms that can bond to 6 carbon atoms is 14. Hence $C_6H_{16}O_2$ cannot be correct. (1 mark)

(d)

```
        H H                                  H  O—H
         \/                                   \/
  H     C      O                       H      C
   \  /   \  /   \                      \   /   \   H
    C       C      H                     C       C/
   /\      /\                           /\      /\
  H  H    H  H                         H  H    H  H
```

and (see second structure above)

(2 marks)
(Total = 8 marks)

Question 31

(a) The products of the reaction are gases and the energy released by the reaction will cause the gases to expand. (2 marks)

(b) From the equation the total mass of reactants = 2 × (34) + 32 = 100 g.
For the maximum load of 2500 kg the masses required are
H_2O_2: 68 × 25 = 1700 kg and N_2H_4: 32 × 25 = 800 kg (3 marks)
(Total = 5 marks)

Question 32

(a) $n(SiO_2)$ = (800 × 1000)/60.09 = 1.33 × 10^4 mol
n(C) = (250 × 1000)/12.01 = 2.08 × 10^4 mol
Molar ratio $n(SiO_2)$: n(C) = 1 : 2, n(C) needed to react with SiO_2 is
2 × 1.33 × 10^4 = 2.66 × 10^4 mol, hence SiO_2 is in excess.
$n(SiO_2)$ reacting = 2.08 × 10^4 ÷ 2 = 1.04 × 10^4 mol
$n(SiO_2)$ remaining = (1.33 – 1.04) × 10^4 = 0.29 × 10^4 mol

Mass (SiO_2) remaining = 0.29 × 10^4 × 60.09 = 17.4 × 10^4 g or 174 kg (3 marks)

(b) n(Si) produced = n(C) ÷ 2 = 2.08 × 10^4 ÷ 2 = 1.04 × 10^4 mol
Mass Si formed = 1.04 × 10^4 × 28.09 = 2.92 10^5 g or 292 kg (2 marks)
(Total = 5 marks)

Question 33

(a) Mass of sodium penicillin administered = 6.0 × 10^{-6} × 50 000 = 0.300 g
n(Na) = n($C_{16}H_{17}N_2NaO_4S$) = 0.300 ÷ 356.4 = 8.42 × 10^{-4} mol (2 marks)

(b) n(N) = n($C_{16}H_{17}N_2NaO_4S$) × 2 = 1.68 × 10^{-3} mol
Mass N = 1.68 × 10^{-3} × 14.01 = 0.0236 g (2 marks)

(c) n(C) = 8.42 × 10^{-4} × 16 = 0.0135 mol
No of C atoms = 0.0135 × 6.02 × 10^{23} = 8.11 × 10^{21} (2 marks)
(Total = 6 marks)

Question 34

(a) n($MgCl_2$) = 0.250 × 0.0500 = 0.0125 mol (1 mark)
(b) n(Cl^-) = 0.0125 × 2 = 0.0250 mol (1 mark)
(c) No. of ions in solution = 0.0125 × 3 × 6.02 × 10^{23} = 2.26 × 10^{22} (1 mark)
(d) Molar mass $MgCl_2$ = 24.3 + 35.45 + 35.45 = 95.2 g mol^{-1}
Mass $MgCl_2$ required = 0.0125 × 95.2 = 1.19 g (1 mark)
(Total = 4 marks)

Question 35

(a) $Mg(OH)_2(s)$ + 2HCl(aq) → $MgCl_2(aq)$ + $2H_2O(l)$ (2 marks)
(b) Mass $Mg(OH)_2$ = (1.20 × 80.0) ÷ 100 = 0.96 g
n($Mg(OH)_2$) = 0.96 ÷ 58.3 = 0.01645 = 0.0165 mol (2 marks)
(c) n(HCl) = 0.0165 × 2 = 0.0329 mol (1 mark)
(d) Volume of HCl required = n(HCl) ÷ c(HCl) = 0.0329 ÷ 0.250
= 0.132 L or 132 mL (2 marks)
(Total = 7 marks)

Question 36

(a) n(NaCl) = 40.0 × 1000 ÷ 58.44 = 684.46 mol
c(NaCl) = 684.46 ÷ 5000 = 0.1369 = 0.137 mol L^{-1} (2 marks)
(b) New concentration of NaCl = 684.46 ÷ 4500 = 0.152 mol L^{-1} (2 marks)
(Total = 4 marks)

Question 37

(a) $Cr(NO_3)_3(aq)$ + 3NaOH(aq) → $Cr(OH)_3(s)$ + $3NaNO_3(aq)$ (1 mark)
(b) n($Cr(NO_3)_3$) = 0.100 × 0.25 = 0.0250 mol and
n(NaOH) = 0.60 × 0.10 = 0.060 mol
n(NaOH) required to react with 0.0250 mol $Cr(NO_3)_3$ = 0.0750 mol
There is insufficient NaOH to react with all of the $Cr(NO_3)_3$ hence $Cr(NO_3)_3$ is in excess.
n($Cr(NO_3)_3$) reacting = 0.0600 ÷ 3 = 0.0200 mol
n($Cr(NO_3)_3$) remaining = 0.0250 – 0.0200 = 0.0050 mol (3 marks)
(c) n($Cr(OH)_3$) formed = n($Cr(NO_3)_3$) reacting = 0.0200 mol
Mass $Cr(OH)_3$ formed = 0.0200 × (52.00 + (17.01 × 3)) = 2.06 g (2 marks)

(d) $n(NO_3^-) = n(Cr(NO_3)_3) \times 3 = 0.0250 \times 3 = 0.0750$ mol
Final volume of solution = 0.100 + 0.600 = 0.700 L
$c(NO_3^-) = 0.0750 \div 0.700 = 0.107$ mol L^{-1} (2 marks)
(Total = 8 marks)

Question 38

(a) n(HCl) = 10.0 × 25.0 = 250 mol
Mass HCl = 250 × 36.46 = 9115 g, i.e. 9.12 kg (2 marks)

(b) Mass of solution = 25.0 × 1000 × 1.16 = 29000 g or 29.0 kg
% composition = (9.12 ÷29.0) × 100 = 31.4 (2 marks)

(c) n(HCl) required = 2.50 × 0.125 = 0.3125 mol
Volume concentrated acid needed = 0.3125 ÷ 10.0 = 0.03125 L
= 31.3 mL (2 marks)

(d) n(HCl) = 0.0500 × 10.0 = 0.500 mol
Volume of dilute solution = 0.500 ÷ 0.500 = 1.00 L
Volume of water needed = 1000 – 50 = 950 mL (2 marks)

(e) Total n(HCl) = (0.200 × 0.60) + (0.300 × 1.60) = 0.600 mol
Total volume = 0.200 + 0.300 = 0.500 L
Final concentration = 0.600 ÷ 0.500 = 1.20 mol L^{-1} (2 marks)
(Total = 10 marks)

Question 39

(a) (i) Molar mass $Al_2(SO_4)_3$ = 342.1 g mol^{-1}
$n(Al_2(SO_4)_3) = 12.83 \div 342.1 = 0.0375$ mol
$c(Al_2(SO_4)_3) = 0.0375 \div 0.250 = 0.150$ mol L^{-1} (2 marks)
(ii) $c(Al_2(SO_4)_3) = 12.83 \div 0.250 = 51.3$ g L^{-1} (1 mark)

(b) $n(Al_2(SO_4)_3) = 0.0500 \times 0.150 = 0.00750$ mol
Volume of diluted solution = 0.00750 ÷ 0.100 = 0.0750, i.e. 75.0 mL
Volume of water needed = 75.0 – 50.0 = 25.0 mL (2 marks)

(c) $c(Al_2(SO_4)_3) = 0.100$ mol L^{-1} hence $c(SO_4^{2-}) = 0.300$ mol L^{-1}
$c(SO_4^{2-}) = 0.300 \times 96.06 = 28.8$ g L^{-1} (2 marks)
Total = 7 marks)

Question 40

(a) v(ethanol) = 15.3 ÷ 0.785 = 19.5 mL (1 mark)

(b) Expected volume of solution = 120 + 19.5 = 139.5 mL (1 mark)

(c) There is a contraction in volume caused by hydrogen bonding between the ethanol and water molecules. Each water molecule can hydrogen bond to two ethanol molecules. (1 mark)

(d) (i) n(ethanol) = 15.3 ÷ 46 = 0.333 mol
c(ethanol) = 0.333 ÷ 0.135 = 2.46 mol L^{-1} (1 mark)
(ii) 15.3 g per 0.135 L = (1 ÷ 0.135) × 15.3 g L^{-1} = 113.3 g L^{-1} (1 mark)
(iii) Assume density of ethanol solution = 1 g mL^{-1}
%m/m(ethanol solution) = 15.3/135 × 100 = 11.3 % m/m (1 mark)
(iv) %m/v(ethanol solution) = (15.3 ÷ 135) × 100 = 11.3% m/v (1 mark)
(v) 1 ppm = 1 g per 10^6 g
15.3 g per 135 g = (10^6 ÷ 135) × 15.3 = 1.133 × 10^5 ppm (1 mark)
(Total = 8 marks)

Question 41

(a) $n(Ca(OH)_2 = 4.50/(40.08 + 32 + 2.02) = 0.0600$ mol,

$n(OH^-) = 2 \times 0.0600 = 0.120$ mol,
$c(OH^-) = 0.120/0.500 = 0.240$ mol L^{-1}. (3 marks)

(b) $2HCl + Ca(OH)_2 \rightarrow CaCl_2 + 2H_2O$;
$n(HCl) = 0.100 \times 0.150 = 0.0150$ mol
Molar ratio $HCl : Ca(OH)_2 = 2 : 1$, $n(Ca(OH)_2) = 0.0150/2 = 0.0075$ mol
Volume $Ca(OH)_2 = 0.0075/0.120 = 0.0625$ L or 62.5 mL. (3 marks)

(c) Mass of $(Ca(OH)_2)$ in 25.0 mL $= 0.025 \times 0.120 \times 74.1 = 0.222$ g
This is in 1000 mL ≅ 1000 g. Hence mass in 10^6 g is
$(0.222 \times 10^6) \div 1000 = 222$ ppm (2 marks)
(Total = 8 marks)

Question 42

(a) $ZnCl_2(aq) + K_2CO_3(aq) \rightarrow 2KCl(aq) + ZnCO_3(s)$ (1 mark)

(b) Molar ratio $ZnCl_2 : K_2CO_3 = 1 : 1$ $\quad n(ZnCl_2) = n(K_2CO_3)$
$n(ZnCl_2) = (0.250 \times 0.050)$ mol $= 0.0125$ mol
$n(K_2CO_3) = (0.500 \times 0.050) = 0.025$ mol, $\quad K_2CO_3$ is in excess.
$n(ZnCO_3) = n(ZnCl_2) = 0.0125$ mol
Mass $(ZnCO_3) = n \times M_r = (0.0125 \times 125.38)$ g $= 1.57$ g (mass of precipitate)
(2 marks)

(c) The potassium ions are spectator ions and all of them remain in the solution.
$n(K^+)$ added $= 2 \times 0.05 \times 0.500 = 0.0500$ mol
Volume of final solution = 50 + 50 = 100 mL
$c(K^+) = n/v = 0.0500/0.100 = 0.500$ mol L^{-1} (2 marks)
(Total = 5 marks)

Question 43

(a) $Fe_2(SO_4)_3(aq) + 6NaOH(aq) \rightarrow 3Na_2SO_4(aq) + 2Fe(OH)_3(s)$ (1 mark)

(b) Molar ratio $Fe_2(SO_4)_3 : NaOH = 1 : 6$
$n(Fe_2(SO_4)_3) = 3.00 \times 0.200$ mol $= 0.600$ mol
$n(NaOH) = 5.00 \times 0.120 = 0.600$ mol

NaOH is the limiting reactant since 0.600 mol $Fe_2(SO_4)_3$ requires 6×0.6 mol NaOH for complete reaction and only 0.600 mol is present.
$Fe_2(SO_4)_3$ is in excess since 0.60 mol NaOH requires only $0.60/6 = 0.1$ mol $Fe_2(SO_4)_3$ for complete reaction (3 marks)

(c) $n(Fe_2(SO_4)_3)$ unreacted $= 0.600 - 0.100$ mol $= 0.500$ mol
$c(Fe_2(SO_4)_3)$ remaining $= 0.500/(0.200 + 0.120) = 1.56$ mol L^{-1} (2 marks)

(d) Molar ratio $NaOH : Fe(OH)_3 = 6 : 2$ i.e. $3 : 1$
0.600 mol NaOH reacts to form $0.600/3 = 0.200$ mol $Fe(OH)_3$
Mass $Fe(OH)_3 = 0.200 \times (55.85 + 48 + 3.03) = 21.4$ g (2 marks)
(Total = 8 marks)

Question 44

(a) $AgNO_3(aq) + KCl(aq) \rightarrow KNO_3(aq) + AgCl(s)$ (1 mark)

(b) Molar ratio $AgNO_3 : KCl = 1 : 1$
$n(AgNO_3) = (1.20 \times 0.0500)$ mol $= 0.0600$ mol
$n(KCl) = (0.800 \times 0.0750)$ mol $= 0.0600$ mol
Since the number of moles of the reactants is the same and the mole ratio is 1:1, neither reactant is in excess. (2 marks)

(c) Silver chloride is the insoluble product.
n(AgCl) = n($AgNO_3$)
Mass AgCl = (0.0600 × (107.87 + 35.45)) = 8.60 g (2 marks)

(d) Ionic equation: $Ag^+(aq) + Cl^-(aq) \rightarrow AgCl(s)$
Spectator ions: K^+(aq) and NO_3^-(aq) (2 marks)
(Total = 7 marks)

Question 45

(a) Mass argon = (105.0 × 10.0 × 39.95) ÷ (8.314 × 300) = 16.8 g (2 marks)
(b) Since mass of gas is unchanged PV/T = constant
New temperature = (60.0 × 20.0 × 300) ÷ (105 × 10) = 342.9 K or 69.8°C (2 marks)
(c) Total mass of argon = 26.8 g and n(Ar) = 26.8/39.95 = 0.671 mol
P = (0.671 × 8.314 × 342.9) ÷ 20.0 = 95.6 kPa (2 marks)
(Total = 6 marks)

Question 46

(a) $n(NO) = 2/3n(Cu) = \frac{2.20 \times 2}{63.55 \times 3} = 0.0231$ mol
Volume NO = (0.0231 × 8.314 × 291) ÷ 99.85 = 0.559 L (559 mL) (2 marks)
(b) n(NO_2) = n(Cu) × 2 = 0.0692 mol
Volume NO_2 = (0.0692 × 8.314 × 298) ÷ 102.0 = 1.68 L (2 marks)
(Total = 4 marks)

Question 47

Since mass of gas is unchanged PV/T = constant, i.e. $\frac{752 \times 15.0}{293} = \frac{100 \times V}{248}$

New volume, $V = \frac{752 \times 15.0 \times 248}{293 \times 100} = 95.5$ L (3 marks)

Question 48

(a) Molar volume = (1.00 × 8.314 × 293) ÷ 101.3 = 24.05 L (2 marks)
(b) (i) density (N_2) = 28.02 ÷ 24.05 = 1.165 g L^{-1} (1 mark)
(ii) density (NH_3) = 17.04 ÷ 24.05 = 0.709 g L^{-1} (1 mark)
(iii) density (NO) = 30.01 ÷ 24.05 = 1.248 g L^{-1} (1 mark)
(c) Actual molar volume (N_2) = 28.02 ÷ 1.165 = 24.05 L mol^{-1} (1 mark)
Actual molar volume (NH_3) = 17.04 ÷ 0.717 = 23.77 L mol^{-1} (1 mark)
Actual molar volume (NO) = 30.01 ÷ 1.249 = 24.03 L mol^{-1} (1 mark)
(d) Small deviations from ideal gas behaviour occur when there are significant attractive forces between molecules. This is the case for NH_3 when hydrogen bonding is possible between the molecules. Attractive forces between the molecules in N_2 and in NO are much smaller and these gases are closer to an ideal gas. (1 mark)
(Total = 9 marks)

Question 49

(a) vol ratio $NH_3 : O_2$ = 4 : 5 thus 6.00 L of NH_3 reacts with 7.50 L of O_2
10.0 L of O_2 would require 8.00 L of NH_3, thus O_2 is in excess. (2 marks)

(b) vol ratio $NH_3 : NO : H_2O$ = 4 : 4 : 6
Thus 6.00 L NO and 9.00 L H_2O are produced. (2 marks)

(c) Volume of O_2 remaining = (10.00 – 7.50) = 2.50 L
Final total gas volume = volume unreacted oxygen + volume products
= 2.50 + 6.00 + 9.00 = 17.50 L (1 mark)
(Total = 5 marks)

Question 50

(a) $N_2(g) + O_2(g) \rightarrow 2NO(g)$ and $2NO(g) + O_2(g) \rightarrow 2NO_2(g)$ (2 marks)

(b) Overall $N_2(g) + 2O_2(g) \rightarrow 2NO_2(g)$
Volume ratio $N_2 : O_2 = 1 : 2$
$V(O_2) = 2 \times 1.5$ L = 3.0 L (2 marks)

(c) Air contains 20% oxygen thus v(air) = 100/20 × 3.0 L = 15.0 L (2 marks)
(Total = 6 marks)

Question 51

(a) Oxygen (1 mark)
(b) $n(Co(NO_3)_3) = 0.980 \div 245 = 0.00400$ mol (1 mark)
(c) $n(Co_2O_3) = 0.332 \div 166 = 0.00200$ mol (1 mark)
(d) $V(O_2) = 72$ mL and $n(O_2) = 0.072 \div 24.05 = 0.00299$ mol
$V(NO_2) = 360 - 72 = 288$ mL and $n(NO_2) = 0.288 \div 24.05 = 0.0120$ mol (2 marks)
(e) The molar ratios are as follows
$n(Co(NO_3)_3) : n(Co_2O_3) = 2 : 1$; $n(NO_2) : n(O_2) = 4 : 1$
$n(Co_2O_3) : n(O_2) = 2 : 3$ $n(Co(NO_3)_3) : n(O_2) = 4 : 3$
$n(Co(NO_3)_3) : n(NO_2) = 1 : 3$ $n(Co_2O_3) : n(NO_2) = 1 : 6$
The balanced equation for the reaction is
$4Co(NO_3)_3(s) \rightarrow 2Co_2O_3(s) + 12NO_2(g) + 3O_2(g)$ (2 marks)
(Total = 7 marks)

Question 52

(a) $n(O_2) = 5 \times n(KMnO_4) \div 2 = (5 \times 0.0250 \times 0.0200) \div 2 = 0.00125$ mol
$V(O_2) = 0.00125 \times 24.05 = 0.0301$ L (30.1 mL) (3 marks)

(b) $n(O_2) = 0.100 \div 32.0 = 0.003125$ mol
$n(KMnO_4)$ required = $(0.003125 \times 2) \div 5 = 0.00125$ mol
Volume of $KMnO_4$ solution required = $0.00125 \div 0.0200 = 0.0625$ L or 62.5 mL (2 marks)

(c) $n(KMnO_4) = 0.0400 \times 0.0200 = 8.00 \times 10^{-4}$ mol
$n(H_2O_2) = 0.0200 \times 0.100 = 20.0 \times 10^{-4}$ mol
$n(H_2SO_4) = 0.0200 \times 1.0 = 200 \times 10^{-4}$ mol
H_2SO_4 is in excess of the other two reactants (only 12.00×10^{-4} mol needed)
Molar ratio $n(KMnO_4) : n(H_2O_2) = 8.00 \times 10^{-4} : 20.0 \times 10^{-4}$
= 2 : 5
This is the molar ratio required by the equation. Hence all of the $KMnO_4$ and H_2O_2 will be consumed.
$n(O_2) = n(H_2O_2) = 20.0 \times 10^{-4}$ mol and $V(O_2) = 20.0 \times 10^{-4} \times 24.05$
= 0.0481 L (48.1 mL) (3 marks)
(Total = 8 marks)

Question 53

(a) Since the gas volumes are measured at the same temperature and presure $n(gas) \propto V(gas)$. Hence $n(CO_2) : n(C_xH_y) = 80 : 20$, i.e. $4 : 1$ and $x = 4$. (2 marks)

(b) $V(O_2)$ reacted = 250 – 130 = 120 mL and $n(O_2) : n(C_xH_y) = 120 : 20$, i.e. 6 : 1. From the equation $x + 0.25y = 6$. Since $x = 4$ then $0.25y = 2$ and $y = 8$. (2 marks)

(c) Molecular formula is C_4H_8 (1 mark)

(Total = 5 marks)

Question 54

No. of α-particles = $3.2 \times 10^{17} \times 10 = 3.2 \times 10^{18}$
$n(He) = (101.3 \times 0.135 \times 10^{-3}) \div (8.314 \times 293) = 5.61 \times 10^{-6}$ mol
No. of α-particles in 1.0 mol = $3.2 \times 10^{18} \div 5.61 \times 10^{-6} = 5.70 \times 10^{23}$. (3 marks)

Question 55

(a) Since P, V and T are the same for both gases $n(X) = n(N_2)$, $1.08/M_r(X) = 0.42/28.02$ and $M_r(X) = (1.08 \times 28.02) \div 0.42 = 72.1$ g mol^{-1} (2 marks)

(b) The most likely formula is C_5H_{12}. If only 4 C were present, then 24 H would be needed to produce a molar mass of = 72.1 g mol^{-1}. 6 C does not leave room for any H. (1 mark)

(Total = 3 marks)

Test: Quantitative Chemistry

Multiple Choice Items

Question	Answer	Comments
1.	D.	The correct equation is $2NO(g) + O_2(g) \rightarrow 2NO_2(g)$
2.	D.	The molar masses (in g mol^{-1}) of these compounds are C_4H_{10} = 58.1; C_3H_9N = 59.1; C_3H_6O = 58.1; $C_2H_4O_2$ = 60.1
3.	A.	n(HCl), in mol, for each answer is (A) = $8.0 \times 0.175 = 1.4$; (B) = $8.0 \div 24.79 = 0.322$; (C) = $8.0 \times 10^{23} \div 6.02 \times 10^{23} = 1.32$; (D) = $8.0 \div 36.45 = 0.219$
4.	A.	Mass of nitrogen present in oxide = 8.8 – 3.2 = 5.6 g $n(N) = 5.6 \div 14 = 0.4$; $n(O) = 3.2 \div 16 = 0.2$ ratio $n(N) : n(O) = 0.4 : 0.2 = 2 : 1$
5.	B.	$n(SO_2) = 60.0/64 = 0.938$ mol; $n(O_2) = 10.0/32 = 0.313$ mol SO_2 is in excess. $n(SO_3)$ produced = $2 \times 0.313 = 0.626$ mol. Mass $SO_3 = 0.626 \times 80 = 50$ g
6.	C.	% O in each compound is CH_4O = 50%; $C_2H_4O_2$, = 53.3%; $C_3H_8O_3$ = 52.2; $C_4H_8O_3$ = 46.2%
7.	C.	Mass of carbon present = $2.18 \times 12 = 26.16$ g Mass hydrogen in compound = 32.0 –26.16 = 5.84 g Ratio $n(C) : n(H) = 2.18 : 5.84 = 1 : 2.67$ or $3 : 8$

Question	Answer	Comments
8.	A	$c_1v_1 = c_2v_2$, $9 \times 0.02 = 1.5 \times v_2$, $v_2 = 0.12$ L or 120 mL. Thus 100 mL must be added.
9.	B.	In each case the amount of CO and O_2 that react to produce CO_2 must be calculated. In (B) 400 mL of CO_2 are produced when 400 mL of CO and 200 mL of O_2 react. Thus the total volume at the start is 400 + 200 + 400 = 1.00 L. For the other cases the volumes of CO and O_2 at the start do not add to 1.00 L. (A) = 1.05 L; (C) = 0.90 L and (D) = 0.95 L.
10.	B.	Mass $NH_3 = 3.70 \times 10^{-4} \times 17 = 6.29 \times 10^{-3}$ g Mass NH_3 in 1.0 L = 6.29×10^{-2} g
11.	C.	Mass of ethanol = $0.900 \times 46.1 = 41.49$ g. Mass of solution = $250 \times 0.932 = 233$ g % composition = $(41.49 \times 100) \div 233 = 17.8$
12.	A.	(A): $n(Cl^-) = 0.05$ and $[Cl^-] = 0.05 \div 0.10 = 0.50$ mol L^{-1}. (B): $n(Cl^-) = 0.03 \times 2$ and $[Cl^-] = 0.06 \div 0.10 = 0.60$ mol L^{-1}. (C): $n(Cl^-) = 0.04 \times 3$ and $[Cl^-] = 0.12 \div 0.10 = 1.2$ mol L^{-1}. (D): $n(Cl^-) = 0.02 \times 4$ and $[Cl^-] = 0.08 \div 0.10 = 0.8$ mol L^{-1}.
13.	D.	80 mL of NH_3 will react with $(80 \times 3) \div 4 = 60$ mL of O_2. All the NH_3 reacts and 20 mL O_2 remains unreacted. Volume of N_2 formed = $(80 \times 2) \div 4 = 40$ mL Volume of H_2O formed = $(80 \times 6) \div 4 = 120$ mL Hence final volume = (20 + 40 + 120) mL = 180 mL
14.	C.	$n(CO_2) = 1.76 \div 44 = 0.04$; $n(H_2O) = 0.90 \div 18 = 0.05$ $n(C) = n(CO_2) = 0.04$; $n(H) = 2 \times n(H_2O) = 0.10$ ratio $n(C) : n(H) = 0.04 : 0.10 = 4 : 10$ Hence empirical formula is C_2H_5.
15.	B.	Since P and T are constant then n(gas) $\propto$ V(gas). O_2 is in excess; 40 mL of O_2 would require 80 mL of CO for reaction. Thus 16 mL of O_2 and all of the CO react. 32 mL of CO_2 are produced and 24 mL of O_2 remain.

Extended Response Answers

Question 1

(a) $n(W) = 154.4 \div 183.85 = 0.8398$ mol (1 mark)

(b) Radius of W atom = 137 pm or 1.37×10^{-8} cm

$$\text{Volume of 1 atom} = \frac{4 \times 3.142 \times (1.37 \times 10^{-8})^3}{3} = 1.077 \times 10^{-23} \text{ mL}$$ (1 mark)

(c) No. of W atoms in block = $8.0 \div 1.077 \times 10^{-23} = 7.4 \times 10^{23}$ atoms (1 mark)

(d) No. of W atoms in 1.0 mol = $7.4 \times 10^{23} \div 0.8398 = 8.8 \times 10^{23}$ (1 mark)

(e) This value is greater than the expected value of 6.02×10^{23}. W atoms are approximately spherical but even when spheres are packed as close together as possible there are tiny spaces left in the structure. Hence in metallic W not all of the available space is occupied by W atoms. The number of atoms in the

block has been over estimated. (In many metals ~74% of the space is actually occupied and for W it is ~68%.)
(1 mark)
(Total = 5 marks)

Question 2

Formula of iron(III) sulfate is $Fe_2(SO_4)_3$.
Molar mass = (55.85 × 2) + (32.06 × 3) + (16.00 × 12) = 399.88

% Fe = (111.7 ÷ 399.88) × 100 = 27.93%
% S = (96.18 ÷ 399.88) × 100 = 24.05%
% O = (192 ÷ 399.88) × 100 = 48.01%
(Total = 3 marks)

Question 3

(a) $n(Cl_2) = PV/RT = (1.23 \times 101.3 \times 6.55) \div (8.314 \times 323) = 0.304$ mol
Mass Cl_2 = 0.304 × 70.9 = 21.6 g
(2 marks)

(b) $n(O_2) = n(Cl_2) \div 2 = 0.304 \div 2 = 0.152$ mol
$V(O_2) = (0.152 \times 8.314 \times 298) \div 101.3 = 3.72$ L
(2 marks)

(c) $n(HCl) = n(Cl_2) \times 2 = 0.304 \times 2 = 0.608$ mol
$c(HCl) = 0.608 \div 0.650 = 0.935$ mol L^{-1}
(2 marks)

(d) n(HCl) in 100 mL = 0.0935 mol
Mass HCl in 100 mL = 0.0935 × 36.46 = 3.41, i.e. %(m/v) = 3.41% (2 marks)
(Total = 8 marks)

Question 4

(a) Since V and T are constant then $P \propto n$, i.e. $P_1/P_2 = n_1/n_2$.
$n(N_2) = 0.1377/28.02 = 0.004914$ mol (= n_1)
$n(X) = (n(N_2) \times 0.97) \div 1.03 = 0.004628$ mol
Molar mass X = 0.2038 ÷ 0.004628 = 44.04 g mol^{-1}
(3 marks)

(b) Possible gases are carbon dioxide, CO_2, propane, C_3H_8, ethanal, C_2H_4O, ethylene oxide, C_2H_4O, dinitrogen oxide, N_2O, or fluoroacetylene, C_2HF.
(1 mark)
(Total = 4 marks)

Question 5

(a) Mass of oxygen = 1.25 – 0.763 – 0.148 = 0.339 g

	C	H	O
Mass (g)	0.763	0.148	0.339
n (mol)	0.763/12.01 = 0.0635	0.148/1.01 = 0.147	0.339/16.0 = 0.0212
÷ smallest	0.0635/0.0212 = 3.0	0.147/0.0212 = 6.93	0.0212/0.0212 = 1.0

Empirical formula = C_3H_7O
(3 marks)

(b) Molar mass of C_3H_7O = 36 + 7 +16 = 59 g mol^{-1}. The actual molar mass of the compound is twice this value. Hence molecular formula is $C_3H_7O \times 2$ or $C_6H_{14}O_2$
(2 marks)
(Total = 5 marks)

Total = 40 marks

Answers: Reactive Chemistry

Multiple Choice Items

Question	Answer	Comments
1.	C.	A precipitation reaction occurs producing insoluble silver chloride. Dissolution separates the ions. Melting NaCl allows the ions to move past one another.
2.	B.	The oxygen only undergoes a change of state. In the other cases a chemical change has occurred.
3.	D.	This is a change of state and therefore a physical change. No new product forms.
4.	A.	Only changes of state are involved in melting and crystallisation.
5.	A.	The changes which occur are easily reversible.
6.	A.	In a chemical change bonds are broken and new bonds form to produce different products. These changes are not easy to reverse and may be impossible.
7.	C.	NaCl and $AgNO_3$ react to produce insoluble AgCl. (A) would give a combustion reaction, (B) an acid-base reaction and (D) a synthesis reaction.
8.	D.	See answer to question 7.
9.	B.	See answer to question 7.
10.	A.	See answer to question 7.
11.	D.	When heated strongly $MgCO_3$ will decompose to MgO and CO_2.
12.	B.	Calcium forms a cation with a 2+ charge. $Ca(OH)_2$ is an ionic solid that is partially soluble in water.
13.	D.	Metal hydroxides do not release a gas when reacted with an acid. Hydrogen carbonates and carbonates only give CO_2. Metals such as zinc produce H_2 gas with acids.
14.	B.	Metal Q displaces the other three metals from solutions of their salts and thus is the most reactive metal. The next most reactive metal is R since it displaces two other metals from solutions of their salts. M is the least reactive since it does not displace any of the other metals.
15.	C.	When heated many metal carbonates decompose to the metal oxide and carbon dioxide. Only oxides very low in the activity series will ecompose further to give the metal and oxygen.
16.	C.	A highly reactive metal would not have been found uncombined and would react with gases in the air and lack strength. Group 1 and 2 metals are generally more reactive than transition metals.

Question	Answer	Comments
17.	C.	Mercury is the least reactive metal (lowest on the activity series).
18.	D.	Many metals will corrode in the presence of oxygen and the absence of water.
19.	B.	Calcium in the most reactive metal in this group and iron is the least reactive.
20.	C.	The most reactive metals are the most difficult to extract from their ores.
21.	D.	Production processes follow scientific discoveries. Nuclear chemistry is the most recent branch of Chemistry and has enabled the production of elements with higher atomic numbers than uranium.
22.	A.	As the metal forms part of a compound, energy is required to overcome chemical bonds and obtain the uncombined metal.
23.	C.	Their low reactivity meant that they were known as elements long before the more reactive metals.
24.	C.	Magnesium is a reactive metal and is therefore found naturally only as its compounds.
25.	B.	Since the metal releases H_2 from HCl it must be more reactive than Cu and Ag. Only metals very low in the activity series, such as Au and Pt do not form an oxide when heated. The metal may or may not displace iron from iron(II) sulfate.
26.	D.	From the information H_2 is more reactive than R; S is more reactive than H_2 and also R. T is more reactive than H_2 but less reactive than S.
27.	A.	The Fe in the steel will react with those cations of metals that are lower in the reactivity series, i.e. Pb^{2+}, Ag^{+} and Cu^{2+}.
28.	D.	From the first experiment, *R* is more reactive than *Q*. From the last two experiments *T* is more reactive than *R* and *Q* since *T* is not displaced from the solution.
29.	A.	This is the activity series of metals.
30.	A.	Zn loses electrons in this reaction ($Zn \rightarrow Zn^{2+} + 2e^{-}$) and reduces sulfur ($S + 2e^{-} \rightarrow S^{2-}$).
31.	D.	The oxidation number of oxygen in each of these species is A = −1; B = −1; C = 0; D = −2.
32.	B.	In IO_3^{-}, the I has an oxidation number of +5. Hence, I needs $4e^{-}$ for reduction to I^{+}.
33.	C.	The changes in oxidation number are in (A) from +2 to +2.5, in (B) +4 to +6, in (C) +6 to −2 and in (D) 0 to +4.

Question	Answer	Comments
34.	D.	The oxidation number of S in the four compounds are (A) +7, (B) +6, (C) +4 and (D) +3.
35.	A.	Al is higher in the reactivity series and is a stronger reductant than Cu (i.e. Al is a more reactive metal) and will oxidise. Oxidation occurs at the anode. The oxidation process will produce electrons and so the Al will be negative.
36.	C.	At the positive electrode, electrons are consumed. The reaction in (B) would occur during recharging of the cell.
37.	C.	The copper half-cell is positive in both cells. The Co and V electrodes are the two reductants. Since the voltage is larger in the Cu/V cell, the vanadium electrode must be at a higher (more negative) potential than the Co half-cell.
38.	A.	The Co half-cell is more negative than Cu by 0.62 V, and the V half-cell is more negative than Cu by 1.52 V. Hence V will be more negative than Co by 1.52 – 0.62 = 0.90 V.
39.	C.	In galvanic cells electrons are produced at the negative electrode. Oxidation occurs at this electrode. From these results Cu is more easily oxidised than *p* and *q* but *r* is more easily oxidised than Cu. Since the voltage from the Cu/*q* cell is greater than that from the Cu/*p* cell *p* is more easily oxidised than *q*.
40.	A.	Since the voltage from the Cu/*q* cell is greater than that from the Cu/*p* cell *p* is more easily oxidised than *q* and *p* will be the negative electrode. The cell voltage will be 1.29 – 0.45 V.
41.	B.	Zinc is a more reactive metal (a stronger reductant) than Fe and will oxidise (corrode) in preference. Oxidation releases electrons and so the Zn will be negative.
42.	B.	The salt bridge **prevents** the reactants from making direct contact. Anions flow into the anode compartment and out of the cathode compartment. Cations go in the opposite direction.
43.	B.	In (A) the oxidation state of Fe changes from +2 to +3. In (B) it changes from +2 to +1. In (C) there is no change in oxidation state and in (D) it changes from 0 to +2.
44.	D.	In this electrochemical cell the equation of reaction will be $Ni(s) + Cu^{2+}(aq) \rightarrow Ni^{2+}(aq) + Cu(s)$ The blue colour due to $Cu^{2+}(aq)$ ions will fade as they react and a reddish solid (Cu) will form on the copper electrode. The green colour due to $Ni^{2+}(aq)$ will become darker and the cell voltage will be 0.34 – (–0.23) = 0.57 V. Ni will be the negative electrode.
45.	D.	In (A) the change in oxidation state is from +6 to +3, in (B) it is from +4 to +2, in (C) +2 to +5 and in (D) +5 to –1.

Question	Answer	Comments
46.	D.	The oxidation state of the Fe has changed from +3 to +2 by gaining one electron.
47.	D.	Since M acts as a cathode the Co electrode will be the anode. Hence E°(Co^{2+}/Co) must be *higher (i.e. more negative)* than that of M. Only Cu and Sn could act as a cathode in this cell. The cell voltage for Co/Co^{2+}//Cu^{2+}/Cu would be 0.62 V. For Co/Co^{2+}//Sn^{2+}/Sn the voltage would be 0.14 V.
48.	A.	The most active metal will have the highest (most negative) E°. The least active metal will have the largest E° (most positive).
49.	D.	Fe^{2+} has been oxidised to Fe^{3+}. The oxidation number of Mn changes from +7 to +2.
50.	A.	E^{o}_{cell} = E°(cathode) – E°(anode) = +1.51 – 0.77 = 0.74 V
51.	B.	For a reaction to occur the E°(oxidant) must be greater than E(reductant).
52.	C.	Since the HCl is at a higher temperature in experiment 2 the CO_2 will be produced at a higher rate and the maximum volume will be reached in a shorter time. At the higher temperature the gas will occupy a larger volume.
53.	C.	This one will not increase the number of collisions between particles and hence the number of successful collisions.
54.	B.	Oxygen in the air reacts with flour in an exothermic process. The fine particles have a large surface area compared with their size. Once started, any reaction between oxygen and flour will thus be very rapid producing large amounts of gaseous products in a short time.
55.	D.	The first and last experiments require the same amount of time despite the concentration of I_2 being doubled.
56.	A.	Increasing the volume of the reaction vessel would decrease the frequency of collisions between reactant particles and hence decrease the frequency of product particles forming.
57.	B.	Addition of an inert gas would not affect the frequency of collisions of the reactant particles and therefore would not affect the reaction rate.
58.	A.	The activation energy is the minimum energy that must be added to the energy of the reactants to break bonds so that the reaction can proceed. Since the energy of the reactants is x, enough energy must be added to increase the energy to w.
59.	B.	(B) will reduce the number of collisions between the reactants and hence the number of successful collisions. The other answers will increase the number of collisions.

Question	Answer	Comments
60.	B.	Explosions occur when large amounts of hot gaseous products are formed very rapidly. The reaction producing these products should be exothermic with a large ΔH and a small activation energy. (B) has the largest ΔH and smallest activation energy. It would therefore require least energy to initiate the reaction but would emit the largest amount of energy.
61.	B.	ΔH is the difference in enthalpy between reactants and products and represents an exothermic reaction
62.	D.	I represents the activation energy of the reaction which would be lowered by the use of a catalyst. Catalysts do not change ΔH for reactions.
63.	B.	A catalyst lowers the activation energy of a reaction. This increases the proportion of successful collisions.

Extended Response Questions

Question 1

(a) $H_3PO_4(aq) + 3NaOH(aq) \rightarrow Na_3PO_4(aq) + 3H_2O(l)$ (2 marks)

(b) $2Na(s) + Cl_2(g) \rightarrow 2NaCl(s)$ (2 marks)

(c) $2HgO(s) \rightarrow 2Hg + O_2(g)$ (2 marks)

(d) $2C_4H_{10} + 13O_2(g) \rightarrow 8CO_2(g) + 10H_2O(l)$ (2 marks)

(e) $2N_2(g) + 3H_2(g) \rightarrow 2NH_3(g)$ (2 marks)

(f) $Al_2O_3(s) + 3H_2SO_4(aq) \rightarrow Al_2(SO_4)_3 + 3H_2O(l)$ (2 marks)

(g) $H_2SO_4(aq) + 2NaHCO_3(s) \rightarrow Na_2SO_4(aq) + 2H_2O(l) + 2CO_2(g)$ (2 marks)

(Total = 14 marks)

Question 2

(a) (i) Synthesis reaction

(ii) $2SO_2(g) + O_2(g) \rightarrow 2SO_3(g)$ (2 marks)

(b) (i) Acid/base reaction

(ii) $Ba(OH)_2(aq) + HCl(aq) \rightarrow BaCl_2(aq) + 2H_2O(l)$ (2 marks)

(c) (i) Precipitation reaction

(ii) $Ba(NO_3)_2(aq) + Na_2SO_4(aq) \rightarrow BaSO4(s) + 2NaNO_3(aq)$ (2 marks)

(d) (i) Acid/carbonate reaction

(ii) $CaCO_3(s) + 2HCl(aq) \rightarrow CaCl_2(aq) + CO_2(g) + H_2O(l)$ (2 marks)

(e) (i) Combustion reaction

(ii) $C_2H_6O(g) + 3O_2(g) \rightarrow 2CO_2(g) + 3H_2O(l)$ (2 marks)

(f) (i) Decomposition reaction

(ii) $2Au_2O_3 \rightarrow 4Au(s) + 3O_2(g)$ (2 marks)

(Total = 12 marks)

Question 3

The relevant equations from the electrochemical series are shown on the next page.

$$Zn^{2+}(aq) + 2e^- \rightleftharpoons Zn(s)$$
$$Fe^{2+}(aq) + 2e^- \rightleftharpoons Fe(s)$$
$$Sn^{2+}(aq) + 2e^- \rightleftharpoons Sn(s)$$
$$Cu^{2+}(aq) + 2e^- \rightleftharpoons Cu(s)$$
$$Ag^+(aq) + e^- \rightleftharpoons Ag(s)$$

Hence the tin will react with the $AgNO_3$ and $CuSO_4$ solutions because Sn is a better reductant than Ag or Cu. However Fe and Zn are better reductants than Sn. Hence no reaction will occur when pieces of tin are placed in solutions of $FeSO_4$ and $ZnCl_2$. The equations for the reactions occurring in the other solutions are

$$2AgNO_3(aq) + Sn(s) \rightarrow 2Ag(s) + Sn(NO_3)_2(aq)$$

$$CuSO_4(aq) + Sn(s) \rightarrow Cu(s) + SnSO_4(aq)$$ (Total = 4 marks)

Question 4

(a) Metal I is more active than metal III, since metal I reacts with cold water but metal III does not. Metal III is more active than $H^+(aq)$ and metal II is less active than $H^+(aq)$ since metal II is less active than Ag^+. Metal IV is less active than metal III. Metal IV is more active than metal II since metal IV reacts with air. Hence the most likely activity series is

metal I > metal III > metal IV > metal II (3 marks)

(b) Metal I: K, Na, Li, Ca (any one of these) (1 mark)
Metal II: Ag, Pt, Au (1 mark)
Metal III: Mg, Al, Zn, Fe (1 mark)
Metal IV: Cu, Hg (1 mark)
(Total = 7 marks)

Question 5

Q is more reactive (better reductant) than P, since Q displaces P from PSO_4. R is more reactive (better reductant) than P, since P cannot displace R from RSO_4. H_2 is more reactive (better reductant) than R. H_2 is also a better reductant than one more metal. This must be P, since if H_2 was a better reductant than Q it would have to be a stronger reductant than P as well.
Thus the order of reductant strengths is Q > H_2 > R > P. (Total = 4 marks)

Question 6

(a) Magnesium is a stronger reductant than nickel and will displace nickel from a solution of nickel chloride. Aqueous nickel ions are green. As the reaction proceeds the concentration of $Ni^{2+}(aq)$ falls and the solution becomes a lighter green. When nickel ions are reduced nickel metal is formed which accounts for the silvery grey solid. Magnesium will also react slowly with water and form small amount of hydrogen. (2 marks)

(b) $Ni^{2+}(aq) + Mg(s) \rightarrow Ni(s) + Mg^{2+}(aq)$ (1 mark)

(c) Reaction of magnesium with water will produce hydrogen gas.

$Mg(s) + 2H_2O(l) \rightarrow Mg(OH)_2(aq) + H_2(g)$ (2 marks)

(d) From the equation in part (b), n(Ni) formed = n(Mg) reacted.
$n(Ni) = 0.880 \div 58.69 = 1.499 \times 10^{-2}$ mol
mass of Mg reacting $= 1.499 \times 10^{-2} \times 24.31 = 0.3645$ g (2 marks)

(e) Some of the Mg has reacted with the water, increasing the mass loss of the Mg. (1 mark)

(f) $n(Ni^{2+})$ at start = 0.200 × 0.150 = 0.0300 mol
$n(Ni^{2+})$ remaining = 0.0300 – 1.499 × 10^{-2} = 0.0150 mol
concentration of Ni^{2+} = 0.0150 ÷ 0.200 = 0.0750 mol L^{-1} (2 marks)
(Total = 10 marks)

Question 7

(a) Z is more reactive (better reductant) than Y and is also more reactive than X. X is more reactive (better reductant) than Y. The order of reactivity (decreasing reductant strength) of metals is Z > X > Y and hence the ease of production from the ores will be the reverse of this order. (3 marks)

(b) Y will be the easiest metal to extract (from Y_2S) and Z will be the most difficult metal to extract. (2 marks)
(Total = 5 marks)

Question 8

(a) $Zn(s) + 2AgNO_3(aq) \rightarrow Zn(NO_3)_2(aq) + 2Ag(s)$ (1 mark)

(b) n(Zn) = 6.537 ÷ 65.37 = 0.100 mol; $n(Ag^+)$ = 0.150 mol
Hence Zn is in excess and only 0.075 mol Zn reacts. All Ag^+ reacts.

Chemical species	Zn(s)	$Zn^{2+}(aq)$	$Ag^+(aq)$	Ag(s)	$NO_3^-(aq)$
Amount (mol)	0.025	0.075	0.0	0.150	0.150

(5 marks)
(Total = 6 marks)

Question 9

(a) Iron is the most reactive metal, silver is the least reactive. These two metals will produce the largest voltage. The iron should be placed in the solution of iron nitrate and the silver in the silver nitrate solution. (1 mark)

(b)

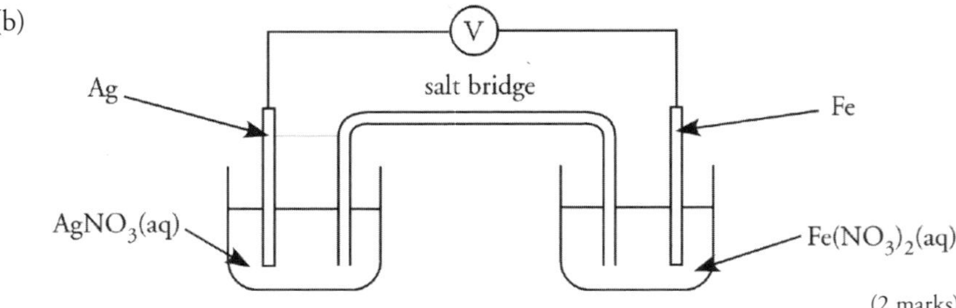

(2 marks)

(c) Fe is the more reactive metal and will be the anode in this cell. The Ag/Ag^+ half-cell will be the cathode.

$E°(cell)$ = $E°(cathode) - E°(anode)$
$E°(cell)$ = 0.80 – (–0.44) = 1.24 V (1 mark)

(d) $Fe(s) \rightarrow Fe^{2+}(aq) + 2e^-$ and $Ag^+(aq) + e^- \rightarrow Ag(s)$

Overall reaction:

$Fe(s) + 2Ag^+(aq) \rightarrow Fe^{2+}(aq) + 2Ag(s)$ (2 marks)

(e) Measured values of the cell potential can differ from the predicted values for the following reasons.

- Non-standard conditions have been used. Standard conditions are 25°C, a gas pressure of 100 kPa and electrolyte concentrations of 1.0 mol L^{-1}. For this cell the student should check that the concentrations are 1.0 mol L^{-1} and the temperature is 25°C (there are no gases involved in this cell).
- The electrodes may be corroded. The student should clean the electrodes with emery paper.
- Using a piece of filter paper soaked in potassium nitrate solution as the salt bridge may increase the internal resistance of the cell. The student should place one of the half-cells in a porcelain pot. Porcelain pots are more effective at allowing cations and anions to move between the half-cells than filter paper soaked in potassium nitrate solution. (2 marks)

(Total = 8 marks)

Question 10

(a) *Physical property:*

- Transition metals are likely to be harder than Group 1 metals.
- Transition metals have higher melting and boiling temperatures than Group 1 metals.
- Magnetism (if the metal is ferromagnetic then it is a transition metal).
- Transition metals are likely to have higher electrical conductivity than Group 1 metals.

Chemical property:

- Group 1 metals are more reactive than transition metals, e.g. Group 1 metals will react with cold water but transition metals do not. Group 1 metals also react more rapidly with oxygen and also react faster with dilute acids.

(2 marks)

(b) The metal selected must form compounds with two different oxidation states; e.g. V, Cr, Mn, Fe, Co, Ni, or Cu. (1 mark)
The pair of compounds must be appropriate e.g. $FeCl_2$ and $FeCl_3$, or $CuCl_2$ and CuCl, or MnO and MnO_2. (1 mark)

(Total = 4 marks)

Question 11

(a) It is expected that the activity of a metal would increase with its atomic radius. The outermost electron or electrons are furthest from the nucleus and less firmly held. Hence the metal atom will more easily lose an electron and thus be more active. (2 marks)

(b) The atomic radius does not completely correlate with these six metals in the activity series. The metals are taken from three different periods in the Periodic Table. When metals from the same period are compared there is a correlation. For example a comparison of Zn and Cu shows that the larger atom is more active. Similarly a comparison of the fifth period metals Sn and Ag shows that Sn with a larger radius is more active. The same is true for Pb and Au. (2 marks)

(c) (i) The smaller the ionisation energy the easier it will be to remove an electron from an atom. Hence the activity of the metal will increase as the ionisation energy decreases. This is generally true going down the same Group in the Periodic Table.

(ii) The lower the electronegativity the less an atom will attract electrons. Hence the greater will be the activity of the metal.

(2 marks)
(Total = 6 marks)

Question 12

(a) (i) Sn^{2+} has been reduced since it gains 2 electrons per Sn^{2+} ion.
(ii) Sn^{2+} is the oxidant as it acquires electrons from the reductant. The reductant donates electrons and is oxidised by the process.
(iii) 2 electrons per tin ion as each ion has 2 positive charges.

(1 + 1 + 1 = 3 marks)

(b) (i) oxide ions: $6O^{2-}(cryolite) \rightarrow 3O_2(g) + 12e^-$
(ii) aluminium ions: $Al^{3+}(cryolite) + 3e^- \rightarrow Al(l)$
(iii) $12e^-$

(1 + 1 + 1 = 3 marks)
(Total = 6 marks)

Question 13

(a) The strongest oxidant will be lowest in the electrochemical series and will be the positive electrode (the oxidant will undergo reduction, i.e. it will consume electrons). The Sn^{4+}/Sn^{2+} half-cell is common to both galvanic cells. While the Sn^{4+}/Sn^{2+} half-cell is positive with respect to the Cd^{2+}/Cd half-cell, it is negative when compared with Fe^{3+}/Fe^{2+}. Thus, the best oxidant must be in the Fe^{3+}/Fe^{2+} half-cell. The best oxidant is Fe^{3+}. (2 marks)

(b) Oxidation occurs at the anode. In galvanic cells the anode is negative. Hence the equations for the reactions occurring are
$Cd(s) \rightarrow Cd^{2+}(aq) + 2e^-$
$Sn^{2+}(aq) \rightarrow Sn^{4+}(aq) + 2e^-$ (2 marks)

(c) Of the three half-cells the Cd^{2+}/Cd half-cell will be the lowest on the electrochemical series and the Fe^{3+}/Fe^{2+} half-cell will be the highest. The likely voltage of a cell constructed from these two half-cells is

$0.55 + 0.62 = 1.17$ V. (1 mark)

(Total = 5 marks)

Question 14

(a) Both oxygen and water are necessary for iron objects to rust. In the desert there is little or no water and deep in the ocean there is little or no oxygen. (2 marks)
(However in the deep ocean sulfate producing bacteria may cause iron to corrode.)

(b) Aluminium forms a surface oxide layer which is strongly bonded to the aluminium beneath it, and which protects the metal from further reaction.
(2 marks)

(c) Sodium reacts violently with water forming sodium hydroxide and hydrogen so cannot be stored in water. (2 marks)

(d) The purposes of alloying gold are to make it harder and more resistant to wear, and to change its colour for use as jewellery by alloying with, for example, copper or platinum. (2 marks)

(Total = 8 marks)

Question 15

(a)

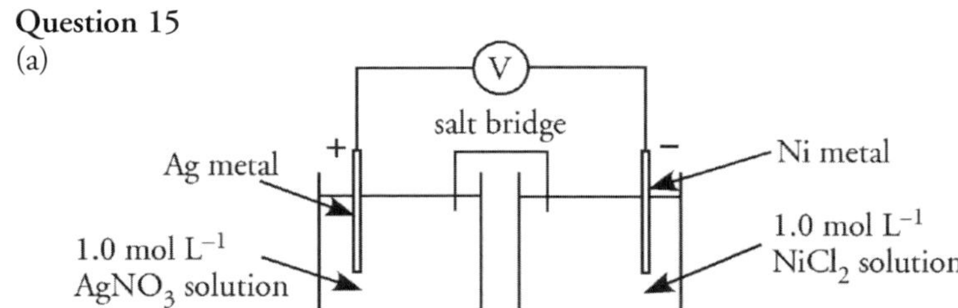

- Correct sketch (1 mark)
- Correct metal in each solution (1 mark)
- Salt bridge (1 mark)
- Ag positive, Ni negative (1 mark)

The polarity of the electrodes can be deduced from the table of standard reduction potentials.

$Ni^{2+}(aq) + 2e^- \rightleftharpoons Ni(s)$ $\quad E° = -0.23$ V

$Ag^+(aq) + e^- \rightleftharpoons Ag(s)$ $\quad E° = +0.80$ V

Ni is a stronger reductant than Ag and will be the source of electrons and hence is the negative electrode. The Ni^{2+}/Ni potential is more negative than the Ag^+/Ag potential. (Alternatively Ag^+ is a stronger oxidant than Ni^{2+} and will consume electrons and be the positive electrode.)

(b) It allows ions to flow between the two half-cells and thus electrons can flow in the external circuit. (1 mark)

(c) KNO_3 (the substance must not react with any of the chemicals in either half-cell.) (1 mark)

(d) At the negative electrode Ni metal is oxidised (this electrode is thus the anode).

$Ni(s) \rightarrow Ni^{2+}(aq) + 2e^-$

At the positive electrode electrons are consumed and Ag^+ is reduced. This electrode is the cathode.

$Ag^+(aq) + e^- \rightarrow Ag(s)$

The overall cell reaction is

$2Ag^+(aq) + Ni(s) \rightarrow Ni^{2+}(aq) + 2Ag(s)$

(3 marks)
(Total = 9 marks)

Question 16

(a) At the negative electrode the reaction occurring is

$Zn(s) \rightarrow Zn^{2+}(aq) + 2e^-$

Hence the mass of the negative electrode (Zn) will decrease.

At the positive electrode the reaction occurring is

$Ni^{2+}(aq) + 2e^- \rightarrow Ni(s)$

Hence the mass of this electrode will increase. (2 marks)

(b) Because of the two electrode reactions given in part (a), $[Zn^{2+}(aq)]$ will increase and $[Ni^{2+}(aq)]$ will decrease. (2 marks)

(c) The salt bridge allows **ions** to flow into or out of the two half-cells and thus maintain the electroneutrality in each cell. Negative ions flow into the Zn half-cell (or positive ions flow out) and positive ions flow into the Ni half-cell (or negative ions flow out). (2 marks)

(Total = 6 marks)

Question 17

Reactants	Predicted reaction Yes/No	Equation
$Fe^{2+}(aq)/Cl_2(g)$	yes	$2Fe^{2+}(aq) + Cl_2(g) \rightarrow 2Fe^{3+}(aq) + 2Cl^-(aq)$
$AgNO_3(aq)/Sn$	yes	$2Ag^+(aq) + Sn(s) \rightarrow 2Ag(s) + Sn^{2+}(aq)$
$SnCl_2(aq)/Cu$	no	
$Cd^{2+}(aq)/Ag(s)$	no	
$Ni^{2+}(aq)/Cd(s)$	yes	$Ni^{2+}(aq) + Cd(s) \rightarrow Ni(s) + Cd^{2+}(aq)$
$Cl^-(aq)/I_2(aq)$	no	

(Total = 9 marks)

Question 18

In the electrochemical series given, Cu^+ is present as both an oxidant and a reductant. In particular Cu^+ is the best reductant and also the best oxidant. Hence the following reaction should proceed:

$$Cu^+(aq) + Cu^+(aq) \rightarrow Cu^{2+}(aq) + Cu(s)$$

This process would be extremely slow in any solid because the Cu^+ ions would only move very slowly, if at all. However, in solution the Cu^+ ions are more mobile and a reaction occurs. (Total = 3 marks)

Question 19

(a) Reduction occurs at the cathode. The standard reduction potentials for these two half-cells are $Co^{2+}/Co = -0.28$ and $Sn^{2+}/Sn = -0.14$. Thus Co is a stronger reductant than Sn and will be oxidised in this cell. Hence Sn^{2+} will be reduced and the tin electrode will be the cathode. (1 mark)

(b) The reactions occurring at the two electrodes are

$Co(s) \rightarrow Co^{2+}(aq) + 2e^-$ and $Sn^{2+}(aq) + 2e^- \rightarrow Sn(s)$

The net cell reaction is: $Co(s) + Sn^{2+}(aq) \rightarrow Co^{2+}(aq) + Sn(s)$ (1 mark)

(c) The cell voltage (potential) is the difference between the two standard reduction potentials, i.e. E°(cell) = E°(cathode) – E°(anode). For this cell, cell potential = $-0.14 - (-0.28) = 0.14$ V (1 mark)

(d) •Non-standard conditions may have been used. Standard conditions are 25°C, a gas pressure of 100 kPa and electrolyte concentrations of 1.0 mol L^{-1}.
•The electrodes may be corroded, i.e. there may be a coating of oxide on the metal.
•If a piece of filter paper soaked in potassium nitrate solution is used as the salt bridge the internal resistance of the cell may have increased. (1 mark)

(Total = 4 marks)

Question 20

(a) Sn/Sn^{2+} and Cu/Cu^{2+} (0.48 V)

(b) Ni/Ni^{2+} and Ag/Ag^{+} (1.03 V)

(c) Zn/Zn^{2+} and Ag/Ag^{+} (1.56 V)

(d) Cd/Cd^{2+} and Au/Au^{+} (2.08 V)

(Total = 4 marks)

Question 21

(a) The copper metal is the cathode, i.e. reduction occurs here. The electrode reaction will be

$$Cu^{2+}(aq) + 2e^{-} \rightarrow Cu(s)$$

Thus copper ions are removed from the solution. The concentration of $Cu^{2+}(aq)$ decreases as does the intensity of the blue colour. (2 marks)

(b) E°(cell) = E°(oxidant) – E°(reductant)
Cu^{2+} is the oxidant and Q is the reductant. Hence the above equation becomes
1.52 = 0.34 – E°(reductant) and E°(reductant) = 0.34 – 1.52 = –1.18 V
From the table of standard reduction potentials Q is Mn. (2 marks)

(Total = 4 marks)

Question 22

(a) $Zn(s) + 2HCl(aq) \rightarrow ZnCl_2(aq) + H_2(g)$ (1 mark)

(b) n(Zn) = 0.26 ÷ 65.4 = 3.98×10^{-3} (n(HCl) = 0.1 which is an excess)
$n(H_2)$ = n(Zn) since it is a 1:1 reaction
Hence mass $H_2 = 3.98 \times 10^{-3} \times 2 = 7.95 \times 10^{-3}$ g (2 marks)

(c) The rate decreased over the time of the reaction. (1 mark)

(d) As the Zn is consumed by the reaction the surface area of the Zn decreases. Reducing the surface area will decrease the rate of the reaction. The HCl is also used up during the reaction and its concentration will also fall. (2 marks)

(e) There are three ways to increase the speed of this reaction:
•raise the temperature, i.e. heat the HCl solution before adding the Zn.
•use a HCl solution with a higher concentration.
•use more finely divided pieces of Zn. (any two for 2 marks)

(f)

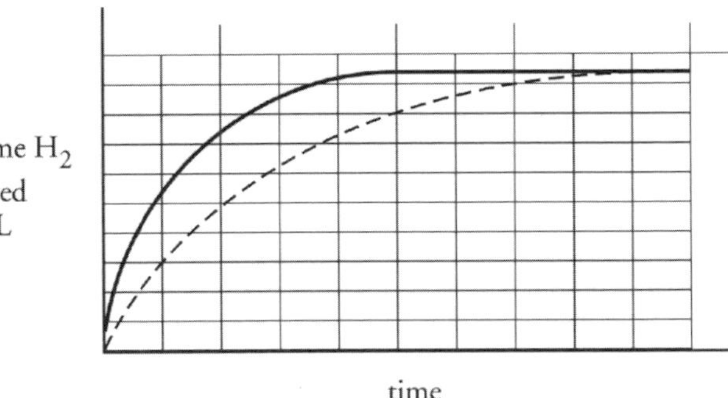

(1 mark)

In the first experiment HCl was in excess and Zn was the limiting reagent (n(Zn) = 0.00398 mol, n(HCl) = 0.100 mol). Zn is also the limiting reagent in the second experiment (n(Zn) = 0.00398 mol, n(HCl) = 0.050 mol). Hence the same volume of H_2 will be produced in the both experiments. Since the concentration of HCl has been reduced it will take longer to produce all of the H_2 gas.

(Total = 9 marks)

Question 23

(a) $CaCO_3(s) + 2HCl(aq) \rightarrow CaCl_2(aq) + H_2O(l) + CO_2(g)$ (1 mark)

(b) n(HCl) = cv = (1.00 × 0.10) mol = 0.10 mol
n($CaCO_3$) = m/(molar mass) = 10.0/(40.08 + 12.01 + 48) = 0.0999 mol

(2 marks)

(c) Molar ratio $CaCO_3$: HCl = 1 : 2
0.1 mol HCl only requires 0.05 mol $CaCO_3$ for complete reaction so since there are 0.0999 mol $CaCO_3$, HCl reacts completely and calcium carbonate is in excess. (1 mark)

(d) Gaseous carbon dioxide is produced, which escapes from the reaction flask.

(1 mark)

(e)

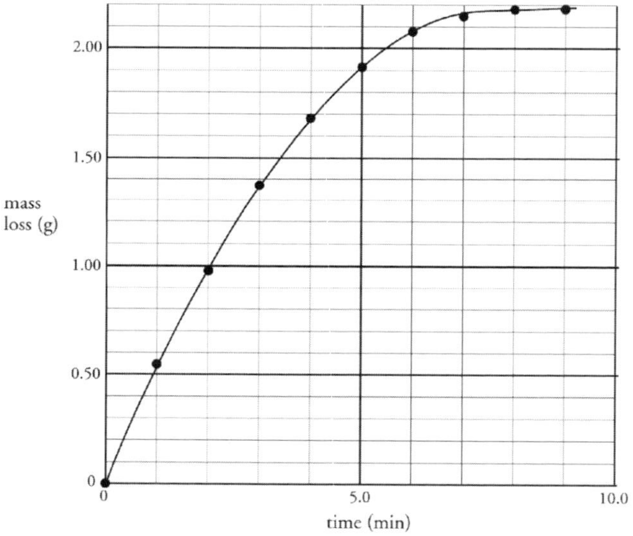

mass loss (g)

2.00
1.50
1.00
0.50
0

0
5.0
10.0

time (min)

(2 marks)

(f) (i) Rate is 0.44 g min^{-1}
(ii) rate is 0.16 g min^{-1} (2 marks)

(g) The rate of reaction decreases with time. (1 mark)

(h) As the acid reacts so the concentration of HCl decreases. (1 mark)

(Total = 11 marks)

Question 24

(a) ΔH = energy of products – energy of reactants
= –305 –(–265) = –40 kJ mol^{-1} (2 marks)

(b) Activation energy of reverse reaction = –230 –(–305) = 75 kJ mol^{-1} (1 mark)

(c)
- When the temperature is increased the molecules move more rapidly and thus there are more collisions per second.
- At the higher temperature more of the collisions will have energy equal to or greater than the activation energy, i.e. the fraction of collisions that are fruitful will be greater. (2 marks)

(d) (i) A catalyst would increase the rate of reaction.

(ii) A catalyst would provide an alternative reaction pathway with a lower activation energy.

(iii) ΔH would not change. ΔH is defined as the difference in energy between the energy of the products and the energy of the reactants. A catalyst does not change these values.

(1 + 1 + 1 = 3 marks)
(Total = 8 marks)

Test: Reactive Chemistry

Multiple Choice Items

Question	Answer	Comments
1.	B.	In 2, 3 and 4 a new product is formed. This does not happen in 1.
2.	C.	Cu and Ag do not react with dilute HCl. Mg reacts with boiling water.
3.	D.	Calcium will react with cold water. Copper and silver do not react with steam.
4.	C.	Pb will only reduce those cations that are lower in the reactivity series, i.e. Ag^+ and Cu^{2+}.
5.	B.	To reduce Sn^{2+} the $E°(M/M^{n+})$ must be more negative than –0.14 V. Since M cannot reduce Zn^{2+} $E°(M/M^{n+})$ must be greater than –0.76 V.
6.	A.	Electrons will be most easily removed from metal I since it has the lowest ionisation energy. Hence it is expected to be the most reactive.
7.	A,	Oxidation is loss of electrons. Metals lose electrons in redox reactions.
8.	C.	Reduction is gain of electrons. Non-metals gain electrons in redox reactions.
9.	D.	Experiment 2 takes place at a faster initial rate but produces less CO_2. Hence less $CaCO_3$ was used. An increase in the concentration of HCl will increase the rate of reaction. In (C) the lower temperature would produce a smaller volume of CO_2 but at a slower rate.
10.	A.	Activation energies are not usually changed by changes in temperature.

Extended Response Answers

Question 1

(a) $NH_4NO_3(s) \rightarrow N_2O(g) + 2H_2O(g)$ (2 marks)

(b) $Hg(l) + 4HNO_3(l) \rightarrow Hg(NO_3)_2(aq) + 2H_2O(l) + 2NO_2(g)$ (2 marks)

(c) $2CuSO_4(aq) + 4KI(aq) \rightarrow 2CuI(s) + I_2(aq) + 2K_2SO_4(aq)$ (2 marks)

(Total = 6 marks)

Question 2

	$Cd^{2+}(aq)$	$Cu^{2+}(aq)$	$Mn^{2+}(aq)$	$Ni^{2+}(aq)$	$Zn^{2+}(aq)$
Cd(s)		Y	N	Y	N
Cu(s)	N		N	N	N
Mn(s)	Y	Y		Y	Y
Ni(s)	N	Y	N		N
Zn(s)	Y	Y	N	Y	

(Total = 4 marks)

Question 3

(a) $E^{o}_{cell} = E°(\text{oxidant}) - E°(\text{reductant})$

Fe is the reductant and Ag^+ is the oxidant.

E°(cell) = +0.80 – (–0.44) volts = 1.24 volts (1 mark)

(b) Overall cell reaction $Fe(s) + 2Ag^+(aq) \rightarrow Fe^{2+}(aq) + 2Ag(s)$ (1 mark)

(c) (i) At the Ag electrode $Ag^+(aq) + e^- \rightarrow Ag(s)$
Mass of Ag deposited = 4.83 – 3.75 = 1.08 g
n(Ag) = 1.08 ÷ 107.9 = 0.0100 mol
At iron electrode $Fe(s) \rightarrow Fe^{2+}(aq) + 2e^-$
n(Fe) reacting = n(Ag) ÷ 2 = 0.00500 mol
Mass Fe reacting = 0.00500 × 55.85 = 0.280 g
Final mass of Fe electrode = 11.57 – 0.28 = 11.29 g (3 marks)

(ii) $n(Fe^{2+})$ in initial solution = 0.200 × 0.500 mol = 0.100 mol
$n(Fe^{2+})$ after reaction = 0.100 + 0.005 mol = 0.105 mol
$c(Fe^{2+})$ = 0.105/0.200 = 0.525 mol L^{-1} (2 marks)

(Total = 7 marks)

Question 4

The relevant equations from the electrochemical series are given below. The chemicals present in the chemistry kit are in bold.

$Zn^{2+}(aq) + 2e^- \rightleftharpoons$ **$Zn(s)$**
$Fe^{2+}(aq) + 2e^- \rightleftharpoons$ **$Fe(s)$**
$Sn^{2+}(aq)$ $+ 2e^- \rightleftharpoons$ **$Sn(s)$**
$Pb^{2+}(aq) + 2e^- \rightleftharpoons$ **$Pb(s)$**
$2H^+(aq)$ $+ 2e^- \rightleftharpoons H_2(g)$
$Sn^{4+}(aq) + 2e^- \rightleftharpoons$ **$Sn^{2+}(aq)$**
$Cu^{2+}(aq)$ $+ 2e^- \rightleftharpoons$ **$Cu(s)$**
$Fe^{3+}(aq)$ $+ e^- \rightleftharpoons Fe^{2+}(aq)$

(a) Either the Cu^{2+} or the Fe^{3+} could be used to oxidise the Sn^{2+}.

$Sn^{2+}(aq) + Cu^{2+}(aq) \rightarrow Sn^{4+}(aq) + Cu(s)$ or
$Sn^{2+}(aq) + 2Fe^{3+}(aq) \rightarrow Sn^{4+}(aq) + 2Fe^{2+}(aq)$ (2 marks)

(b) The only reagent that could reduce the Fe^{3+} without reducing the Cu^{2+} is copper metal.

$Cu(s) + 2Fe^{3+}(aq) \rightarrow 2Fe^{2+}(aq) + Cu^{2+}(aq)$ (2 marks)

(c) In theory any of the metals Zn, Fe, Sn, or Pb could be used to prepare a sample of hydrogen. However, in practice only Zn or Fe would give a fast enough reaction to produce the hydrogen in a reasonable time.

$Zn(s) + 2H^{+}(aq) \rightarrow Zn^{2+}(aq) + H_2(g)$ or
$Fe(s) + 2H^{+}(aq) \rightarrow 2Fe^{2+}(aq) + H_2(g)$ (1 mark)
(Total = 5 marks)

Question 5

(a) Y is a stronger reductant than Cu by 0.45 V. Z is a stronger reductant than Cu by 1.10 V. Hence Z is a stronger reductant than Y. Cu is a stronger reductant than X. Hence the order of half-cells is

$Z^{2+}/Z > Y^{2+}/Y > Cu^{2+}/Cu > X^{+}/X$ (3 marks)

(b) Since Y^{2+} is a stronger oxidant than Z^{2+} the Y^{2+}/Y will be the positive half-cell. The EMF will be the difference between the voltages that the half-cells produce with the Cu^{2+}/Cu half-cell, i.e. $1.10 - 0.45 = 0.65$ V (2 marks)
(Total = 5 marks)

Question 6

(a) –2 (b) –1 (c) +3 (Total = 3 marks)

(Total = 40 marks)

Answers: Drivers of Reactions

Multiple Choice Items

Question	Answer	Comments
1.	B.	Since ΔH is negative this is an exothermic reaction. Energy is given out to the surroundings. The energy of the products is less than the energy of the reactants.
2.	A.	The temperature of the water falls when the reaction is endothermic since the reaction absorbs energy from the surroundings, i.e. the water. ΔH is given a +sign for endothermic reactions. Alternative (A) shows the correct symbols of state.
3.	B.	For an endothermic reaction the products have more energy than the reactants and the enthalpy change is positive. The activation energy of a reaction is not linked to the enthalpy change of the reaction.
4.	A.	The combustion of fuels is an exothermic reaction in which heat energy is given out. The products therefore have less chemical energy than the reactants, as some energy has been lost to the surroundings.
5.	C.	For *complete* combustion all of the C atoms and H atoms are converted into CO_2 and H_2O, i.e. (A). Incomplete combustion produces H_2O and either CO and/or C. (B) is a dehydration reaction and (D) is a partial oxidation.
6.	B.	The equations for the combustion of these fuels are $\frac{1}{2}CH_4 + O_2 \rightarrow \frac{1}{2}CO_2 + H_2O$ $2/5C_2H_2 + O_2 \rightarrow 4/5CO_2 + 2/5H_2O$ $1/3C_2H_4 + O_2 \rightarrow 2/3CO_2 + 2/3H_2O$ $1/5C_3H_8 + O_2 \rightarrow 3/5CO_2 + 4/5H_2O$
7.	B.	Reaction II is a combustion reaction for which ΔH is negative. The other three are endothermic reactions. Reaction I involves breaking the bonds in an ionic lattice, reaction III is the removal of an electron and reaction IV is bond breaking.
8.	C.	This is an endothermic reaction, since the temperature of the water falls. No value is given for the calorimeter constant hence only the energy change of the water can be calculated. Energy *lost* by the water = 4.18 × 100 × (19.1 – 12.9) = 2592 J or 2.592 kJ. n(NH_4HCO_3) = 7.91 ÷ 79.1 = 0.100 mol. For 1.00 mol reacting the energy change is +25.9 kJ.
9.	D.	Energy required from hexan-1-ol = 152 ÷ 0.45 = 337.8 kJ n(hexan-1-ol) = 337.8 ÷3984 = 0.0848 mol Mass hexan-1-ol = 0.0848 × 102.2 = 8.66 g
10.	B.	n(CH_3OH) = 1000 ÷ 32 = 31.25 mol Energy supplied to car = 31.25 × 726 × 0.30 = 6806 kJ Distance travelled = 6806 ÷ 2000 = 3.4 km.

Question	Answer	Comments
11.	C.	The decomposition of Fe_2O_3 will absorb energy. Energy absorbed = 825 ÷ 1.5 = 550 kJ.
12.	B.	During complete combustion both carbon and hydrogen are fully oxidised so the products are carbon dioxide and water. If incomplete combustion occurs carbon monoxide and water or carbon and water are produced.
13.	B.	Combustion of 1 mol of C_2H_5OH consumes 3 mol of O_2 and produces 2 mol of CO_2, 3 mol of H_2O and 1368 kJ. The values for CH_3OH are 1.5 mol of O_2, 1 mol of CO_2, 2 mol of H_2O and 726 kJ.
14.	A.	n(hydrocarbon) = 1.00/(molar mass) for each fuel. Energy released = Heat of Combustion × n(hydrocarbon) $n(CH_4)$ = 1.0/16 = 0.0625 mol Energy released = 890 × 0.0625 kJ = 55.63 kJ The values for the other fuels are C_2H_6 = 52 kJ, C_3H_8 = 50.5 kJ and C_4H_{10} = 49.6 kJ.
15.	D.	The products are at a lower energy and more stable than the reactants. Since ΔH = energy of products – energy of reactants, ΔH will be negative. The energy released is given to the surroundings.
16.	D.	This is an exothermic reaction. $n(CO_2)$ = 11 ÷ 44 = 0.25 mol From the equation the production of 3 mol of CO_2 releases 2208 kJ. Hence heat released is 0.25 × 2208 ÷ 3 kJ.
17.	C.	When 1 mole of each of the fuels is burnt the energy released is $\Delta H_c(C_2H_5OH)$ = 29.6 × 46.1 = 1365 kJ mol^{-1}; $\Delta H_c(C_8H_{18})$ = 47.8 × 114.2 = 5459 kJ mol^{-1}; $\Delta H_c(C_4H_{10})$ = 49.5 × 58.1 = 2876 kJ mol^{-1}; $\Delta H_c(C_3H_8)$ = 50.3 × 44.1 = 2218 kJ mol^{-1}.
18.	D.	Since the reaction is exothermic the energy of the products must be lower than that of the reactants by 74 kJ mol^{-1}. The top of the curve must be 32 kJ mol^{-1} higher than the energy of the reactants.
19.	D.	$n(C_4H_{10}O)$ = 1.50 ÷ 74.1 = 0.02024 mol Heat energy given to water = 1530 × 0.02024 = 30.97 kJ Temperature rise of water = $\frac{30.97 \times 1000}{4.18 \times 300}$ = 24.7°C Final temperature of water = 20.7 + 24.7 = 45.4°C
20.	C.	Molar mass of 1-propanol = 60 g mol^{-1} $\Delta H_c(C_3H_7OH)$ = 2021 ÷ 60 = 33.68 kJ g^{-1}
21.	A.	Heat energy given to water = $\frac{4.18 \times 250 \times 16.0}{1000}$ = 16.72 kJ

Question	Answer	Comments
21(cont).	A.	$n(CH_3OH) = \frac{125.58 - 124.38}{32} = 0.0375$ mol $\Delta H_c = 16.72 \div 0.0375 = 446$ kJ mol^{-1}
22.	B.	Energy given to solution = $(4.20 \times 100 \times 24.0) = 1008$ J n(Zn) = 3.27/65.3 = 0.0501 mol; $n(CuSO_4) = 1.0 \times 0.1 = 0.1$ mol, which is an excess. ΔH for reaction = –10.08/0.0501 = –201 kJ mol^{-1} Since the temperature rises ΔH is negative.
23.	B.	Since the solution has absorbed energy the temperature will fall. The formation of 1 mole of $CaBr_2$ would absorb 110 kJ. The absorption of 5.5 kJ will occur when 5.5/110 mol of $CaBr_2$ forms. This is $(5.5 \times 200)/110$ g.
24.	B.	$n(Ba(OH)_2) = 31.53 \div 315.3 = 0.100$ mol $n(NH_4CNO) = 6.0 \div 60 = 0.100$ mol Molar ratio from the equation is 1:2, hence only 0.050 mol of $Ba(OH)_2$ is used. The heat absorbed is $0.050 \times 75 \times 1000 = 3750$ J. Temperature *change* in the calorimeter will be $3750 \div 150$, i.e. 25°C and the final temperature will be 20 – 25 = –5°C.
25.	D.	The formation of 1 mol of methanol and 1 mol of water will release 48 kJ. The reaction of 3.0 g of hydrogen would release 24 kJ.
26.	A.	Exothermic reactions have a negative ΔH. The products are more stable than the reactants and thus at a lower energy. Hence the products have stronger bonds.
27.	C.	When a reaction occurs the bonds in the reactants are broken and bonds in the products are formed. The difference in these two terms is ΔH for the reaction. Since the combustion of H_2 is exothermic the formation of O–H bonds must release more energy than it takes to break the bonds in H_2 and O_2. To break the bonds in 2 mol of H_2 and 1 mol of O_2 requires $(2 \times 436) + 498 = 1370$ kJ. Energy released when 2 mol of H_2O is formed from 4H and 2O is $1370 + (2 \times 241)$ (since 2 mol of H_2O is formed) = 1852 kJ. This energy results from the formation of 4 O–H bonds (in 2 mol H_2O) Bond energy for one O–H bond is $1852 \div 4 = 463$ kJ mol^{-1}.
28.	C.	The energy change for the reaction $NO_2 \rightarrow NO + \frac{1}{2}O_2$ is 90 – 33 = +57 kJ mol^{-1}. For the reverse reaction the energy change will change sign, i.e. it will be –57 kJ mol^{-1}. The equation in the question is double the one above, hence the energy change will be double.
29.	D.	From Hess's law: ΔH(reaction I) = ΔH(reaction II) + ΔH(reaction III)

Question	Answer	Comments
29(cont).	D.	$-84 = +52 + \Delta H$(reaction III) and ΔH(reaction III) = $-84 - 52 = -137$ kJ mol^{-1}
30.	D.	This is the only reaction where the energy decreases. In the other three reactions the products have higher energy than the reactants.
31.	C.	Equation (3) is obtained if equation (2) is reversed, doubled and added to equation (1) doubled. Hence $\Delta_c H(3) = 2 \times (-890) + 2 \times 282 = -1216$ kJ mol^{-1}
32.	B.	The energy needed to break the bonds in H_2 and Br_2 is $+436 + 193 = 629$ kJ mol^{-1}. The energy released when each H–Br bond forms is -366 kJ mol^{-1}. The energy change for the reaction is $(-2 \times 366) + 629 = -103$ kJ mol^{-1}.
33.	C.	The energy change for $H_2S(g) \rightarrow 2H(g) + S(g)$ is the same as $H_2S(g) \rightarrow 2H(g) + S(s)$ followed by $S(s) \rightarrow S(g)$ and then $H_2(g) \rightarrow 2H(g)$, i.e. $+21 + 277 + 436 = +734$ kJ mol^{-1}. However this is the energy to break two H–S bonds.
34.	C.	In crystals of sodium chloride the ions are arranged in a regular lattice, i.e. they are highly ordered and will have a lower entropy than the salt solution. In the other three cases the entropy increases because the system becomes more disordered.
35.	A.	There are gas molecules in the products than in the reactants, hence the system is more disordered. In the other three cases the number of gas molecules decreases.
36.	C.	ΔS = S(products) – S(reactants) = $304 - (2 \times 240)$ $= -176$ J mol^{-1} K^{-1}. Since the number of gas molecules has decreased it is expected that the entropy would decrease.
37.	B.	The activation energy influences the speed of the reaction. The change in the amount of disorder in the system is the entropy change and the change in heat content is the enthalpy change.
38.	A.	ΔS = S(products) – S(reactants) = $(2 \times 257) - 205 - (2 \times 248)$ $= -187$ J mol^{-1} K^{-1}. A decrease in the number of gas molecules causes a decrease in entropy.
39.	B.	ΔS = S(products) – S(reactants) $= [(2 \times -138) + 137] - [(2 \times -316) + (2 \times 106)] = -139 - (-420)$ $= +281$ J mol^{-1} K^{-1}.
40.	C.	$\Delta G = \Delta H - T\Delta S = -92 - (-298 \times 0.199) = -92 + 59.3$ $= -33$ kJ mol^{-1}.
41.	A.	Increasing the temperature will increase $T\Delta S$. Since ΔS is negative ΔG will change from -33 to more positive values. At ~450°C ΔG will be $+52$ kJ mol^{-1}.

Extended Response Questions

Question 1

(a) *Methane:*

Molar mass CH_4 = (12.01 + 4.04) = 16.05 g mol^{-1}
16.05 g methane produces 890 kJ of energy
Energy produced by 1000 g methane = (1000/16.05) × 890 = 5.55 × 10^4 kJ

Propane:

Molar mass (C_3H_8) = (36.03 + 8.08) = 44.11 g mol^{-1}
44.11 g propane produces 2220 kJ of energy
Energy produced by 1000 g propane = (1000/44.11) × 2220 = 5.03 × 10^4 kJ

Octane:

Molar mass (C_8H_{18}) = (96.08 + 18.18) = 114.26
114.26 g octane produces 5470 kJ of energy
Energy produced by 1000 g octane = (1000/114.26) × 5470 = 4.79 × 10^4 kJ

(1 + 1 + 1 = 3 marks)

(b) *Methane:*

890 kJ energy is produced when 44.0 g CO_2 forms
1000 kJ energy is produced when (1000/890) × 44.0 = 49.4 g CO_2 forms

Propane:

2220 kJ energy is produced when (44.0 × 3) g CO_2 forms
1000 kJ energy is produced when (1000/2220) × 132.0 = 59.5 g CO_2 forms

Octane:

5470 kJ energy is produced when (44.0 × 8) g CO_2 forms
1000 kJ energy is produced when (1000/5470) × 352 = 64.4 g CO_2 forms

(1 + 1 + 1 = 3 marks)
(Total = 6 marks)

Question 2

(a) $2C_8H_{18}(l) + 19O_2(g) \longrightarrow 8CO_2(g) + 4CO(g) + 4C(s) + 18H_2O(l)$
or $C_8H_{18}(l) + 9\tfrac{1}{2}O_2(g) \longrightarrow 4CO_2(g) + 2CO(g) + 2C(s) + 9H_2O(l)$

(3 marks)

(b) The three equations are

$C_8H_{18}(l) + 12.5O_2(g) \longrightarrow 8CO_2(g) + 9H_2O(l) \quad \Delta H = -5470 \text{ kJ mol}^{-1}$ (1)
$C_8H_{18}(l) + 8.5O_2(g) \longrightarrow 8CO(g) + 9H_2O(l) \quad \Delta H = -3207 \text{ kJ mol}^{-1}$ (2)
$C_8H_{18}(l) + 4.5O_2(g) \longrightarrow 8C(s) + 9H_2O(l) \quad \Delta H = -2323 \text{ kJ mol}^{-1}$ (3)

From reaction (1): when 8 mol of CO_2 are formed, 5470 kJ are released.
Thus when 4 mol of CO_2 are formed, 5470 × (4/8) = 2735 kJ are released

From reaction (2): when 8 mol of CO are formed, 3207 kJ are released.
Thus when 2 mol of CO are formed, 3207 × (2/8) = 801.8 kJ are released

From reaction (3): when 8 mol of C are formed, 2323 kJ are released.
Thus when 2 mol of C are formed, 2323 × (2/8) = 580.8 kJ are released

Energy released by reaction in part (a) = 2735 + 801.8 + 580.8 = 4118 kJ

(3 marks)
(Total = 6 marks)

Question 3

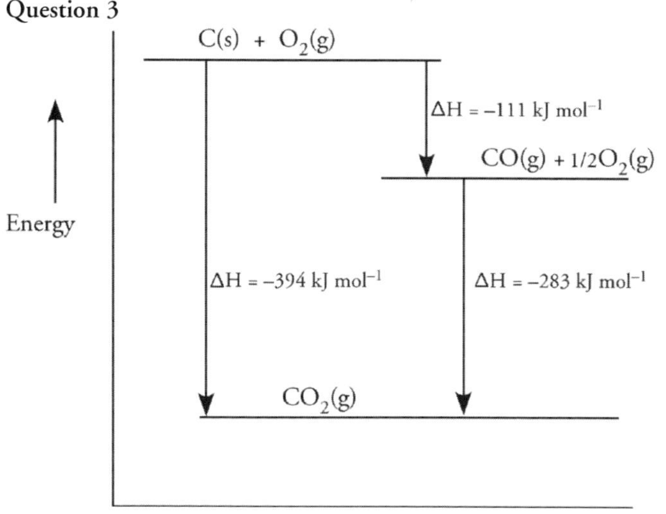

(Total = 3 marks)

Question 4

(a) *ammonium nitrate:*

temperature change = (20.10 – 16.98) °C = 3.12°C

$n(NH_4NO_3)$ = 4.192/(28.02 + 4.04 + 48) = 0.0524 mol

0.0524 mol causes a temperature fall of 3.12°C, hence this reaction is endothermic.

Heat energy absorbed = 4.18 × 100 × 3.12 = 1304 J or 1.304 kJ

Heat of solution = +1.304/0.0524 = +24.9 kJ mol^{-1} (2 marks)

potassium hydroxide:

temperature change = (29.04-20.55) °C = 8.49°C

n(KOH) = 3.496/(39.1 + 16 + 1.01) = 0.0623 mol

0.0623 mol causes a temperature rise of 8.49°C, hence this reaction is exothermic.

Hear energy released = 4.18 × 100 × 8.49 = 3549 J or 3.549 kJ

Heat of solution = –3.549/0.0623 = –57.0 kJ mol^{-1} (2 marks)

(b)
- No heat loss or gain to the surroundings occurs.
- The solids dissolve completely.
- The polystyrene cup, stirrer and thermometer absorb a negligible amount of energy. (1 mark)

(c) Any of the assumptions mentioned in (b) may be incorrect e.g. energy exchange with the surroundings may occur. (1 mark)

(d) $NH_4NO_3(s) \xrightarrow{water} NH_4^+(aq) + NO_3^-(aq); \Delta H = +24.9 \text{ kJ mol}^{-1}$

This reaction is endothermic.

(2 marks)

$KOH(s) \xrightarrow{water} K^+(aq) + OH^-(aq)$ $\Delta H = -57.0 \text{ kJ mol}^{-1}$

This reaction is exothermic.

(2 marks)

(e)

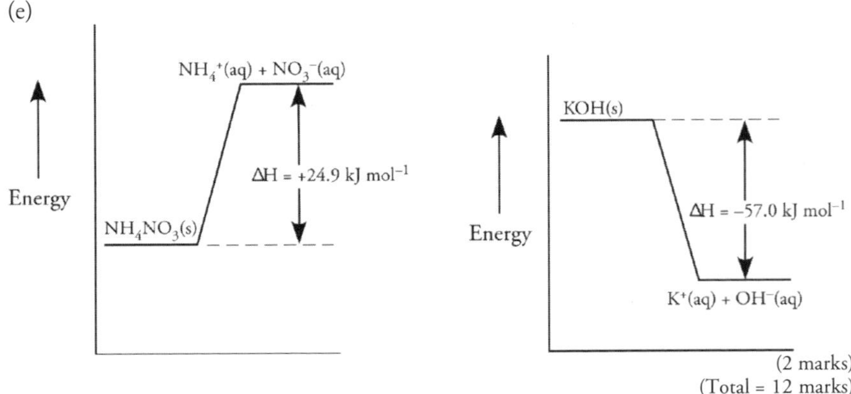

(2 marks)
(Total = 12 marks)

Question 5

(a) $2C_6H_{14}(l) + 19O_2(g) \rightarrow 12CO_2(g) + 14H_2O(l)$ (2 marks)

(b) Mass of C_6H_{14} = volume × density = (1000 × 0.660) g = 660 g
n(C_6H_{14}) = 660/(86.20) mol = 7.66 mol
Heat of combustion = 4163 kJ mol^{-1}
Heat energy released by 1.00 L = (4163 × 7.66) kJ = 3.19×10^4 kJ (3 marks)
(Total = 5 marks)

Question 6

Molar mass of glucose = (72.06 + 12.10 + 96.0) = 180.2 g mol^{-1}
180.2 g glucose supplies 2800 kJ of energy
n(glucose) needed = 13500 ÷ 2800 = 4.82 mol
13,500 kJ is supplied by 4.82 × 180 g glucose = 868.7 g glucose
Mass of glucose required per day = 868.7 g (Total = 2 marks)

Question 7

(a) Complete combustion of 2 mol of CH_4 would release 2 × 890 = 1780 kJ.
Complete combustion of 2 mol of methanol releases 1452 kJ.
The first experiment would release the most energy. (1 mark)

(b) For the first reaction $\dfrac{\text{energy released}}{\Delta H} = \dfrac{n(CO_2)}{1}$

Hence n(CO_2) = 1000 ÷ 890 = 1.12 mol

In the second reaction $\dfrac{\text{energy released}}{\Delta H} = \dfrac{n(CO_2)}{2}$

Hence n(CO_2) = 1000 × 2 ÷1452 = 1.38 mol

The combustion of methanol will release more CO_2 to produce the same amount of energy as methane. (2 marks)
(Total = 3 marks)

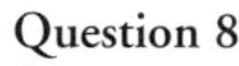

Question 8

(a)

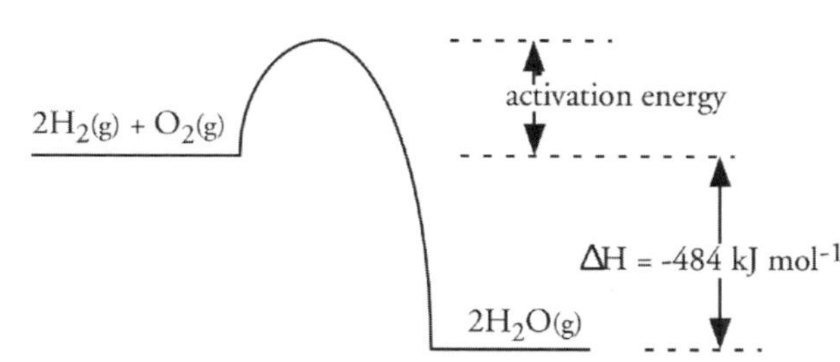

(3 marks)

(b) In an exothermic reaction, the products are at lower energy and have stronger bonds than the reactants. (1 mark)

(c) When steam is converted into water, $H_2O(g) \rightarrow H_2O(l)$, energy is released. Hence the reaction $2H_2(g) + O_2(g) \rightarrow 2H_2O(l)$

will release more energy than the reaction $2H_2(g) + O_2(g) \rightarrow 2H_2O(g)$

(2 marks)
(Total = 6 marks)

Question 9

(a) The total volume of solution being heated is 100 mL, while the temperature increase is 2.80°C (23.80 – 21.00).
Energy change in the reaction = 4.18 × 100 × 2.80 = 1170 J. (1 mark)
This amount of energy is released by 0.05 × 0.4 = 0.02 mol of acid (and base). (1 mark)

For 1 mol of acid, the amount of energy released is $\frac{1170}{0.02}$ = 58 520 J = 58.5 kJ. (1 mark)

Hence $\Delta H = -58.5\ \text{kJ mol}^{-1}$ (negative sign since temperature rises). (1 mark for correct sign)

(b) Polystyrene foam is a good insulator, so temperature changes during the reaction can be recorded with some accuracy (i.e. without significant gain or loss of energy from or to the surroundings). (1 mark)

(c) NaOH is the limiting reagent for the calculation.
n(NaOH) = 0.05 × 0.800 = 0.04 mol (1 mark)

Since 58.5 kJ is released by 1 mol of NaOH, 0.04 mol will release 58.5 × 0.04 = 2.34 kJ of energy.

Energy released (in J) = 4.18 × volume of solution × temperature rise

Temperature rise = $\frac{2.34 \times 1000}{4.18 \times 100}$ = 5.6°C (1 mark)

(Alternatively, it could be argued that the same volume of solution needed to be heated as in the first experiment, but with twice the amount of acid and alkali. The temperature rise would therefore be twice as great, assuming that the specific heat capacity of the solution was unchanged.)

(d) Heat released by reaction = (4.18 × 100 × 2.48)/1000 = 1.037 kJ
Equation for reaction is $NH_3(aq) + HCl(aq) \rightarrow NH_4^+(aq) + Cl^-(aq)$
Hence both reactants completely react.
$n(NH_3) = n(HCl) = 0.0500 \times 0.400 = 0.0200$ mol

ΔH for neutralisation = $-1.037/0.0200$ = -51.8 kJ mol^{-1}. (2 marks)

(e) The two reactions are different $H^+(aq) + OH^-(aq) \rightarrow H_2O(l)$ and $NH_3(aq) + H^+(aq) \rightarrow NH_4^+(aq)$. Hence different values are expected. (1 mark)

(Total = 10 marks)

Question 10

(a) Heat supplied to water = $4.18 \times 300 \times (49.6 - 16.7) = 41256.6$ J
= 41.3 kJ (1 mark)

(b) Heat produced by Bunsen = $\dfrac{41.3 \times 100}{65}$ kJ = 63.5 kJ (1 mark)

(c) $CH_4(g) + 2O_2(g) \rightarrow CO_2(g) + 2H_2O(g)$ (1 mark)

(d) n(CH_4) burnt = $\dfrac{PV}{RT} = \dfrac{115 \times 1.54}{8.314 \times 289.7} = 0.07353$ (1 mark)

This amount of gas released 63.5 kJ

1 mol of gas should release = $\dfrac{63.5}{0.07353}$ = 863.6 kJ (1 mark)

ΔH for reaction is -864 kJ mol^{-1} (1 mark)

(Total = 6 marks)

Question 11

(a) (i) The energy of the reactants should be placed at zero and the energy of the products should be at -20 kJ. (2 marks)

(ii) The top of the energy barrier for the uncatalysed reaction will be 210 kJ above the energy of the products, i.e. at +190 kJ. (1 mark)

(iii) The top of the energy barrier for the catalysed reaction must be less than +190 kJ but greater than zero. (1 mark)

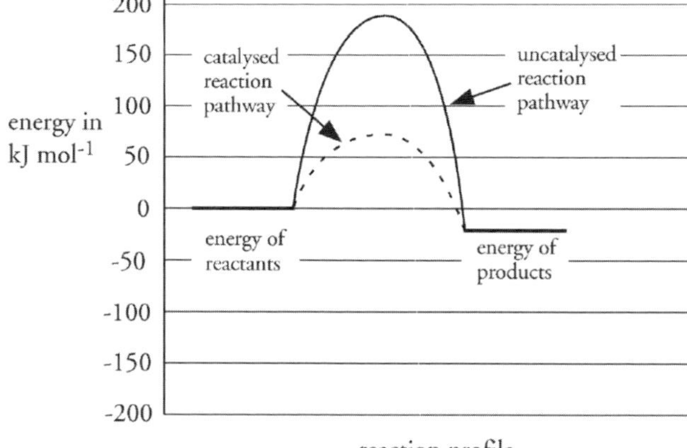

(b) n(CH_3CHO) needed = $1000 \div 20.0 = 50.0$ mol
Mass CH_3CHO = $50.0 \times 44.1 = 2205$, i.e. 2210 g (2 marks)

(Total = 6 marks)

Question 12

(a) Metals are better conductors of heat than glass. Less heat will be wasted heating the container. (1 mark)

(b) Mass methanol used = $35.674 - 34.396 = 1.278$ g

n(methanol) = 1.278 ÷ 32 = 0.0399 mol (2 marks)

(c) Heat given to water = 4.18 × 300 × 11.8 = 14.80 kJ (1 mark)

(d) Heat of combustion = 14.80 ÷ 0.0399 = 371 kJ mol^{-1} (1 mark)

(e) Any two of

- incomplete combustion of methanol
- heat lost in heating the container
- heat lost to the air
- heat lost from the container

(2 marks)

(Total = 7 marks)

Question 13

(a)

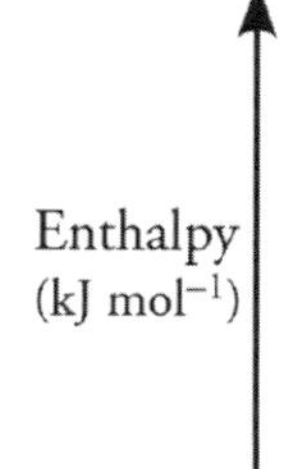

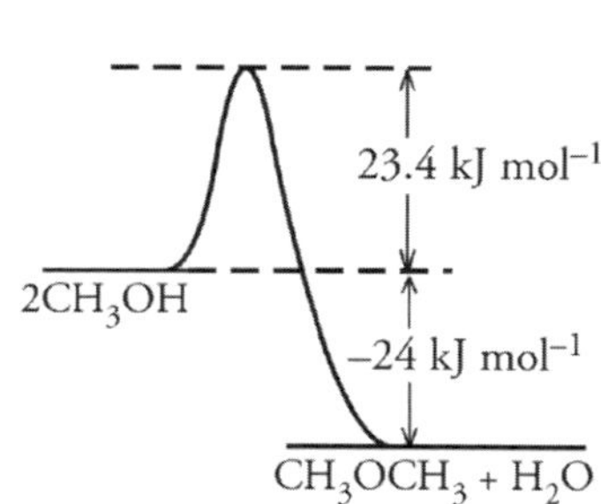

(3 marks)

(b) Advantages:

•It is a renewable fuel (provided the methanol is produced from renewable sources).

•It will have a lower sulfur content than fossil fuels.

•Since it rapidly undergoes complete combustion, the exhaust gases will contain less CO and there will be less carbon particles produced.

Disadvantages:

•It is a gas at room temperature and it will need to be compressed for storage on a vehicle. The fuel tank must withstand high pressures.

•It may be more expensive than equivalent fuels from crude oil since there are several steps in the production process (bio-waste to methane, methane to methanol and methanol to dimethyl ether).

•Since dimethyl ether contains some oxygen, combustion will produce less energy than combustion of petrodiesel (its heat of combustion will be lower).

(2 marks)

(Total = 5 marks)

Question 14

There are two C–C bonds in C_3H_8, two H–O bonds in each H_2O and two C=O bonds in each CO_2.

Energy required to break the bonds in C_3H_8 = (2 × 346) + (8 × 414) = 4004 kJ
Energy required to break the bonds in O_2 = 5 × 498 = 2490 kJ
Total energy required in bond breaking = 6494 kJ
Energy released when bonds form in $3CO_2$ = 3 × 2 × 804 = 4824 kJ
Energy released when bonds form in $4H_2O$ = 4 × 2 × 463 = 3704 kJ
Total energy released by bond formation = 8528 kJ
Heat of combustion C_3H_8 = Energy absorbed – Energy released = 6494 – 8528
= –2034 kJ mol^{-1} (Total = 4 marks)

Question 15

Reaction III will result if Reaction I is reversed and then followed by Reaction II. The enthalpy change will be

$+169 + (-157) = +12$ kJ mol^{-1} (Total = 2 marks)

Question 16

(a)

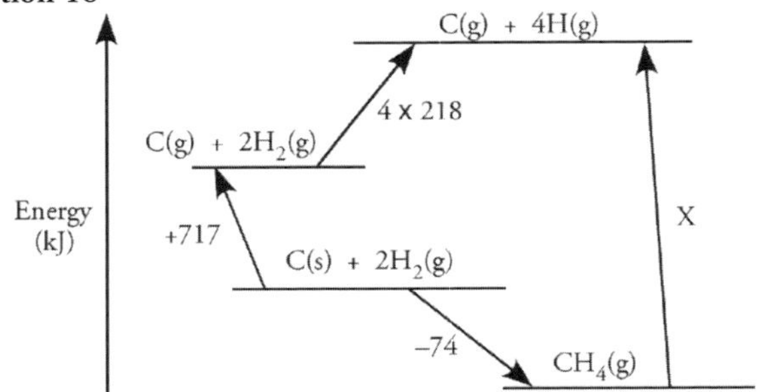

(2 marks)

(b) $X = +74 + 717 + (4 \times 218) = 1663$ kJ mol^{-1} (1 mark)

(c) There are four C–H bonds in CH_4. To break all four bonds requires 1663 kJ. To break one C–H bond requires $1663 \div 4 = 416$ kJ. (2 marks)

(Total = 5 marks)

Question 17

(a) The energy change to produce H_2O_2(g) from H_2(g) and O_2(g) is $-188 + (+52) = -136$ kJ mol^{-1}

The energy required to produce 2H(g) and 2O(g) from H_2(g) and O_2(g) is $+436 + (+498) = +934$ kJ mol^{-1}

Enthalpy change for the reaction $H_2O_2(g) \rightarrow 2H(g) + 2O(g)$ is

$934 - (-136) = 1070$ kJ mol^{-1} (3 marks)

(b) To break the two O–H bonds requires $2 \times 463 = 926$ kJ
Energy required to break O–O $= 1070 - 926 = +144$ kJ mol^{-1} (2 marks)

(Total = 5 marks)

Question 18

(a) The entropy is expected to increases since gases have higher entropies than solids. Hence ΔS should be positive. (1 mark)

(b) $\Delta S^{o}_{298} = \Sigma S(\text{products}) - \Sigma S(\text{reactants}) = (14.2 + 65.3) - (28.0 + 0)$
$= +51.5$ J mol^{-1} K^{-1} (2 marks)

(c) $\Delta G = -278.3 - (298 \times 0.0515) = -294$ kJ mol^{-1} (2 marks)

(d) This reaction will be spontaneous since ΔG is negative. (1 mark)

(Total = 6 marks)

Question 19

(a) $\Delta S = \Sigma S(\text{products}) - \Sigma S(\text{reactants}) = (186 + 660) - 428$
$= +418$ J mol^{-1} K^{-1}

$\Delta G = +270 - (298 \times 0.418) = +145 \text{ kJ mol}^{-1}$ (3 marks)

(b) At 25°C this reaction is non-spontaneous because ΔG is positive. For a spontaneous reaction to occur ΔG must be negative. When $\Delta G = 0$ the reaction will on the point of changing from non-spontaneous to spontaneous.

$0 = +270 - (T \times 0.418)$ and $T = 270 / 0.418 = 646$ K

The temperature should be greater than 646 K (2 marks)

(Total = 5 marks)

Question 20

(a) $\Delta S = 240 - (198 + 262) = -220 \text{ J mol}^{-1} \text{ K}^{-1}$ (1 mark)

(b) $\Delta S = (428 + 378) - (615 + 220) = -29 \text{ J mol}^{-1} \text{ K}^{-1}$ (1 mark)

(c) $\Delta S = 428 - (396 + 205) = -173 \text{ J mol}^{-1} \text{ K}^{-1}$ (1 mark)

(d) $\Delta S = 230 - (220 + 131) = -121 \text{ J mol}^{-1} \text{ K}^{-1}$ (1 mark)

(e) $\Delta S = [(4 \times 214) + (6 \times 189)] - [230 + (7 \times 205)]$
$= +325 \text{ J mol}^{-1} \text{ K}^{-1}$ (1 mark)

(f) $\Delta S = 240 - (186 + 0.5 \times 205) = -48.5 \text{ J mol}^{-1} \text{ K}^{-1}$ (1 mark)

(Total = 6 marks)

Question 21

(a) CO_2 is a gas and will have a higher entropy than the two solids. Magnesium carbonate contains more atoms than magnesium oxide, which means that it is more complex and has a higher entropy. (2 marks)

(b) (i) $\Delta S = 27 + 214 - 66 = +175 \text{ J mol}^{-1} \text{ K}^{-1}$ (1 mark)
(ii) $\Delta G = +100 - (298 \times 0.175) = +47.9 \text{ kJ mol}^{-1}$ (1 mark)

(c) Since ΔG is positive this reaction will be non-spontaneous at 25°C. (1 mark)

(d) (i) $T = 100 / 0.175 = 571$ K (1 mark)
(ii) If $MgCO_3$ is heated to 571 K it will start to decompose and produce CO_2 and MgO. (1 mark)

(Total = 7 marks)

Question 22

(a) $\Delta S = (70 + 0.5 \times 205) - 144 = +28.5 \text{ J mol}^{-1} \text{ K}^{-1}$ (2 marks)

(b) $\Delta G = -95 - (298 \times 0.0285) = -104 \text{ kJ mol}^{-1}$ (2 marks)

(c) At 25°C ΔG for this reaction is negative. Hence the reaction is expected to be spontaneous. Since the reaction does not occur it is most likely that the activation energy for the reaction is large. At 25°C the molecules of H_2O_2 do not have enough energy to react. (1 mark)

(Total = 5 marks)

Test: Drivers of Reactions

Multiple Choice Items

Question	Answer	Comments
1.	A.	A fuel is a substance that releases energy when it reacts with oxygen, i.e. the reaction is exothermic. In exothermic reactions the energy of the products is less than that of the reactants.
2.	C.	Catalysts provide an alternative reaction pathway with a lower activation energy than other pathways.
3.	B.	The bond energy is the enthalpy change for the reaction $HCl(g) \rightarrow H(g) + Cl(g)$. This is equivalent to $HCl(g) \rightarrow ½H_2(g) + ½Cl_2(g)$ followed by $½H_2(g) + ½Cl_2(g) \rightarrow H(g) + Cl(g)$. Bond energy = (+184 + 436 + 242) × 0.5 = 431 kJ mol^{-1}
4.	B.	n(gas) is same for all four fuels since T & P are the same and the same volume of gas is used each time. If 1 mol of each gas were burnt, then the energy released would be CH_4 = 890; C_2H_6 = 1560 kJ; C_2H_2 = 1300 kJ; CO = 233 kJ.
5.	A.	The heat energy released when 1 g of each gas reacts is CH_4 = 890 ÷ 16 = 55.6 kJ; C_2H_6 = 1560 ÷ 30 = 52 kJ; C_2H_2 = 1300 ÷ 26 = 50 kJ; CO = 233 ÷ 28 = 8.32 kJ.
6.	C.	n(pentan-1-ol) = 1500 / 3331; Ratio n(H_2O) : n(pentan-1-ol) = 12 : 2, i.e. 6 : 1 Mass H_2O = (1500 / 3331) × 6 × 18 = 48.6 g
7.	C.	n(butan-1-ol) = 2.00 / 74.1 Energy released = (2.00 / 74.1) × 2676 = 72.2 kJ Mass of water = (72.2 × 1000) ÷ (4.18 × 20.0) = 864 g
8.	D.	Energy released = 100 × 4.18 × (31.1 – 20.2)/1000 = 4.556 kJ n(Mg) = 0.243 /24.3 = 0.0100 mol; n(HCl) = 0.100 mol Hence HCl is in excess and all of the Mg reacts. ΔH = –4.556 ÷ 0.0100 = –456 kJ mol^{-1} (Sign is negative since energy is released.)
9.	D.	Gases have higher entropies than other materials. The entropy of $C_6H_{12}O_6$ will be greater than that of C_2H_5OH since it is a more complex molecule.
10.	B.	n($(NH_4)_2S_2O_8$) = 22.82 / 228.2 = 0.100 mol Energy absorbed from water = 0.100 × 37.0 = 3.70 kJ Δt = 3700 ÷ (4.18 × 100) = 8.85°C Final temperature = 19.5 – 8.9 = 10.6°C
11.	B.	The three esters given in the table differ in formulae by a CH_2 group. The differences in ΔH_c are 653 and 652 kJ mol^{-1}. The difference in formulae between methyl heptanoate and methyl stearate is 11 × (CH_2). Hence ΔH_c should increase by

Question	Answer	Comments
11(cont).	B.	11 × 652.5, i.e. -7178 kJ. ΔH_c for methyl stearate is -7178 + 4863 kJ mol^{-1}.
12.	D.	Heat released = n(compound) × heat of solution The compound releasing the smallest amount of energy will produce the smallest temperature rise. For the four examples the heat released is A = (1.00 × 23.6)/23.9 = 0.987 kJ B = (1.00 × 44.5)/40.0 = 1.11 kJ C = (1.00 × 57.6)/56.1 = 1.02 kJ D = (1.00 × 71.6)/149.9 = 0.478 kJ

Extended Response Answers

Question 1

(a) (i) $n(CuSO_4) = 8.00 \div 159.6 = 0.0501$ mol
Energy released = 100 × 4.18 × (27.3 – 18.6) / 1000 = 3.64 kJ
ΔH (reaction I) = –3.64 ÷ 0.0501 = –72.6 kJ mol^{-1}
(Sign is negative since energy is released, i.e. the temperature rises)
(3 marks)

(ii) $n(CuSO_4.5H_2O) = 10.00 \div 249.7 = 0.0400$ mol
Energy absorbed = 100 × 4.18 × (18.6 – 18.1) / 1000 = 0.209 kJ
ΔH (reaction II) = +0.209 ÷ 0.0400 = +5.2 kJ mol^{-1}
(Sign is positive since energy is absorbed, i.e. the temperature falls)
(3 marks)

(b) From Hess's Law, $\Delta H + \Delta H$ (reaction II) = ΔH (reaction I)
ΔH = –72.6 – 5.2 = – 77.8 kJ mol^{-1} (2 marks)
(Total = 8 marks)

Question 2

(a) The sign of the entropy change is expected to be positive since gas molecules are formed from a molecule in the liquid phase. Also seven molecules are produced from one molecule. (2 marks)

(b) ΔS = +467 + (6 × 220) – 752 = 1035 J mol^{-1} K^{-1} (2 marks)

(c) $\Delta G = \Delta H - T\Delta S$ = +660 – (298 × 1.035) = +352 kJ mol^{-1} (2 marks)

(d) Since ΔG is positive the reaction will be non-spontaneous. (1 mark)

(e) $0 = \Delta H - T\Delta S$, i.e. $T = \Delta H / \Delta S$ = 660 ÷ 1.035 = 638 K
When the temperature is slightly higher than 638 K the reaction will become spontaneous. (2 marks)
(Total = 9 marks)

Question 3

Reaction IV ≡ 2 × (*Reaction I*) + 3 × (*Reaction II*) + reverse of *Reaction III*

ΔH(*Reaction IV*) = (–394 × 2) + (–286 × 3) – (+1560)
= –788 – 858 + 1560 = –86 kJ mol^{-1} (Total = 3 marks)

Question 4

Energy needed for bond breaking = (946 × 0.5) + 498 = 971 kJ
Energy produced by bond formation = 2 × 469 = 938 kJ
ΔH = 971 – 938 = +33 kJ mol^{-1} (Total = 3 marks)

Total = 35 marks

Notes

Notes

Notes

Notes

Notes

Notes

Notes